The IBM PC-DOS Handbook

The IBM® PC-DOS Handbook

Richard Allen King

Berkeley · Paris · Düsseldorf SYBEX®

Cover art by David Gauger
Art by Gaynelle B. Grover
Layout by van Genderen Studio

Library of Congress Card Number: 83-61387
ISBN 0-89588-103-9
First Edition 1983
Printed in the United States of America
10 9 8 7 6 5 4 3 2 1

To Janet

Table of Contents

3   53

Disk Description and Usage

4   67

PC-DOS and the Keyboard

5   83

Output to the Monochrome and Color/Graphics Monitors

6   105

The Serial and Parallel Ports

7   115

Dates and Times in PC-DOS

11   161

Your PC-DOS Files

12   181

Batch Operations, or Bye Bye Repetition

13   193

The Monochrome and Color/Graphics Screens

17   241
Tables and Maps

Appendix A: 275
The Difference between MS-DOS and PC-DOS

Appendix B: 281
Differences between PC-DOS Versions 1.0, 1.05, and 1.1

Appendix C: 285
Creating Programs Using the Debugger

Acknowledgements

I would like to thank Dr. Rudolph S. Langer, who suggested the subject of this book and from whom I learned most of my better programming practices (the others are mine); Ron Shafer, of AAO Computer Services Inc., for assistance in providing access to MS-DOS; Bob Good, for reviewing the manuscript and providing helpful suggestions; Salley Oberlin and Barbara Gordon, for their valuable editorial improvements, good humor, and courier services; and my wife Janet, whose support has been unflagging and generous.

Richard Allen King

June 1983

Introduction

This is a book written for people who know a little about computers. It assumes that you are using an IBM Personal Computer with the PC-DOS operating system, and that you need a rapid way of knowing more about some of the tools and features you have to work with.

If you intend to write programs that will run within PC-DOS (and MS-DOS), then the first half of the book, Chapters 1 through 8, is for you. It shows you the bare necessities of programming the 8086/8088. Then it shows you the functions your program can call within PC-DOS, along with the structures (files and programs) and devices (keyboard, screens, disks, and serial and parallel ports) on which the functions operate. Throughout the first eight chapters, where ROM BIOS (the basic input/output system installed within the IBM PC) provides better service than PC-DOS, the ROM BIOS function calls are described as well. Reading the first half of the book gives a programmer, both first-time and experienced, the background to proceed with confidence.

If you want to become adept at using PC-DOS at the command level, the second half of the book, Chapters 9 through 16, gives you quick access to the features and capabilities of this operating system. For instance, in the section on using the keyboard in Chapter 9, you will see how to use a single key (F3) to recall the last command, instead of having to retype it. The user-oriented half of the book also shows how to use batch operations, how to set up a filing system, the differences you need to be aware of between the monochrome and color/graphics capabilities, how to redirect output to a parallel printer, and a variety of other useful information.

A number of tables and maps exist that have been designed to give an "at a glance" view of important elements of the system. These tables appear within the text wherever necessary, but to save hunting around for the relevant illustration at a later date, any major map or table has been reproduced in the tables and maps chapter—Chapter 17. Much useful information has been transferred to the tables, so riffling through different manuals for that useful table you once noticed possibly has been reduced to looking in Chapter 17.

You are encouraged to skip the whole technical/programming (first) half of the book with no qualms at all, if that suits your purpose. The second half, Chapters 9 through 16, covers a lot of what you need to know to make PC-DOS work for you. You can drive a car all over North America without knowing much at all about what is under the hood.

This book is written to save you a lot of time searching around in the IBM manuals. Key features described there in obscure places are brought to light here and placed in their logical context. Nonetheless, we assume that you have available the Disk Operating System manual for the IBM PC. If you have the Technical Reference manual, so much the better. It will be useful for the more complex programming tasks that you might someday undertake, although information needed from the Technical Reference manual is usually supplied here. This book is not supposed to replace the DOS manual; it is an extension and clarification of it. For instance, the basic DOS commands, CHKDSK through TYPE (ASSIGN through VOL in version 2.0), are described well in the DOS manuals, so they are not described in detail here. Instead, the PC-DOS Command Summary, with notes on each command as appropriate, is provided in Chapter 17.

HOW TO USE THIS BOOK

If you want to find out all you can about a subject, read the chapter with the relevant title and look up all appropriate index entries. This type of organization allows the author to avoid the repetition that would occur if it were necessary to exhaustively include everything on a subject in one central location.

Once you have read this introduction and Chapter 1, feel free to move to any chapter that interests you. The book has independent chapters on each subject. It need not be read from beginning to end, as if it were a tutorial.

Wherever appropriate, references to the relevant pages of the Disk Operating System and Technical Reference manuals have been provided. The page numbers refer to the second edition (May 1982) of the version 1.10 DOS manual, and the revised edition (July 1982) of the Technical Reference manual. If you have first editions of those manuals, try looking at slightly lower page numbers if what you seek is not on the page(s) referenced. If you have the later, reorganized edition of the Technical Reference manual, only the appendix page numbers will be useful.

CONVENTIONS USED IN THE BOOK

All numbers are expressed in decimal (base 10) unless they are followed by an H, as in 21H, in which case they are hexadecimal (base 16). Numbers that are self-evidently hexadecimal (numbers that contain letters) are not necessarily followed by an H.

The use of K when referring to memory sizes and disk capacities indicates the number 1024. So 64K, a convenient way of referring to the space addressable by 16 bits, means 65,536.

The word *disk* refers to both diskettes and the fixed disk. Where information relevant only to the fixed disk is presented, the phrase *fixed disk* or *hard disk* is used.

The name of a file in PC-DOS terminology consists of a filename of one to eight characters, or a filename (of one to eight characters), followed immediately by a period and a filename extension of one to three characters. In this book *file name* (note the space) refers to the whole name of the file, which is either *filename* without an extension, or *filename.extension*. This may seem pedantic, but the distinction is useful later on.

Where you see [2.0], it means that the immediately preceding item is available only in PC-DOS version 2.0 (or later). Versions 1 refers to both versions 1.0 and 1.1. You will see comparisons made between versions 1 and version 2.0.

We are about done with the introductory section, save to tell about the history and origins of PC-DOS, then summarize each of the chapters.

THE HISTORY OF PC-DOS

In 1980 Seattle Computer Products needed an operating system to support their board-level 8086 microprocessor for S-100 systems. The ancestor of PC-DOS was born that summer, and they named it QDOS. As happens with most software, the PC-DOS we now know and love has come a long way from the original operating system, although it owes its basic structure to that dim past progenitor.

Tim Paterson is the programmer who wrote QDOS. Being a programmer of sensitivity and humor, he called it QDOS because that's what it was—a quick-and-dirty operating system. Quick and dirty are characteristics of the origins of a few fine (and many more not so fine) products. By the end of 1980 QDOS had become 86-DOS, not only because programmers' humor is not favored by those who sell, but also because 86-DOS was significantly better than QDOS and deserved another name.

Microsoft had earlier bought rights to the 86-DOS software. When IBM decided to venture into the microcomputer business, it chose Microsoft as one of the possible developers of an operating system for its line of personal computers. Within multiple shrouds of secrecy, a team of Microsoft's programmers, using 86-DOS as a base, developed the now-revealed PC-DOS on a prototype PC. By May 1981 that team included Tim Paterson. Just before the release of the IBM PC, Microsoft closed its grip on 86-DOS by purchasing exclusive rights to it from Seattle Computer, renaming it MS-DOS at the same time.

Tim Paterson stayed with Microsoft to the completion of version 1.1, did a little planning for version 2.0, then returned to Seattle Computer in April 1982.

Now that you know the origins of PC-DOS, please do not leap to the phone to call Microsoft with your queries and suggestions. IBM bought the operating system from Microsoft, and has taken it over as a product of its own. It may be that IBM can alter and expand PC-DOS as it wishes, with no obligation to let Microsoft know of the changes. IBM is now solely responsible for all of PC-DOS. However, so far (up to the release of version 2.0) Microsoft says that as far as the applications software interface (function calls) is concerned, PC-DOS and MS-DOS are the same.

The valuable information behind all this history is that Tim Paterson, the creator of 86-DOS, chose his operating system interface conventions to match those used in CP/M. Independent software builders had by that time written a large variety of applications to run under CP/M. It was important to Seattle Computer Products' marketing of its 8086 card that the predominant suppliers of existing software written for CP/M would find it relatively easy to take advantage of the 8086's superior capabilities.

Perhaps the most rewarding aspect of Tim Paterson's work, for himself as well as for us, was that he was able to provide an operating system freed of the limitations inherent in CP/M, and that he got some of his operating-system-capabilities wish list taken care of. The result is a system that is a marked improvement over CP/M—competent instead of irritating in its handling of error conditions, friendly to the user, and now, with version 2, well on its way to becoming an all-purpose, sophisticated operating system.

SUMMARIES OF THE CHAPTERS

Chapter 1 is an introduction to operating systems in general and to PC-DOS in particular. The capabilities of PC-DOS are described from the point of view of the programmer and applications user. Relevant aspects of the 8086/8088 architecture are introduced first. This is followed by an overview of the utility routines that PC-DOS makes available to programs via function calls. The software components that make up PC-DOS are also discussed.

Chapter 2 discusses files in PC-DOS: their structures and capacities, the tools available for file creation and deletion, and data entry and manipulation. The tree-structured file access mechanisms of version 2.0 are discussed, as well as the file control block file access strategy of versions 1. Chapter 2 also covers the use of file allocation tables for the allocation of disk space to files.

Chapter 3 gives a thorough description of the use of disk space in PC-DOS, including how the disk is organized into numbered sectors, what the capacities of the variously formatted disks are, a description of the disk access functions, and how the first few sectors of a disk are used for holding the PC-DOS software components.

Chapter 4 talks about the issues involved in getting single characters and strings of characters from the keyboard. It shows you how to make use of the keyboard access functions provided by PC-DOS. The key reassignment feature of version 2.0 is also described.

Chapter 5 introduces the two different display types (monochrome and color/graphics) available with the IBM PC. It describes how to use both the PC-DOS and the ROM BIOS functions to address them, and the differences between them. The screen control sequences provided in version 2.0 are also described.

Chapter 6 introduces the serial and parallel port handling capabilities; they exist as function calls within PC-DOS and ROM BIOS, and as part of the MODE command.

Chapter 7 is about dates and times in PC-DOS: their different representations, the function call used to access them, and how PC-DOS and ROM BIOS maintain the time and date.

Chapter 8 is about version 2.0 of PC-DOS. It discusses version 2.0 from a programmer's point of view. Version 2.0 function calls are described in each chapter as appropriate, but the new features of version 2.0 that do not have a home in other chapters of the book are shown here.

Chapter 9 begins the second half of the book with a discussion of PC-DOS at the user's level. Chapter 9 is a grab-bag of useful introductory information. Included is a brief comparison of PC-DOS with CP/M, a note on what parts of the DOS manual are most important to read, how PC-DOS makes use of the IBM PC's keyboard, how PC-DOS handles disk errors, and a note on the expanded capabilities of version 2.0.

Chapter 10 is a quick look at EDLIN, the PC-DOS editor with characteristics that endear it to so few.

Chapter 11 talks about files from a user's point of view. It discusses how to set up a filing system and how to choose file names. It also talks about file capacities and the tree-structured filing system available in version 2.0.

Chapter 12 is all about batch operations, i.e., how to use the PC's batch capability to save you much repetition and to have the PC perform sequences of commands without your intervention.

Chapter 13 gives the user's view of the two types of displays: monochrome and color/graphics. It discusses the differences between them, color selection on the color/graphics display, and how well programs written for one type of display adaptor will run on the other.

Chapter 14 shows you how to use the serial port to redirect output from the parallel printer port to letter-quality printers attached to the serial port, and how to connect with information retrieval services.

Chapter 15 shows you how to use DEBUG: what it can do for you, how to patch a program using DEBUG, and how to use it to look around PC-DOS.

Chapter 16 tells you all about the new features introduced with version 2.0: pipes and filters, I/O redirection, hard disk support, print spooling, and much more.

Chapter 17 is the tables and maps chapter. In this chapter you will find most of the tables, figures, memory maps, and command summaries that you may need as you use PC-DOS.

Appendix A discusses the differences between MS-DOS and PC-DOS. Appendix B talks about the differences between PC-DOS versions 1.0, 1.05, and 1.1. Appendix C shows you how to create short programs using the debugger. This might save you buying the Macro Assembler.

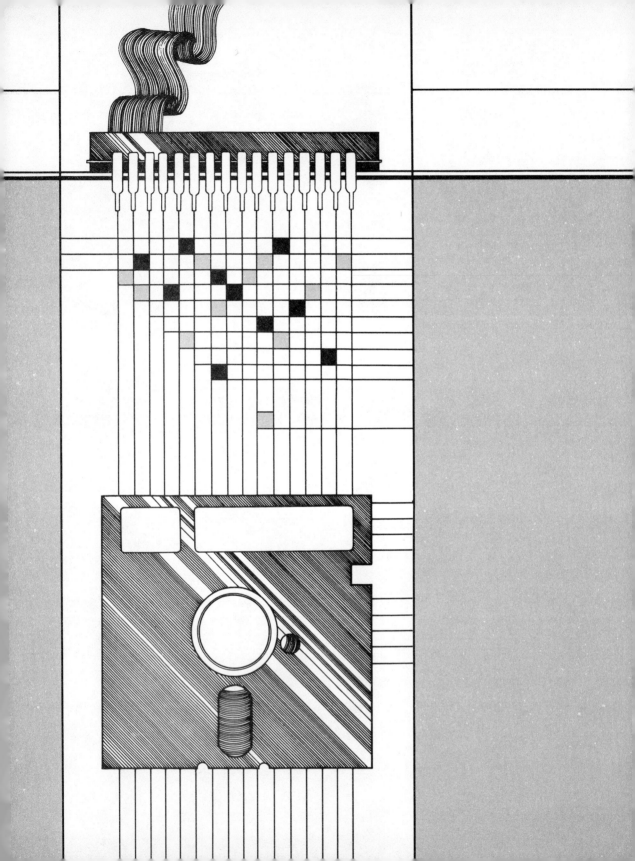

PC-DOS—A First View

INTRODUCTION

By the end of this chapter, you will have a feel for the range of what PC-DOS can do for you as a programmer, and you will have enough background knowledge to make good use of the information in the chapters that follow.

Like other chapters, this one begins with a short summary of the topics covered. To give a perspective on PC-DOS, we start the chapter with a brief introduction to operating systems, then examine the fundamentals of PC-DOS. We introduce ROM BIOS, a small piece of an operating system built into the hardware of the IBM PC. Next comes a description of some of the features of the 8086/8088 microprocessor that you will need to know about in order to work with PC-DOS. You will see how memory is addressed and how registers are used, and you will learn about interrupt vectors, program segment prefixes, and a few other things essential to programming for the PC. After this preparation, we introduce function calls, the method by which programs can take advantage of all the utility routines PC-DOS provides. A list of the functions is presented so you can get a feel for the scope of what is available. We outline the major software components of PC-DOS at the end of this chapter.

A reminder about the organization of this book: The first half, Chapters 1 through 8, is about the nitty-gritty of programming. You will need the first half when you design and write the code for a program. If you have not programmed for the PC before, then the second half of the book (beginning with Chapter 9) would be a useful place to start.

OPERATING SYSTEMS

An operating system is a set of software tools that are designed to make it easy for people and programs to make optimum use of a computer. People who use computers have different levels of needs and interests. For the sake of convenience we will separate these people into two groups: users and programmers.

The *user* wants a convenient set of commands to manage files of data or programs, copy diskettes, and run application packages such as the WordStar and VisiCalc programs.

The *programmer* needs a set of tools that can help him put together and debug programs. He or she needs program editors, assemblers, compilers, linkers, and a debugger. In addition, a programmer's life is made easier when a program can use routines within the operating system for doing some of the frequently needed (and sometimes complex) tasks required of any program, such as file manipulation and transfer of data to and from the various devices attached to the computer.

PC-DOS is an operating system for both users and programmers. It does not have all the features of an advanced operating system (such as UNIX), but it does have the basic facilities in versions 1, and some advanced features are included in version 2. You can do a lot with either version.

PC-DOS FUNDAMENTALS

PC-DOS is an operating system for the IBM Personal Computer. The name DOS is used instead of OS, because the programs that make up the operating system are designed around the concept that files are to be found on the disk. The system needs a disk before any useful action can take place.

This operating system, PC-DOS, provides a variety of functions whereby a program can conveniently use the hardware it runs on. It also provides a set of tools for the user and programmer (often the same person) to keep track of programs and data, execute programs, and design and build new programs.

These are the fundamental capabilities of PC-DOS:

For the User

1. Management of disk-based files. A set of user commands, CHKDSK through TYPE (ASSIGN through VOL in version 2.0), provides the disk and disk file management capabilities.

2. The batch feature, whereby groups of command sequences can be saved, then executed at will without having to respecify them.

3. The maintenance of time and date.

4. The print-screen capability, whereby the image of the screen can be sent to the printer on command. There is also a mode where whatever appears on the screen is echoed to the printer on a line-by-line basis.

5. The MODE command for changing the number of columns on the screen, for specifying parameters associated with the printer and the serial port, and for redirecting output destined for the parallel printer to the serial port.

6. In version 2, I/O redirection, pipes, filters, a form of print spooling, and the ability to print an image of the color/graphics display.

For the Programmer

1. Utility routines, accessed by function calls, for handling character input and output to and from the keyboard, monochrome or color/graphic displays, disk, and printer.

2. Function calls for file creation and deletion, data entry and access, and disk access. These are the components of the disk file management capability.

3. Function calls for time and date management.

4. A standard methodology for program initiation, program termination, and Ctrl Break character handling.

5. Program development tools: the linker, the debugger, and EDLIN, an extremely elemental editor.

The function calls are described a little later in the chapter. For now, let's look at some software that is not part of PC-DOS, but that PC-DOS uses a lot.

PC-DOS AND ROM BIOS

ROM BIOS is a piece of operating system software built into the PC hardware. It is resident in read-only memory (ROM) on chips in the IBM PC. It does what the name, basic input/output system, implies: it handles the basic input and output functions for the IBM PC. Like PC-DOS, it contains routines to respond to function calls, and it does useful work for whomever calls those functions. PC-DOS uses many of the ROM BIOS functions, and ROM BIOS in some areas is more powerful than PC-DOS. If you are programming for the PC, it doesn't make any sense to look at PC-DOS without looking at ROM BIOS.

In addition to I/O support, ROM BIOS contains

- the primary PC bootstrap,
- routines that test and report errors in all the currently configured components of the PC,
- a set of patterns for generating the first 128 ASCII characters when the display is operating in graphics mode,
- time-of-day maintenance routines, and
- the print screen utility.

ROM BIOS is useful only to programmers, not directly to users. It contains no features for accepting user commands, and it has no file handling capabilities.

The connection between PC-DOS and ROM BIOS is intimate but not indissoluble. PC-DOS uses a number of the features of ROM BIOS. PC-DOS could be rewritten to ignore the existence of BIOS and still appear to the user and programmer to be the same system. The question of interest to programmers is this: If ROM BIOS is in any way better than PC-DOS, why not use ROM BIOS instead? The answer is that if you expect your programs to be portable from PC-DOS to MS-DOS, they should not use ROM BIOS.

Fully portable programs can be moved from computer to computer without difficulty. Portability from one machine to another is achieved when the language used to write the program is machine independent, and when the operating system provides a buffer between the program and the unique characteristics of the hardware it runs on. Clearly, 8088 assembly language is not machine independent, but PC-DOS has established a set of conventions for handling I/O. Programs that are to be portable between PC-DOS and MS-DOS, and between one version of PC-DOS and the next, have to use these DOS conventions.

ROM BIOS on occasion offers better facilities than PC-DOS for making use of the unusual features of the IBM PC. For example, the IBM PC has two types of display adaptors; ROM BIOS has better functions for accessing them than does PC-DOS. Wherever ROM BIOS is better, it is mentioned in the relevant discussions in this book.

FEATURES OF THE 8086/8088

We cover here the essentials of what you need to know about the 8088 microprocessor. It is assumed that you have some experience or knowledge of programming at the assembly language level, or will be learning more about it soon from another book. To be able to program within PC-DOS, you will need to know how memory is addressed, how registers are used, how to use interrupt vectors, and the purpose of a program segment prefix.

Memory Addressing and the Segment:Offset Format

The main microprocessor in the IBM PC (the 8088) handles addresses in the segment:offset format. This occurred because the 8086/8088 has a one-megabyte address space—1,048,576 bytes; it takes 20 bits to address one megabyte, so, clearly, more than one 16-bit word must be used to specify an address. The architects of the 8086/8088 resolved the problem of how best to use registers to address the memory by coming up with the segment:offset format. The segment register addresses a 64K chunk (segment) within the one-megabyte address space, and the offset register points within the 64K segment.

By convention, an address is expressed in hexadecimal digits, 4 bits to a digit. 20 bits can be expressed in five hex digits, so a 20-bit absolute address can be written as, say, B0000H (which is the address of the character in the top left corner of the monochrome screen). The absolute address B0000H expressed in segment:offset format is B000:0.

You will become accustomed to the segment:offset form of addressing quite quickly; for those who are not familiar with it, here is more information about segments, followed by examples of converting segment:offset addresses to absolute addresses.

More on the Segment:Offset Format

A segment of memory contains up to 64K (65,536) bytes and always begins at a paragraph boundary. A paragraph is 16 bytes long and begins at an absolute address that is a multiple of 16, so the address of a paragraph boundary always has the four low-order bits (the last hex digit) equal to zero.

You can view the segment part of a segment:offset address as a count of the number of paragraphs away from absolute address 00000H (the first location in memory). (Again, once you become familiar with segment:offset form, you probably will forget this interpretation of the segment portion of the address, and just consider it as a starting point somewhere in the one-megabyte address space.) If you multiply the segment address by the length of a paragraph, i.e., shift it left by one hex digit, you will find the absolute address of the segment.

The offset portion is a 16-bit address that refers to a byte anywhere within the area of memory whose starting address is defined by the segment register.

Converting Segment:Offset to Absolute Address

To convert an address in the segment:offset format to an absolute address, take the digits to the left of the colon, shift them left one digit, and add the offset. Let's look at some examples.

Conversion Examples   The address in ROM BIOS of the word that holds the keyboard flag is 40:0017. Shift the segment portion, 40, left one digit to get 400. Add the offset, 0017, to get 417H, the absolute address of the keyboard flag. As another example, the address of the 8K ROM BIOS chip is F000:E000. Its absolute address is FE000H.

To illustrate a slightly more complex example, programs are loaded at offset 100H in the code segment. When you call DEBUG, the segment registers (see below) are set to the location of the program segment prefix (04D5:0000 in version 1.1). The program begins at 04D5:0100, which is absolute address 4E50H.

Segment Registers in the 8086/8088

Of the sixteen registers in the 8086/8088, four are set aside to be used as segment registers: the code segment register, CS; the data segment register, DS; the stack segment register, SS; and the extra segment register, ES. The address of the current instruction is expressed by CS:IP, a combination of the code segment (CS) and the instruction pointer (IP). Similarly, the stack pointer is SS:SP, and the address of data is expressed by DS:DX. These are not the only valid combinations, as you will see when you look at the descriptions of the functions provided by PC-DOS.

Byte Registers in the 8086/8088

We have seen how some of the registers of the 8086/8088 are used. It is time to round out our knowledge of registers so that we can understand how PC-DOS uses them.

Each general-purpose register contains 16 bits, one word. Clearly, it is often convenient to deal in bytes rather than words. The 8086/8088 architecture allows for that by providing a way to specify that instructions operate only on either the low- or the high-order byte of a register. The four general-purpose registers (AX, BX, CX, and DX) can be addressed this way. The fairly obvious ways of referring to each half of those registers are AH and AL, BH and BL, CH and CL, and DH and DL.

Let's look at another aspect of the 8086/8088 architecture that contributes to the organization of PC-DOS, interrupt vectors.

Interrupt Vectors

The 8086/8088 design supports software interrupts. Designers of earlier computers came up with the idea that some small part of memory should be set aside to contain the addresses of the various routines that handle hardware interrupts. Programmers quickly saw the potential in this (that there was a fixed address to go to get a particular function accomplished), chatted avidly with the chip designers, and now we have locations set aside for software interrupts.

The first 1024 (400H) memory locations in the 8086/8088 are reserved for interrupt vectors. Each vector is the 4-byte address of the routine that services that interrupt. Of the 256 vectors, some (the first 16) are devoted to hardware interrupts; most are available for software interrupts. ROM BIOS and PC-DOS between them use most of the next 32 vectors (up to about 30H).

Programs may change the contents of these vectors at will. Some are set at the time of system initialization. Each program can have its own way of handling a particular interrupt or function; if it does it will redirect the appropriate vector to its own code. However, interrupt vectors that point to ROM BIOS tend to remain the same, because ROM BIOS provides many useful utilities.

Chapter 17 shows the first 40 vectors. The "Interrupt Vectors" section shows two sets of tables for interrupt vectors, giving their purpose and their initialized values. The values are shown to help you look around ROM BIOS, PC-DOS, and BASICA, and to see where these programs take on the servicing of different interrupts.

Page 3-3 of the Technical Reference manual, in a table entitled Interrupt Vector Listing, gives the names and addresses of the ROM BIOS routines that service some of these interrupts. Page 3-22 of the same manual contains Table 31, BASIC and DOS Reserved Interrupts, which provides more information on the use BASIC makes of the interrupt vectors.

The memory devoted to interrupt vectors allows for 256 separate vectors. PC-DOS already (version 2) provides 100 different functions that a program can call, so to restrict its use of the vector space, PC-DOS channels most of its function calls through interrupt 21H. The AH register is used to distinguish one request from another. Now let's examine a feature of program organization in PC-DOS, the program segment prefix.

Program Segment Prefixes

Each program that PC-DOS runs is given a program segment prefix (PSP). This is an area of memory, 256 (100H) bytes long, that serves as a communications area between the program and PC-DOS. The name *program segment prefix* is used somewhat in defiance of correct English. The communications area begins at location zero of the segment allocated to the program, and it is a prefix to the program itself, which begins at offset 100H within the segment (the PSP extends from 0H to FFH).

The PSP is used to contain a variety of useful information, including the size of the program segment (at offset 6), the addresses to which control passes under a number of different termination conditions, buffer space for the command line that brought the program to life (whose beginning coincides with the default disk buffer address), and a couple of tiny file control blocks, formatted to match the disk drive designators and file names of any arguments that were included in the command line. A diagram of the program segment prefix can be found at the end of Chapter 17. The existence of the PSP explains why programs loaded into their segments begin at offset 100H instead of offset zero. PC-DOS creates the PSP when loading programs. The PSP does not exist on the disk.

Now let's look at function calls, through which a program can ask PC-DOS to perform a great variety of tasks.

FUNCTION CALLS IN PC-DOS

PC-DOS makes use of the interrupt vectors 20H through 27H. Interrupt 21H is called the function request interrupt, and it is through this vector that most of your program's function calls will be made. The other vectors are for controlling the terminations of programs and for reading from and writing to the disk without reference to PC-DOS files (the disk access functions are described in Chapter 3).

In the area of function calls, PC-DOS and MS-DOS are the same. If you write a program that runs successfully under PC-DOS, and it does not use ROM BIOS or directly access any unique features of the IBM PC, it should run well under MS-DOS. Let's see how programs can make use of these functions.

Calling Functions

To call a function, set the registers so that the function you are calling will know what to do, then simply execute the INT instruction. This is a two-byte instruction of the form

INT nn

where nn (in hex) is the number of the interrupt vector. The machine language for INT is CD; the two hexadecimal bytes that form the interrupt 21H function request are CD 21.

Calling Functions from BASIC

You can also call PC-DOS functions from BASIC programs. The BASIC that comes with PC-DOS is quite comprehensive in its capabilities, but now and again it is useful to be able to use one of these function calls. Appendix C of the BASIC manual describes how to call machine language subroutines from BASIC. Don't be put off by the first sentence of the appendix; you can create small machine language subroutines (using DEBUG) and use the BASIC CALL statement to execute them without much difficulty. Passing arguments to the subroutine is a little more complex, since it requires that you understand how to use the stack.

Let's look at the functions that PC-DOS provides within interrupt 21H.

Interrupt 21H Functions

Of the 87 different functions provided (in version 2.0) under interrupt 21H, 13 are used internally and exclusively by PC-DOS, and the other 74 can be called by your program to do something useful. (The actions of functions used internally by PC-DOS are not necessarily exclusively controlled by the value of the registers on entry, so they cannot be used by programs that are not part of the PC-DOS operating system.)

These functions are not grouped in any strict form; it seems that new functions are assigned numbers as the need arises. If you have a function number but do not know what it does, you can look it up in Appendix D of the DOS manual. In the following table the functions are grouped alphabetically by what they do for us, rather than in numerical order. These are the groups:

- Break detection control [2.0]
- Character device I/O
    Display (standard output device [2.0])
    File or device I/O [2.0]
    I/O control channel access [2.0]
    Keyboard (standard input device [2.0])
    Printer (alias parallel port) I/O
    Serial (alias asynchronous port) I/O
- Country-dependent information [2.0]
- Date and time
- Disk access (DTA access is found in file access)
- EXEC (load and/or execute another program) [2.0]
- File and directory access, versions 1
- File and directory access, version 2.0 [2.0]
- Memory management functions [2.0]
- Program termination
- Vector access
- Verify read after write
- Version number access [2.0]

Please take some time now to read through the following list of functions and their brief descriptions. When you are aware of the tools you have to work with, designing a program becomes much more rewarding, and it is more likely to lead to success. The function number, in hex, appears to the right of a brief description of the function. If you want to know more about one or a group of functions, use the index to find where it is described in more detail.

Break Detection Control [2.0]

More extensive Ctrl Break checking is either on or off; this is controlled by function 33H (and by the BREAK command).

Character Device I/O

A variety of functions exist for sending and receiving characters to and from the devices on the system. In versions 1 each function is device specific. Version 2 includes I/O redirection, and the functions can apply to devices other than those for which they were originally intended.

Display (Standard Output Device [2.0])

Output, with Ctrl Break detection	02H
Output, without Ctrl Break detection	06H
String output	09H

File or Device I/O [2.0]

Read CX characters into DS:DX buffer [2.0]	3FH
Write CX characters from DS:DX buffer [2.0]	40H

I/O Control Channel Access [2.0]   This is a general-purpose function for investigating the status of a device, and for reading and writing to the I/O control channel.

I/O control, AL dictates subfunction [2.0]   44H

AL	Function
0	Get device information
1	Set device information
2	Read CX bytes into DS:DX buffer
3	Write CX bytes from DS:DX buffer
4	Read CX bytes from BL drive number
5	Write CX bytes to BL drive number
6	Get input status
7	Get output status

Keyboard (Standard Input Device [2.0])

Input, with Ctrl Break detection	01H
Attempt input (if DL = FF)	06H
Input, without echo or Ctrl Break detection	07H
Input, without echo but with Ctrl Break detection	08H
Get string into DS:DX + 2	0AH
Check status (AL = FF if character ready)	0BH
Clear buffer, invoke 1, 6, 7, 8, or A above	0CH

Printer (Alias Parallel Port) I/O

Output character in DL	05H

Serial (Alias Asynchronous Port) I/O

Wait for input character	03H
Output character in DL	04H

Country-Dependent Information [2.0]

Get currency symbol, date format, etc. [2.0]   38H

Date and Time Access

These functions get and set the system time and date. The function that accesses a file's time and date is shown in "File Access Functions in Version 2.0." The time and date formats are discussed in Chapter 7.

Get date into CX:DX   2AH
Get time of day into CX:DX   2CH
Set date from CX:DX   2BH
Set time of day from CX:DX   2DH

Disk Access

Most disk accesses will be generated by the file access functions. These access functions are available for more unusual circumstances.

Disk reset, flush file buffers   0DH
Read CX sectors into DS:BX   Interrupt 25H
Select default disk drive   0EH
Write CX sectors from DS:BX   Interrupt 26H

The EXEC Function [2.0]

Execute (or load) a program/process [2.0]   4BH
Terminate a process (EXIT) [2.0]   4CH
Get completion code of terminated process [2.0]   4DH

File Access Functions in Versions 1.0, 1.1, and 2.0

As you can see, the majority of function calls in PC-DOS have something to do with file access. The following set of functions is available in all versions, and requires the use of correctly prepared file control blocks that specify block numbers, record numbers, and record lengths.

Whole file access
Create a file   16H
Open a file   0FH
Close a file   10H
Delete a file   13H
Rename a file   17H

Sequential record access

Read a record	14H
Write a record	15H

Random record access

Read single record	21H
Read multiple records	27H
Write single record	22H
Write multiple records	28H

Finding files in the directory

Search for first entry	11H
Search for next entry	12H

File size

Read the file size	23H
Change the file size	28H, CX = 0

Utilities

Set the disk transfer address (DTA)	1AH
Parse the file name	29H
Read after write verify	2EH
Set random record field in the FCB	24H

File Access Functions in Version 2.0

These functions are available in version 2. The functions are for accessing any address within the address space of a file (the block/record concept is irrelevant) and for manipulating files within a tree structure of files.

Whole file access

Create a file [2.0]	3CH
Open a file [2.0]	3DH
Close a file [2.0]	3EH
Delete a file [2.0]	41H
Rename a file [2.0]	56H

Reading and writing data

Read from a file (or device) [2.0]	3FH
Write to a file (or device) [2.0]	40H
Set address within file [2.0]	42H
Read file (or get/set device) status [2.0]	44H

File handle manipulation

Get another file handle for the same file [2.0]	45H
Point existing file handle to another file [2.0]	46H

Finding files in the directory

Search for first entry [2.0]	4EH
Search for next entry [2.0]	4FH

Directory manipulation

Make a directory [2.0]	39H
Remove a directory [2.0]	3AH
Change to another directory [2.0]	3BH
Get current directory [2.0]	47H

Utilities

Get the disk transfer address (DTA) [2.0]	2FH
Get the disk parameters (free space, etc.) [2.0]	36H
Get or set a file's attribute [2.0]	43H
Get the read-after-write verify state [2.0]	54H
Get and set the file's date and time [2.0]	57H

Memory Management Functions [2.0]

These version 2 functions allocate and deallocate memory in units of paragraphs (16 bytes).

Allocate BX paragraphs [2.0]	48H
Change size of allocated memory block [2.0]	4AH
Free allocated block (segment in ES) [2.0]	49H

Program Termination

The first two functions are identical in effect. The third (4CH) is part of version 2 and should be used instead of the first two. The fifth (31H) is also part of version 2 and should be used instead of interrupt 27H.

Terminate, no completion (error) code	INT 20H
Terminate, no completion (error) code	00H
Terminate, return completion code [2.0]	4CH
Terminate, stay resident	INT 27H
Terminate, stay resident (KEEP) [2.0]	31H

Vector Access

Two central routines for accessing the interrupt vectors are offered:

Get interrupt vector value [2.0]	35H
Set interrupt vector	25H

Verify Read after Write

It is possible to tell PC-DOS to read and check for accuracy anything that it writes to disk, using these functions (or the VERIFY command):

Get verify status [2.0]	54H
Set verify status on or off	2EH

Version Number Access [2.0]

Get the version number (0 if prior to 2.0) [2.0]	30H

All these functions are described in the first half of the book, in the appropriate chapters. The descriptions show how your program can call the function, as well as the results (normal and abnormal) of calling the function.

The functions report their status on return in various ways. In versions 1, the AL register is often used to pass error or completion codes. In version 2, an attempt has been made to standardize error reporting; the carry bit is used to indicate whether an error occurred (set if error), and the AX register value corresponds to an entry in a table of errors, which is shown in the Function Call Error Return Table in Chapter 17.

A FEW MORE NOTES

A few more notes are left to be covered before we can move on. One word that may not have a meaning for you in the context of PC-DOS is *clusters*. A cluster is a unit of allocation of disk space. A cluster is a whole number of sectors; the number depends on the capacity of the whole disk. When files expand and contract, clusters are added or removed from the file.

There is a difference between file name and filename. It is explained in the Introduction, which precedes Chapter 1. If you haven't read that yet, you should. It contains information that is applicable throughout the book, including such things as what the difference is between filename and file name. I'd hate to see the difference unappreciated, because it took a lot of effort on the part of the editors and typesetters of this book to maintain the difference.

Let's now look briefly at the programs that make up PC-DOS. The file structures, disk layout, and data I/O are all described in the chapters that follow.

THE COMPONENTS OF PC-DOS

PC-DOS consists of four separate components: the disk bootstrap and the three files IBMBIO.COM, IBMDOS.COM, and COMMAND.COM. Appendix B of the DOS manual provides information on the organization of these programs, and it describes how they work together during system initialization and command interpretation. An outline is provided here.

The Disk Bootstrap

The disk bootstrap is found on the first sector of every PC-DOS diskette, and on the first sector of the partition allocated to PC-DOS on the fixed disk. It is put there by the FORMAT command.

When the IBM PC is powered on, after ROM BIOS completes its equipment check routines, and assuming all is well, ROM BIOS reads the first sector of the disk (the disk bootstrap) into memory at location 7C00H and executes it. The disk bootstrap program takes over from there. Its task is to load IBMBIO.COM into 600H. The disk bootstrap checks that it recognizes what it read as IBMBIO.COM and continues from there to read in IBMDOS.COM following IBMBIO.COM. If it does not recognize the program it reads into 600H, it puts out a message saying that the disk is not a system disk, please load another, then hit a character to continue. The disk bootstrap has served its purpose once IBMBIO.COM and IBMDOS.COM are in memory.

IBMBIO.COM

IBMBIO.COM is the interface between the heart of the operating system and the I/O capabilities of the IBM PC. Because ROM BIOS exists in the PC, IBMBIO.COM is largely an interface between IBMDOS.COM (the heart of PC-DOS) and the PC's ROM BIOS. If you use DEBUG to look at the first few locations of IBMBIO.COM, you will see a series of JMP instructions that branch to routines for keyboard input, character output, RS-232 serial port I/O, output to the printer, and time-of-day handling.

IBMDOS.COM

IBMDOS.COM is the program containing the code for the file management and disk buffering management capabilities of PC-DOS. It also contains the code for the various utility functions that PC-DOS (and MS-DOS) provide for programs.

COMMAND.COM

COMMAND.COM is the command processor. It is the program that sends the system prompt to the display and looks at and interprets the characters typed at the keyboard. The command processor exists as two separate parts: one that is always resident, next to IBMDOS.COM, and another that is loaded into the high part of memory and may be overlaid by programs that occupy or use most of the memory available in the PC.

SUMMARY

This chapter has provided introductory information about PC-DOS. An outline of the general purpose of PC-DOS has revealed that PC-DOS is an operating system that can be used with ease and success by programmers as well as by people who mostly need to run application software. The necessary background information on the 8086/8088 microcomputer has been covered: how its address space is addressed, how its registers are used, and the software interrupt feature. The IBM PC's ROM BIOS has been introduced, as well as the four software components of PC-DOS. Brief notes have been presented on the purpose of all the functions that programs running under PC-DOS can call. If you want to get to know PC-DOS at the user level, turn to Chapter 9. Otherwise, let's explore the heart of PC-DOS, its file management system.

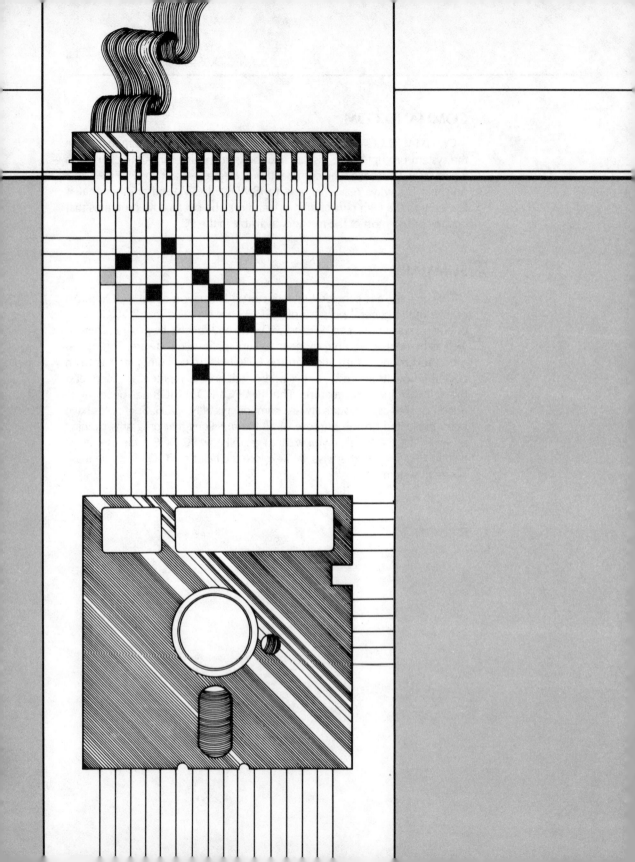

Files in PC-DOS

INTRODUCTION

This chapter tells you about the two separate strategies for file handling and data access in PC-DOS. Versions 1.0 and 1.1 share file handling and data access techniques that are based on file control blocks and records within files. Version 2.0 adds a completely new set of function calls, which base file handling on an ASCII string that designates the file, and data access on an address within the file's address space.

We begin the chapter with a very brief outline of files in PC-DOS. This outline includes notes on file capacities and the file access features common to versions 1.0, 1.1, and 2.0. After this discussion of common features, we devote a major section of the chapter to the file access functions introduced with versions 1.0 and 1.1.

After versions 1 file handling has been described, we examine the different, additional strategy for file and data access that has been introduced in version 2.0.

We then discuss how, in all three versions, disk space is allocated to a PC-DOS file using the file allocation tables. By the end of this chapter, you will feel comfortable working with any of the PC-DOS file handling capabilities. Let's begin with the outline of the PC-DOS filing system, so you can make a comparison with other filing systems.

AN OUTLINE OF FILES IN PC-DOS

A file in PC-DOS can be as large as you wish. A file has a theoretical maximum size of about four billion characters. (Four bytes are used to indicate the size of a file, giving a possible file size of 4,294,967,296 characters.) The file size need not be prespecified; it expands as necessary. The file naming scheme is not too restrictive—an eight character filename and a three character filename extension. There is no mechanism for continuing files across disk boundaries.

The Capacities of PC-DOS Files

Since PC-DOS versions 1 do not accommodate hard disks or other expanded capacity media, we are limited to a maximum of 160,256 bytes per file for a single-sided diskette, 322,560 bytes per file for a double-sided diskette.

Version 2.0 includes hard disk support. If you have either a PC with an extension chassis or an XT, a 10MB hard disk is available, so files can be very large. Version 2.0 also supports diskettes with nine sectors per track, thus increasing the maximum file size to 179,712 bytes for single-sided diskettes, and 362,496 bytes for double-sided diskettes.

PC-DOS File Attributes

Each file in PC-DOS has an attribute. The attribute is a one-byte flag, which is maintained in the directory entry for a file. The purpose of the file attribute is to enable files to be marked so that they receive special handling by the operating system. For instance, IBMBIO.COM and IBMDOS.COM are two files that exist on disks containing PC-DOS, but their names never show up in a directory listing. That is because their attribute marks them as hidden files.

Versions 1 allow for three different file attributes: hidden file (02), system file (04), and normal file (00). Version 2 expands the range of possible meanings for the attribute byte (see Figure 2.4).

PC-DOS File Access Function Calls

All PC-DOS file access capabilities are found within interrupt 21H. The particular function that you want carried out is selected by setting the AH register and the appropriate argument registers, then executing interrupt 21H. On return, if the function provides any status information, register AL contains it. (Note: The absolute disk read and write capabilities lie outside interrupt 21H, but they operate on files only by accident or by special design.)

The structure of a PC-DOS file as it exists on the disk, as well as the allocation and deallocation of disk space (measured in units of clusters) to a file as it expands and contracts, are described near the end of this chapter, in the section "Allocation of Disk Space to a PC-DOS File." Let's see how versions 1.0 and 1.1 approach file handling and data access.

AN OVERVIEW OF VERSIONS 1 FILE HANDLING AND DATA ACCESS

The system of files and file access implemented within PC-DOS versions 1 is simple and adequate. PC-DOS versions 1 neither supply nor expect a specific system of organizing groups of files, except that a single-sided diskette cannot contain more than 64 files, and a double-sided diskette cannot contain more than 112 individual files.

A file and its current state are described by a file control block (an FCB) external to that file. (See the section "File Control Blocks".) The same file may, in theory, be accessed in turn by several FCBs—each having its own idea of the structure and current state of access of the file.

The access mechanisms use the block and record concepts, where the block is 128 records of whatever size you choose, up to a maximum of 64K bytes. Access may be either sequential or at random.

Note that this method of file access is unchanged in version 2.0. (A program that uses versions 1 file access calls will run fine in version 2.0, with one possible exception. If a program uses the file allocation table (FAT) address supplied by function 1BH, it may have trouble when running in version 2.0, because version 2.0 returns a pointer to a byte containing the FAT identification byte, not the address of the FAT itself.)

THE STRUCTURE OF A PC-DOS FILE—VERSIONS 1

A file is a series of data bytes, organized logically into records within blocks. A block is a group of 128 logically contiguous records. A record is a group of logically contiguous bytes, up to 64K (65,536) bytes in length.

The concept of having blocks of records in a file can be useful, but the choice of 128 as the number of records within a block is arbitrary and restrictive—it deprives the concept of most of its usefulness. At least there is flexibility in the choice of record length, or else we would be stuck with a design feature that is almost two decades out of date. The block/record structure is important, because file access capabilities provided by the

PC-DOS routines are in these units. Let's examine file control blocks, so we can work with this file structure.

FILE CONTROL BLOCKS

A file control block is the interface between the PC-DOS file access mechanisms and the file of raw data on the disk. The FCB contains information on the structure of the file, its name and length, and the current address of both sequential and random access operations. An FCB does not contain information about the location of the file on diskette—this information is contained in the diskette directory and in the file allocation table.

Before creating, reading, or, in fact, making any access to a file, a file control block frame must exist for that file. FCBs are very necessary. For example, you need an FCB to step through the entries in a directory.

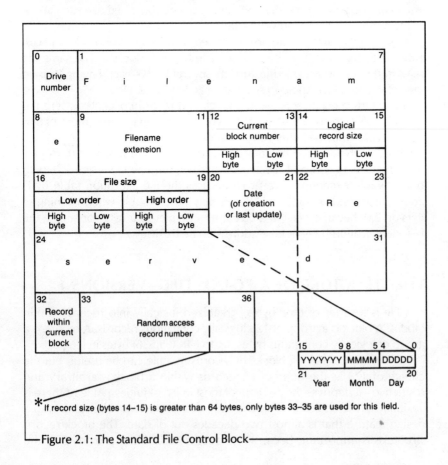

*If record size (bytes 14–15) is greater than 64 bytes, only bytes 33–35 are used for this field.

Figure 2.1: The Standard File Control Block

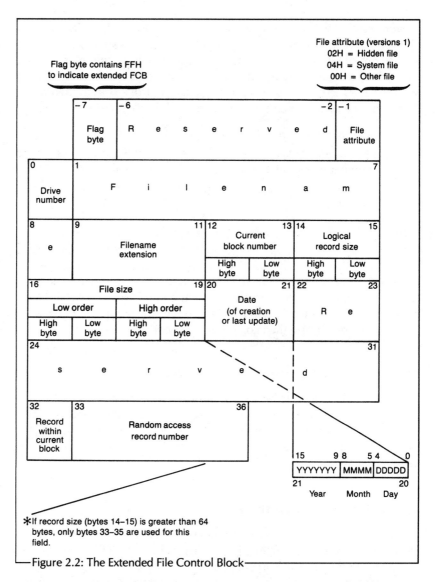

Figure 2.2: The Extended File Control Block

Two types of FCBs exist: standard and extended. The standard FCB is thirty-seven bytes long. It is shown in Figure 2.1. The extended FCB is simply a standard FCB with a seven-byte prefix to indicate that the file described has special attributes (a nonzero attribute byte). Figure 2.2 shows an extended file control block, with the three different attributes that versions 1 accept.

Note the odd arrangement of the high- and low-order bytes in the current block, logical record size, and file size fields of the FCB. The random access record number field is handled strangely as well.

File control blocks do not necessarily have all fields filled in at any one time. They are pieced together from your program and by the routines within the INT 21H function calls that take file control blocks as arguments. The fields that control access to the contents of the file are

1. the logical record size (bytes 14–15),
2. the current block number (bytes 12–13) and the current record number within the block (byte 32) for sequential access, and
3. the random record number (bytes 33–36), which is used for random access.

In the following file access descriptions, we will see under what circumstances you need to supply the fields and when they are filled in by PC-DOS. (Note: The individual fields of the FCB are further described on pages E-8 and E-9 of the DOS version 1.1 manual.) Before we look at file access (and now that you know what a file control block looks like), you need a place to create a file control block. But first we have to apologize for a little poor English, and then go ahead and use it.

Unopened File Control Blocks

The text below often refers to "an unopened file control block." When an FCB contains only the disk drive, the filename, and the filename extension, it is the FCB of an unopened file. The DOS manual somewhat ungrammatically calls this an "unopened FCB," and we shall adopt the same convention.

Choosing a Home for the File Control Block

To create an FCB, you need memory space. A standard offered by PC-DOS is at location 5C in the program segment prefix (PSP). However, in keeping with the ideas that freedom and flexibility are desirable, that your program may need to manipulate more than one file at a time, and that a symmetric and systematic layout of FCBs is preferable to scattered FCBs, you could choose not to use the standard FCB address of 5C offered by PC-DOS.

Instead, you could set aside within your program space for a small set of FCBs, each with enough room to become an extended FCB should the need arise. An area of 4 × EXFCBlen bytes, where EXFCBlen is the length of an extended FCB, is sufficient for four FCBs. This may avoid any fiddling around caused by the effects of the FCB outgrowing its previous space allocation, as has happened to the spaces allocated at 5C and 6C in the program segment prefix. The only times use of the FCB at 5C can be recommended are (1) during a search for a file using functions 11H or 12H, (2) when deleting a file using function 13H, and (3) perhaps when the program is first called. When your program is called, PC-DOS will try to make filenames out of the first two arguments on the command line, putting them at 5C and 6C as embryo FCBs. It's nice for the operating system to be so helpful, but irritating because the file name at 6C is in the middle of the FCB starting at 5C, and when you use the 5C FCB it overflows into the default disk access buffer at 80H. Your program can create FCBs from ASCII strings or command lines, using function 29H, which puts unopened FCBs wherever you want.

After that plug for a systematic approach to positioning file control blocks, let's move on to the function calls, which enable you to work with the PC-DOS file system.

ACCESSING A FILE AND ITS DATA IN PC-DOS VERSIONS 1

To make any file access activity occur, all we have to do is make an adjustment to some field(s) in the FCB, set some registers, then call the appropriate function. Let's look briefly at the subject of register settings.

Register Settings for Function Calls

In the descriptions that follow, most of our discussion examines the contents of the file control block and how, why, and when the various fields within the FCB are adjusted. The register contents on the call to the file access functions are discussed only briefly, because they vary little from one call to another.

The function to be called is specified in the AH register. The DS:DX registers point to the file control block. The CX register is used in the random block read and write routines for a record count.

Now that we know which registers to use when calling file access functions, let's see which functions we have available.

Versions 1 File Access Functions

Figure 2.3 summarizes the file access calls with their function numbers. Remember that these functions are present in version 2.0 and return the

Purpose	Function Number
Whole file access	
Create a file	16H
Open a file	0FH
Close a file	10H
Delete a file	13H
Rename a file	17H
Sequential record access	
Read a record	14H
Write a record	15H
Random record access	
Read single record	21H
Read multiple records	27H
Write single record	22H
Write multiple records	28H
Finding files in the directory	
Search for first entry	11H
Search for next entry	12H
File size	
Read the file size	23H
Change the file size	28H, CX = 0
Utilities	
Set the Disk Transfer Address (DTA)	1AH
Parse the file name	29H
Read after write verify	2EH
Set random record field in the FCB	24H

Figure 2.3: Summary of Versions 1 File Access Functions

same results. To make a comparison with the function calls that make up the new file access strategy provided by version 2.0, see Figure 2.5.

The function calls within interrupt 21H provide for two different levels of file access: (1) finding files and (2) working with a single file. First we will examine the function calls for working with a single file—opening, reading, writing, and closing a file. After that we will examine the function calls for creating files and finding and altering directory entries for a file; lastly, we will look at the utility functions.

WORKING WITH A SINGLE FILE

Here we describe the set of tools you can use when working with a single file. A file can be opened and closed; its contents can be accessed sequentially or at random. If a file is accessed at random, either single or multiple records can be read or written. Let's see how to open a file that already exists.

Opening a File—Function 0F

A file must be opened before any data transfer can take place. An unopened FCB containing a drive specification, a filename, and a filename extension is all you need to open a file. To open the file, put the address of the FCB in DS:DX, the value F in AH, and execute interrupt 21H. If you have reason to use an extended FCB, DS:DX must point to the first byte of the FCB prefix (the flag byte).

The open function looks for the file name in the directory, returning FF in AL if it can't find it. If it finds the file name in the directory, it supplies values for four fields in the FCB. It also modifies the drive number field if it was set to 0 (default drive number) prior to the open command.

The open function zeroes the current block number (bytes 12–13), sets the logical record size to a default value of 80H (128 decimal), and reads the file size and the date from the directory entry for the file. The open function does not set byte 32, the record number within the block, nor does it set bytes 33–36, the record number relative to the beginning of the file—the field that is used for random access. It would seem natural to initialize both the current block and the current record within the block to zero to give sequential access a good start, but your program has to make either one or both settings; the open function does not do it for you.

Reading from and Writing to a File

PC-DOS will read from or write to open files only. Once the file is open, you are only three steps away from transferring data: a record size needs to be specified, either the two current record fields or the one random record field needs to be set, and a disk transfer address (DTA) needs to be provided.

Those three steps cover a lot of ground, so we should proceed in an orderly way. First we will discuss the record size and record selection fields of the FCB. Then we will examine the function for setting the DTA. After that we will cover the functions that do the reading and writing, and examine the meaning of the status indicators on return from the function.

The Record Size Field

The logical record size field (bytes 14–15) of the FCB is set to a default value of 80H (128 decimal) by the open and create functions. If you are happy with that, no change needs to be made. If not, alter the word at byte 14 in the FCB to the value you want. This could vary from 1, a single byte per record, to a very large number of bytes per record, say 64K. Practicality dictates the upper limit.

The Current Block and
Current Record Fields under Sequential File Access

The current block and current record size fields need to be set at the beginning of sequential file access. They are bytes 12–13 and byte 32 of the FCB. The current block is set to zero by the create and open functions. If you want sequential access to begin at other than block zero, set this field to the block of your choice.

The current record field, byte 32, is not initialized except by your program. Set it to zero to start sequential access at the beginning of the file; set it to the value of your choice (in combination with the current block number) to begin access at any location other than the first record.

Each successful sequential file access (via functions 14H and 15H) increments the current record field. When the current record reaches 128, the current block field of the FCB is incremented. As long as sequential access continues in this mode, no further setting of these two fields by your program is necessary.

The Current Block and
Current Record Fields under Random File Access

There is a connection between the current and random access fields of the FCB that you need to be aware of: the random file access functions translate the random record field into the current block and record fields. When a random access is performed, the sequential access mechanism loses its place in the sequence.

The Random Record Field

The random record field, at bytes 33–36 in the FCB, directs the file routines to the nth record in the file, where n is specified by the random record field.

This field is *not* changed by the single-record random read and write activities (functions 21H and 22H in interrupt 21H). It *is* changed by the random block read and write functions (27H and 28H). These routines take a record count (in CX). At the end of the transfer, the random record field is updated to match the address of the next record. (Note: The concept of dividing the file into blocks of 128 records does not have any relevance to random access. The random record field specifies the nth record from the beginning of the file. The use of "block" in "random block write" is unfortunate. All it means in this context is that more than one record can be read at a time.)

One other way of changing the random record field is to call function 24H. Function 24H sets the random record field based on the values of the current block and current record fields. One last reminder—any random access will set the current block and current record fields, i.e., the fields that drive the sequential access mechanisms.

Now that we have seen the three different types of record access (sequential, single-record random, and random block access), let's see how to tell PC-DOS what part of memory to use as a record(s) buffer.

Setting the Disk Transfer Address (DTA)—Function 1A

A disk transfer address is a disk buffer address. It's a memory location to read into or write from. The read and write routines won't read or write data beyond the end of the segment specified by the DTA, nor wrap to the beginning of it, so make sure the DTA has enough space between the offset portion of its address and the end of its segment to accommodate your largest record.

The disk transfer address is set by a call to function 1A (INT 21H) with DS:DX being the DTA. Version 2.0's file access system also uses this function to set disk transfer addresses. In addition, version 2.0 has function 2FH, which gets the DTA. It's always a good idea to be able to read anything you have written.

Reading a Record
under Sequential File Access—Function 14H

The file has been opened, and the logical record size field (bytes 14–15) has been set, either by the open function to 80H or by your program to another value. The current block field has been zeroed by the open function and perhaps reset by your program. The current record field has been set, and the DTA setting function has been called with your buffer address. Now, to read a record from the file, set DS:DX to point to the FCB, set AH = 14H, and execute interrupt 21H. On return, if AL = 0, the transfer was made successfully and the record number (current block, current record) was incremented. If there were any problems, AL would contain one of the following nonzero error codes:

01   End of file, no data in record
02   DTA's available segment space not large enough, i.e., buffer too small; transfer terminated early
03   End of file, partial record read, filled with zeros

Writing a Record under
Sequential File Access—Function 15H

The differences between this and the read function are the direction of transfer, the setting of AH to 15H before execution of interrupt 21H, and the return codes in AL, which are as follows:

00   Successful write
01   Diskette full
02   Record larger than DTA's available segment space, i.e., disk buffer too small

A read-after-write check facility is available whenever you need confirmation that the data recorded is just what you want. See the descriptions of function 29H (which sets the verify state) in "Versions 1 Utility Functions" and function 54H (which reads the verify state) in "Version 2.0 Utility Functions," later in this chapter.

Reading Records under
Random File Access—Functions 21H and 27H

There are two major differences between random and sequential file access. The random record field of the FCB controls which record is accessed, and in random file access a choice must be made between reading single records or blocks of records.

The random read function (21H) reads a single record, while the random block read function (27H) reads the number of records specified by CX. As we noted before, during random access the records are numbered from zero, starting from the beginning of the file, and the current block number is irrelevant.

As with sequential access, before a successful random record file access can be made, the file must be open, the logical record size set and the DTA specified. In addition, the random record number field in the FCB (bytes 33–36) must be set. For a random block read, CX must be set to the number of records to read; it must not be set to zero!

Random Read (Single Record)—Function 21H   For a single record random read, set DS:DX to point to the FCB, set AH to 21H, and execute interrupt 21H. On return AL will provide one of the following codes as status information:

00 Transfer successful

01 End of file, no more data is available

02 DTA's segment space is inadequate, transfer has ended prematurely

03 End of file, a partial record is available, filled out with zeros

Random Block Read (Multiple Records)—Function 27H   For a multiple record random read, set DS:DX to point to the FCB, set CX to the number of records to be read, set AH to 27H, and execute interrupt 21H. On return AL will provide status information:

00   Transfer successful

01   End of file after reading a whole number of records

02   As many records as possible were read before disk buffer space was exhausted

03   End of file, the last record read is a partial record

FCB Fields Changed by Random Reads   The current block and current record fields that drive sequential access are always set by random access. This may seem odd, but there are semiplausible justifications for it. When the single record access function 21H is used, the current block and current record fields are set to the sequential equivalent of the random record address. For multiple record access via function 27H, they are set to the sequential equivalent of the record that follows the last of the group of records accessed.

Writing Records under
Random Record Access—Functions 22H and 28H

The preparation for the random record write is the same as that for the random record read, except for the difference in the value of AH.

Random Write (Single Record)—Function 22H For a single record random write, set DS:DX to point to the FCB, set AH to 22H, and execute interrupt 21H. On return, AL provides status information:

    00   Successful transfer

    01   Diskette full

    02   DTA of inadequate length, transfer ended

Random Block Write (Multiple Records)—Function 28H For a multiple record random write, set DS:DX to point to the FCB; set CX to the number of records to be written; set AH to 28H; and execute interrupt 21H. On return, AL provides status information:

    00   Successful transfer

    01   Insufficient disk space, no records written

NOTE: Do not call this function with a CX of zero! This function has a special purpose when CX = 0 on entry—it changes the file size! This capability is no doubt convenient in other circumstances, but it could lead to unfortunate results if the routine that computed CX (the number of records to write) came up with zero. In fact, a civilized and flexible (but sadly inexperienced) program may want to call the write function with a CX of zero, expecting no records to be written. Using CX = 0 to change a file length is a bit like defining NUL: to be an erase-all function. Using function 28H to change the file size is described in the section "Changing the Length of a File."

Closing a File—Versions 1

Files need to be closed before the program terminates, to ensure that data which belong to the file but still are in memory buffers are flushed to the disk (or other devices) and that the directory entry is correctly updated. This applies to files that are being changed by either the sequential or random write functions.

Before updating the directory entry, the close function checks that the file name in the FCB is still in the same place in the directory, and only proceeds if that is the case.

The file closing function call is 10H. To close a file, you put the address of an opened FCB in DS:DX, set AH to 10H, and execute interrupt 21H. On return, AL provides status information:

    00   File successfully closed

    FF   File name not found in correct position on the directory; directory not updated

If AL returns an FF, your program could execute its own version of the error retry facility (the Abort, Retry, Ignore? message) provided by PC-DOS, to give the user a chance to change diskettes.

FINDING, CREATING, AND DELETING FILES—VERSIONS 1

This section describes the function calls that find and operate on the directory entries for files. First we will discuss the functions that look for specific file names in the directory, then we will discuss the create, delete, and rename functions. A note on the utility that tells you the file size is tucked in at the end of this section.

As with any file access operation within PC-DOS, a file control block is an essential prerequisite to doing anything useful. As usual, the address of the FCB is passed to the function in DS:DX.

Finding Files in the Directory

The file name as written by the user may contain the question mark (?) or asterisk (*) characters. Function 29H, which parses command lines looking for file names, will translate the asterisk character into as many question mark characters as necessary. This slight diversion into user-specified file names has been taken to show that when looking for a file name in the directory, allowance has to be made for finding more than one match with it. Because of this, two functions are allocated to finding file names in the directory: search for the first entry and search for the next entry.

Searching for the First Entry—Function 11H

This function does just what the title implies, and more. It uses an unopened file control block, which consists of the disk drive number, a filename, and a filename extension. Either of the filename fields may contain question marks.

This function steps through the disk directory and returns when it finds the first matching file name. In addition, a valid, unopened FCB is created at the disk transfer address. This feature is convenient, because the original unopened FCB you supplied cannot be used for accessing the file unless you are willing to abandon the search for further matches. The newly created FCB at the disk transfer address is, in fact, a copy of the disk directory entry, suitably offset from the DTA to make it into an acceptable FCB. This is the FCB to use to access the file found by the search. The next function call description, search for the next entry, sheds more light on this.

To search a disk directory for the first matching file name, set the DTA to an address where an FCB can be usefully created, point DS:DX to an unopened FCB, set AH to 10H, and execute interrupt 21H.

On return, if AL = 0, a valid, unopened FCB will exist at the disk transfer address. It will be a standard or extended FCB, to match the one supplied via DS:DX. The disk directory entry has been placed at FCB address one; the disk drive number has been placed at FCB address zero; and the prefix has been supplied (if necessary) to match the prefix that DS:DX pointed to before the call. This is the FCB to use to access the file. If AL = FF on return, however, no matching entry was found.

If you want to find files with nonzero attribute bytes (for example, hidden or system files), you need to use an extended FCB that includes the relevant attribute bit settings.

Searching for the Next Entry—Function 12H

The DOS manual thoroughly describes the purpose of this function. It is used to find the next matching directory entry only after the search for the first entry function has been successful. The calling parameters and return values (AL = 0 for success, and AL = FF for none found) are the same as those in function 11H.

The reason that the FCB that is pointed to by DS:DX cannot be used for file access is that it is used by these stepping functions to keep track of their place in the directory. Disk operations would cause the searching functions to lose their place.

Renaming a File—Function 17H

The function to rename a file needs the usual unopened FCB to find the file(s) whose name is to be changed. On finding a candidate, the file name beginning at DS:DX + 11H replaces the file name in the directory. (Note: I've not yet managed to use this function to change a set of files called fred1, fred2, fred3 into alfred1, alfred2, alfred3 in one function call. If you find a way, please let me know.) To change a file's name, set DS:DX to point to a modified FCB, where the new file name exists at DS:DX + 11H, set AH to 17H, and execute interrupt 21H. On return, AL = 0 indicates success. AL = FF indicates either that no match was found or that the rename operation would have created a file name identical to one already existing in the directory, and it refused to do that.

Creating a File—Function 16H

To create a file you must start with an unopened FCB. PC-DOS will do the work of putting together an unopened FCB for you. COMMAND.COM creates unopened FCBs at 5C and 6C when the program is called, and you may be able to use one of these. If you have available a command line with the file name in it, you can use function 29H, described later, to create an unopened FCB. COMMAND.COM puts a copy of the command line at 81H when the program is called.

Once you have the FCB, put its address in DS:DX, set AH to 16H, and execute interrupt 21H. The create file function will then look for a free (or matching) directory entry, initialize it to a zero length file, open that file, and return with AL = 0. You get no warning that you may be destroying an existing file; it is up to you to have used other functions, such as attempting to open the file, if you care about that not happening. If the directory is full and the file does not already exist, no file will be created and AL will equal FF on return.

If you want the file to be marked with one or more special attributes (say, hidden and system), an extended FCB (rather than a standard FCB) must be used. Here DS:DX contains the address of the first byte of the prefix (FCB address minus seven), which is the first byte of the extended FCB.

Note that the create function provides an opened file.

Deleting a File—Function 13H

Again, an unopened file control block (extended or standard) is needed to delete a file. This function deletes from the directory all files that match the filename and filename extension in the FCB.

The file name may contain the wild-card question mark (?) in place of any of the characters in the filename or filename extension. If the file name does contain wild-card characters, all files that match will be deleted. This function does not operate like the search functions, where only the first matching file is processed.

To delete a file, set DS:DX to point to the unopened FCB; set AH to 13H; and execute interrupt 21H. On return, if a matching directory entry or entries were deleted, AL = 0. If no match was found, AL = FF.

Reading the File Size—Function 23H

A file's diskette directory entry contains the file's size in bytes. While a file is open, its size is maintained in the file size field of the FCB, also in terms of number of bytes. However, versions 1 file access strategy deals in records, not bytes, so function 23H returns the file size in terms of the number of records in the file, based on the logical record size in the FCB. An unopened FCB must contain a file name that uniquely identifies the file you are interested in, because the file size returned belongs to the file with the first matching entry in the directory. The file size is returned in the random record field of the FCB, bytes 33–36. To read the file size in terms of number of records in the file, set DS:DX to point to the FCB, set AH to 23H, and execute interrupt 21H. On return, AL = 0 if a match was found and the file size supplied; AL = FF if no matching entry was found.

Changing the Length of a File—Function 28H, CX = 0

This utility is provided as a subset of the random block write function (28H). Its action is to change the length of a file to the product of the random record field and the logical record size fields of an opened FCB. If you want to set the file size to a number of bytes, set the logical record size in the FCB to 1.

To use this function to change the length of a file, set CX to zero. Then set DS:DX to point to the FCB, set AH to 28H, and execute interrupt 21H.

If the length is reduced, the disk space allocation routines release clusters that become free. If the length is increased, additional clusters are allocated as necessary. However, if the disk becomes full, AL = 01 on return, and the increase in length is not made.

For more on the allocation and deallocation of disk space to a file, see "Allocation of Disk Space to a PC-DOS File" near the end of this chapter.

VERSIONS 1 UTILITY FUNCTIONS

The three remaining function calls that do not fit into any of the above categories are described here. One of them, the file name parsing function, which creates an FCB from a file name, is most useful. Of the other two, one sets and resets the read-after-write verify capability, and the other sets the random record field of the FCB, based on the value of the current block and current record fields.

Parsing the File Name—Function 29H

This utility extracts the file name and disk drive designator from a command line to make a ready-to-use, unopened, standard FCB.

The action of the parse function is controlled by the bit setting in AL. (This function is described on pages D-18 and D-19 in the DOS version 1.1 manual.) The normal setting for AL on entry is 0F. DS:SI points to the command line to parse, ES:DI points to the place to create the FCB. To call the function, set AH to 29H and execute interrupt 21H.

On return, AL does not provide the whole story. If it equals FF, the drive specifier in the command line was invalid. If AL = 00 or 01, the operation was successful, but the FCB has to be checked to see whether the first byte of the filename (ES:DI + 1) is other than a blank. If AL = 01, the file name contained one or more wild-card characters (* or ?). DS:DI is stepped along the command line and points to the first character after the file name on return.

The Read-after-Write Verify Capability—Function 2E

Function 2E permits toggling of the read-after-write verify operation. For data that is vital to the state of health of the nation, or planet, where you must be sure you have done whatever you can to ensure its correct recording on the disk, use this capability. Unless you use large block transfers, the time it takes to write to disk when read-after-write is enabled is on average close to triple the time it takes to write to disk when read-after-write is not enabled. The IBM PC's disk write failure rate is normally very low. However, this function could be useful if your PC is operating in a very noisy electrical environment.

To turn on read-after-write verification, three register settings are necessary. Set DL = 0, AL = 01, AH = 2E, and execute interrupt 21H.

To turn off the verify operation, set both DL and AL equal to zero; set AH equal to 2E; and execute interrupt 21H. Version 2.0 includes the complement to this function: function 54H, which gets the verify state. Function 54H returns AL = 0 if verify is off and AL = 1 if verify is on.

Setting the
Random Record Field in the FCB—Function 24H

This utility converts the file address found in the sequential access fields of the FCB to a random record file address. To use it, set DS:DX to point to an opened FCB, set AH = 24H, and execute interrupt 21H. The random record field will be set to the same file address as the current block and current record fields.

VERSION 2.0 FILE HANDLING AND DATA ACCESS

Version 2.0 brings us a tree-structured filing system. This is an exciting development, and it moves PC-DOS into the ranks of powerful and productive operating systems.

If tree-structured (or hierarchical) systems of data organization are unfamiliar to you, Chapter 11, "Your PC-DOS Files," will be useful. We will assume in this part of the book that you know about tree structures.

With version 2.0 you can forget all about file control blocks. All you need to know to get data out of a file is

- the file name,
- the path (through the tree structure to the file), and
- the address within the file at which the data begins.

You can see that this is a much more simple and flexible arrangement than all that fiddling with file control blocks.

In version 2, the concept of a file handle has been introduced. Once a file has been opened, the PC-DOS file access functions that operate only on opened files expect to be passed a sixteen-bit file handle instead of the path and file name. A file handle is a short way of identifying a file (or device).

The additional file access functions in version 2.0 have been written to make it easier for programs to accommodate I/O redirection. The read and write functions will read from and write to devices as well as files. In fact, devices are treated as if they were files; devices also have file handles.

Before we look at how to use the version 2.0 function calls, let's examine some of the new aspects to file access in a little more detail, and see how some existing conventions have been changed or expanded.

The File Name

The file name is carried over from versions 1. In versions 2.0, it has the same format (an eight-character filename, optionally followed by a period and a three-character filename extension), except that the four characters

$$\backslash \ | \ < \ >$$

cannot be used within the file name.

The Path

The path is a series of directory names separated by backslashes (\ ). Each directory name takes you down another level in the tree, arriving eventually at the file. The path begins at the root directory if the first character of the path is a backslash. For example:

\clothes\shoes\brown

may be the path to a directory of files for brown shoes on a disk devoted to personal possessions. Where the current directory is

\clothes

a path to the same directory of brown shoe files is

shoes\brown

The format for directory names is the same as for file names—eight characters, period, three characters, although the directory name extension is not often used.

The total length of any path (from the root directory to the directory containing the file of interest) cannot exceed 63 characters.

A path is limited to a single disk. Unless a disk drive designator precedes the path name, the default drive is used.

The Address of the Data

A file in version 2.0 is considered to be an address space. Your programs specify an address within the file, then read or write data at that address. The organization of the data in the file is thus freed from any constraints (such as blocks and records) imposed by the operating system. (Note: This form of file space addressing can be crudely simulated in versions 1 by using the random access feature with a logical record size of one.)

When a program reads or writes data to a file, the address increments by the number of bytes read or written.

Register Use Conventions

The file functions use one of two possible forms of file identification: either (1) an ASCII string containing a drive designator, the path, and the file name (we will call this the path string); or (2) a sixteen-bit file handle.

The address of the path string (which must be terminated with a 00 byte) is passed in DS:DX. File handles are passed to functions in the BX register and received from functions in the AX register. File attributes and byte counts are passed in the CX register.

Error Reporting

Instead of each function call returning error conditions in a manner unique to itself, error condition reporting and interpretation has been unified.

The basic error indicator for the functions introduced with version 2.0 is the carry flag. The preexisting functions still return a nonzero value in AL, or do whatever they do to indicate error conditions.

In version 2.0, if the carry flag is set on return, AX contains the error code. The meaning of the errors returned in AX may be found by reference to a common table of error conditions. The Function Call Error Return Table in Chapter 17 shows the error return codes and their meanings.

This centralization of meaning has minor disadvantages. Several of the file access functions will, on occasion, return error 5, meaning that access has been denied. It is nice to know that it failed, but a little more information about why it failed would be helpful.

Access Modes

Version 2 has introduced the idea of an access mode. The access mode is only applicable when the file is open. You can use it to specify whether you want a file opened for reading, for writing, or for both reading and writing. The ability to specify an access mode gives you additional control over the use of the file, beyond that specified by the attribute byte.

The access mode is specified at the time the file is opened using the open function (3DH). (A newly created file always has an access mode of read/write.) These are the three access modes:

Mode	Meaning
0	Open file for reading
1	Open file for writing
2	Open file for both reading and writing

Once the file has been opened with a restrictive access mode (read-only or write-only), the only way to access it differently is to close the file and re-open it with another access mode. Except for newly created files, the access mode will not override the effect of a read-only attribute byte. A request to open a file having a read-only attribute with access mode 1 or 2 will fail.

Attribute Bytes

Version 2 has expanded the range of possible meanings for the attribute byte in a directory entry. In version 2, directory entries exist for entities

Byte	Attribute Meaning
00	Normal read/write file
01	Read-only file
02	Hidden file
04	System file
08	Root directory entry containing volume label
10	Directory entry containing a subdirectory
20	The file's archive (dirty) bit

Figure 2.4: Attribute Byte Values for Files and Directory Entries

other than files, and the range of values for a file attribute has increased. Figure 2.4 shows the new list of attributes.

Now that we have learned about some of the basics of version 2's filing system, let's examine the functions we have to work with.

VERSION 2.0 FILE HANDLING FUNCTIONS

The functions supplied in version 2.0 for the new form of file handling are shown in Figure 2.5 on the next page. We will examine them group by group.

WHOLE FILE ACCESS—VERSION 2.0

The functions that operate on whole files are create, open, close, delete, and rename.

Creating a File—Function 3C

The create function creates a new file or truncates an existing file to zero length. As with versions 1, if you care about the possibility of destroying the contents of existing files, your program needs to confirm that a file does not exist before attempting to create it.

To create a new file or zero the length of an existing file, put the ASCII path string address in DS:DX, the file attribute in CX, set AH equal to 3C, and execute interrupt 21H. This function opens the file if the creation was successful, and it returns the file handle for that file in AX. Further reference to the file must be made using the returned file handle.

After a successful file creation, the access mode is set to read/write, even if the attribute specified in CX was read only.

Opening a File—Function 3D

A file can be opened with one of three access modes: reading, writing, or both reading and writing. The access mode is passed in AL.

Purpose	Function Number
Whole file access	
Create a file	3CH
Open a file	3DH
Close a file	3EH
Delete a file	41H
Rename a file	56H
Reading and writing data	
Read from a file (or device)	3FH
Write to a file (or device)	40H
Move the read/write address pointer	42H
Get file (or get/set device) status	44H
File handle manipulation	
Get another file handle for the same file	45H
Point existing file handle to another file	46H
Finding files in the directory	
Search for first entry	4EH
Search for next entry	4FH
Directory manipulation	
Make a directory	39H
Remove a directory	3AH
Change to another directory	3BH
Get current directory	47H
Utilities	
Get the Disk Transfer Address (DTA)	2FH
Get the disk parameters (free space, etc.)	36H
Get or set a file's attribute	43H
Get the read-after-write verify state	54H
Get and set the file's date and time	57H

Figure 2.5: Summary of Version 2.0 File Access Function Calls

To open a file, set DS:DX to point to the ASCII string containing drive, path, and file name; put the access mode of your choice in AL; set AH equal to 3D; and execute interrupt 21H. On return, if the carry is set, the error code is in AX. If the carry is not set, the file was successfully opened and the file handle for the file is in AX.

Closing a File—Function 3E

You need a file handle to close a file. To close a file, put the file handle in BX, set AH equal to 3E, and execute interrupt 21H.

The only error returned is code 6, which means that the file routines did not recognize the file handle. If the handle is recognized, the file buffers are flushed to disk and the file is closed.

Deleting a File—Function 41H

The delete file function uses the ASCII drive, path, and file name string. To delete a closed file, point DS:DX to the ASCII string, set AH to 41H, and execute interrupt 21H. An opened file cannot be deleted.

An error code 5 will occur if the file you are trying to delete has the read-only attribute. When this happens, the file's attribute byte must first be changed to 0 (using function 43H), then the delete file function called again.

Renaming a File—Function 56H

Renaming a file requires two ASCII drive, path, and file name strings. The drive, if used, must be the same in both strings.

To rename a file, point DS:DX to the file's current path and file name string, point ES:DI to the new path and name, set AH equal to 56H, and execute interrupt 21H.

With this function, a file can be detached from one directory and added to another directory. In effect, the file can be moved freely within the tree. This function will not move a file from one disk drive to another.

READING AND WRITING DATA—VERSION 2.0

The version 2.0 data transfer functions work for both files and devices. Three functions are provided: one for reading, one for writing, and one for setting the address at which the reading and writing will occur. A fourth function, status checking, can be used as an alternative way of detecting end-of-file conditions.

Reading from a File—Function 3F

To read from a file in version 2.0, a program must specify the number of bytes to be read and the address of the buffer into which the data will be read.

The address within the file from which to begin to read (the read/write pointer) need not be set unless random access is desired. The read/write pointer can be set by the set address function (42H). When the file is opened, the address is set to zero. Each read or write action adjusts the pointer by the number of bytes read or written.

To read from a file, put the file handle into BX, put the buffer address into DS:DX, put the number of bytes to read into CX, set AH equal to 3F, and execute interrupt 21H.

On return, the number of bytes read is in AX. When the end of the file is reached, the carry is not set. The way to detect the end of the file (when reading) is to examine the AX register on return. If the AX value is not the number of bytes called for (AX not equal to CX), end of file has been reached. The next read will get no more bytes.

Writing to a File—Function 40H

Writing to a file in version 2.0 is a simple operation. To write to a file, put the number of bytes to write into CX, put the buffer address from which to write into DS:DX, put the file handle into BX, set AH equal to 40H, and execute interrupt 21H. The file will expand as necessary, unless the disk becomes full. The disk-full condition can be detected by comparing the value returned in AX, which is the number of bytes actually written, with the number of bytes the function was instructed to write. The read/write pointer is incremented by the number of bytes written.

Moving the Read/Write Address Pointer—Function 42H

Use this function to set the address at which random access reading and writing is to occur. The function accepts both absolute and relative pointer movement instructions, depending on the value of AL on entry. If AL = 0, the function interprets the value in CX:DX as an absolute address. If AL = 1, the address is set to the sum of the current address plus the value in CX:DX.

To set the read/write pointer, set AL to the absolute or relative adjustment control, set CX:DX to the address (absolute) or offset (relative), set the file handle into BX, set AH equal to 42H, and execute interrupt 21H. On return, the new value of the read/write pointer can be found in DX:AX. This function can be used to expand the file.

File Length Determination

The set address function has an ancillary mode of operation, which can be used to determine the length of a file. If AL = 2 on entry, the pointer is moved to the end of file plus the offset. If the offset is zero, on return DX:AX will contain the address of the end of the file. If the offset is greater than zero, on return DX:AX will point beyond the end of the file. Since the file is not expanded in this ancillary mode of operation, why the function would accept a nonzero offset is a mystery.

Get File Status—Function 44H

The I/O control function for devices can be used as an alternative method of monitoring whether the end of the file has been reached.

Function 44H is mostly used for device I/O control. It has eight subfunctions, three of which have meaning when the function is used on files. Subfunction 6 returns input status, subfunction 7 returns output status. For both subfunctions, a return value in AL of FF means that the end of the file has not been reached. AL contains a zero when the end of the file has been reached.

TRADING FILE HANDLES

Version 2.0 contains two functions for dealing with file handles. They both provide ways for getting a second file handle for a file. The first function (45H) provides an entirely new handle, while the second function (46H) detaches a handle from one file and gives it to another.

Get a New File Handle for a File—Function 45H

To get an additional file handle for a file, put its file handle into BX, set AH equal to 45H, and execute interrupt 21H. On return, AX contains another file handle for the same file.

Programs that use these separate file handles for the same file must be written carefully. They must not try to use the two (or more) file handles as if they were for totally different files. All the file handles converge to the same table of a file's status information, which includes the read/write address pointer. For example, if two more or less independent parts of the same program are using different file handles for the same file, they should use the absolute mode of read/write pointer movement. If the two parts of the program independently make relative adjustments to the same address pointer, they will not be reading and writing data in the right places.

Point a File Handle to Another File—Function 46H

This is the other way of getting two file handles for the same file. The same cautions apply as for function 45H. To attach a file handle that belongs to one file to another file, put the file handle of the file you are willing to abandon into CX, put the other file handle into BX, set AH equal to 46H, and execute interrupt 21H. On return both file handles point to the same file. If the file to be abandoned was opened, this function closes it before attaching its handle to the other file.

FINDING FILES IN A DIRECTORY—VERSION 2.0

The two functions covered in this section, search for first entry and search for next entry, correspond to functions 11H and 12H, their counterparts in the FCB-related file access mechanism of versions 1. The information that is returned when a matching file is found is returned in the current DTA (disk buffer), formatted as follows (the DTA address offsets are decimal values):

DTA Address	Content
0–20	Reserved for subsequent access calls
21	Attribute found
22–23	File's time
24–25	File's date
26–27	Low-order file size
28–29	High-order file size
30–42	Name of file terminated by zero byte

The last field (30–42) will be shorter than 13 bytes if the file name is less than twelve bytes.

Search for the First Entry—Function 4E

To find the first matching entry, point DS:DX to the ASCII string containing the drive, path, and file name; put the relevant attribute into CX; set AH equal to 4EH; and execute interrupt 21H. On return, the first 43 bytes of the DTA will be set as noted in the preceding section.

Search for the Next Entry—Function 4F

To find the next matching entry, set AH equal to 4FH and execute interrupt 21H. The information in the current DTA is used to search for the next matching file.

MAKING, REMOVING, AND CHANGING DIRECTORIES

Like files, directories can be created and deleted. Also, a program needs the ability to move its basis of operations from one directory to another. The following four functions provide the equivalent of four user-level commands: MKDIR, RMDIR, CHDIR (when used to change to another directory), and CHDIR with no arguments (when used to display the current directory).

Making a Directory—Function 39H

To make a directory, point DS:DX to the ASCII string containing the drive and path that terminates with the name of the new directory; set AH equal to 39H, and execute interrupt 21H.

On return, if an error code 5 is indicated (access denied), the function was asked to create a copy of an existing directory and refused to do so.

Removing a Directory—Function 3A

To remove an existing directory, point DS:DX to the ASCII string containing the drive and path, set AH equal to 3AH, and execute interrupt 21H.

PC-DOS will not allow you to remove a directory that contains any files or subdirectories, nor will it allow you to remove the root directory!

Changing the Current Directory—Function 3B

This is the equivalent of the CD path command, where the current directory becomes the one specified in the command. To change the current directory, set DS:DX to point to the ASCII string containing the drive and path, set AH equal to 3BH, and execute interrupt 21H.

Getting the Current Directory—Function 47H

This function is the equivalent of the CD (CHDIR) command with no arguments. To get the current directory for a specific drive, put the drive number (0 = default, 1 = first drive, etc.) into DL, and point DS:SI to a 64-byte buffer where the function is to put the full path (but not the drive) of the current directory.

VERSION 2.0 UTILITY FUNCTIONS

Five utility functions related to file access have been supplied in version 2.0. Three of them relate to already existing functions; two are new. Of those related to versions 1 functions, two read settings that versions 1 functions could set but not read (the DTA and the read-after-write verify state), and one supplies disk parameter information without giving away the address of the file allocation table.

Get the Disk Transfer Address—Function 2F

Function 1A sets the disk transfer address. Version 2.0 supplies a function that will read it. To get the DTA, set AH equal to 2FH and execute interrupt 21H. On return, ES:BX contains the current disk transfer address.

Get the Read-after-Write Verify State—Function 54H

Function 2E allows you to set and reset the read-after-write verify state. Function 54H allows a program to read it. To read the read-after-write verify state, set AH equal to 54H and execute interrupt 21H. On return, AL = 0 if verify is off; AL = 1 if verify is on.

Functions 2EH and 54H are equivalent to the user-level VERIFY command.

Get the Disk Parameters—Function 36H

Function 1BH in versions 1 returns the address of the file allocation table. Programs can then compute the free space on the disk by looking into the allocation table.

In version 2.0, that same function returns a pointer to a byte containing a copy of the first byte of the file allocation table. In version 2.0 the file allocation tables for hard disks are not resident in memory, so it is no longer possible to hand out a pointer to them. Function 36H supplies immediately what had to be computed in versions 1. To get the disk parameters, set DL to the drive number, set AH equal to 36H, and execute interrupt 21H.

On return, if the drive designator was valid (AX returned not equal to FFFF), DX contains the total number of clusters on the drive, BX contains the number of free clusters, AX contains the number of sectors per cluster, and CX contains the number of bytes per sector. This is all you ever need to know about a disk.

Get or Set a File's Attribute—Function 43H

To get a file's attribute, set AL equal to zero, point DS:DX to the drive, path, and file name ASCII string, set AH equal to 43H, and execute interrupt 21H. The file's attribute is returned in CX.

To use this function to set a file's attribute, set AL equal to one and put the attribute in CX. The other arguments are the same.

Get and Set a File's Date and Time—Function 57H

In version 2.0, programs have the priviledge of being able to set the date and time that is stored in a file's directory entry. Versions 1 could read the date and time (just the date in version 1.0) from the FCB, but not set them. This function will either read or set the date and time, according to the value of AL on entry. If AL = 0, the date and time are read. If AL = 1, the date and time are set.

To access a file's date and time, pass the file handle in BX, set AL as needed, set AH equal to 57H, and execute interrupt 21H. The date is passed in DX, the time is passed in CX. The file's date and time are updated automatically by PC-DOS. Use of this function is not compulsory; PC-DOS updates the file's date and time each time something is written to the file.

ALLOCATION OF DISK SPACE TO A PC-DOS FILE

Disk space is allocated to a newly created or expanding file under control of the file allocation routines. These routines use the file allocation table (FAT) as a map of the occupied and available clusters on a diskette.

A cluster on a single-sided diskette is a single sector, 512 bytes. A cluster on a double-sided diskette is a unit of two contiguous sectors, 1024 bytes. A cluster on a fixed disk is also two contiguous sectors, but version 2.0 provides for other values. Function 36H can be used to find the cluster size in sectors and the number of bytes in a sector. (Function 36H is an improved version of function 1BH.)

On double-sided disks the clusters occupy both sides on one track before moving on to the next track. Any file greater than four clusters (eight sectors) will occupy parts of both sides of a double-sided diskette.

The file allocation table contains 12-bit entries (which can be represented in 3 hex digits) for each of the allocatable clusters on the diskette. Three hex digits are sufficient to address 4096 clusters, far more than are needed for the available diskette space in PC-DOS version 1.1. A brief computation— 320×1.5 bytes = 480 bytes—shows that less than 512 bytes will suffice for the mapping of all possible clusters on a single- or double-sided, eight-sector diskette. For convenience of access, a full sector is used for each copy of the file allocation table. The two FATs are found at sectors one and two, where sector zero is the first sector on the diskette.

In version 2.0, the FAT has to record the allocation of 360K bytes of diskette space, and megabytes of hard disk space. For nine-sector-per-track diskettes, the FATs are each two sectors long. The size of the fixed disk's FATs are established when the FDISK command defines the area of the disk that will be devoted to PC-DOS.

The file allocation routines use the FAT to keep track of the chain of clusters that make up a file. The address of the first cluster is kept in the directory entry for that file (at bytes 26–27). All file access routines use this as an index into the FAT to find the address of the next cluster, where in turn the address of the next cluster is found, and so on. The chain is terminated by a cluster value of FFx, where $8 <= x <= F$. The chain of clusters in the FAT is lengthened or shortened to match changes in the file size as they occur. When a file is shortened and clusters become free, their locations in the FAT are set to zero.

The allocation routines mark the position of unreadable clusters on the disk by FF7 entries in the FAT.

Given the file allocation table scheme for keeping track of the contents of a file on disk, if the FAT goes bad, the entire contents of the disk become unavailable. With this in mind, the system designers chose to keep two copies of the FAT on the disk, immediately following the boot sector.

Byte	Disk Type
FF	Double sided, eight sectors per track
FE	Single sided, eight sectors per track
FD	Double sided, nine sectors per track
FC	Single sided, nine sectors per track
F8	Fixed disk

Figure 2.6: Disk Type Indicated by First FAT Byte

The distinction between single- and double-sided diskettes is carried in the FAT. The first few sectors of each diskette are not allocatable clusters (they are the boot, the two FAT sectors, then the directory sectors), so the first two FAT entries are free for other purposes. Figure 2.6 shows the correspondence between the first byte of the FAT and the disk type. The second and third bytes are always FFFF.

SUMMARY

We have examined the two different types of file access strategies provided in PC-DOS: the file control block oriented type, available in versions 1.0, 1.1, and 2.0; and the path, file name, and address-space type, available in version 2.0. We have examined in detail all of the file access functions involved in both access strategies. We have seen how the file allocation tables are used to distribute the available disk space to files as they need it.

The access method in version 2.0 is recommended, because it is simpler to use and less restricted in concept. Microcomputer operating systems are ever improving. The file handling capabilities in version 2.0 demonstrate one such significant advance.

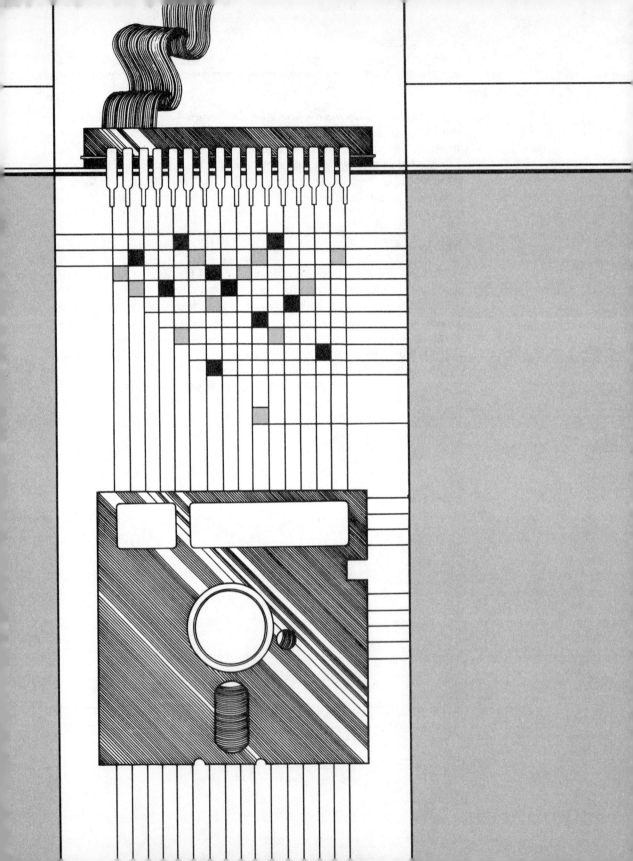

Disk Description and Usage

INTRODUCTION

This chapter describes how the diskettes and fixed disks are used by PC-DOS. It shows how the disks are divided into sectors, tracks, and sides, and explains how each one is numbered. In addition, it provides a list of the essential PC-DOS files found on a PC-DOS disk, describes their positions on both single- and double-sided diskettes, and examines the capacity of the space remaining for user files and programs. The file-independent disk access functions available in PC-DOS are described briefly, and the chapter concludes with notes on programming for nonstandard disk drives.

DISKETTE SECTOR LAYOUT IN PC-DOS

In this section we will examine the configuration of tracks and sectors on single- and double-sided diskettes for both versions 1 and version 2.0. We will also examine the sector layout for the IBM 10MB fixed (or hard) disk. Whenever the configurations differ between versions, two different values will be given, with versions 1 given first. Now for a few facts:

- A *sector* contains 512 bytes (half a K).
- There are eight or nine sectors in a diskette track. Versions 1 have eight sectors per track. Version 2.0 normally has nine sectors, but eight may be specified to maintain compatibility with versions 1.
- In versions 1 a diskette track contains 4096 bytes (4K).
- In version 2.0 a diskette track contains either 4096 bytes, or, more often, 4608 bytes (4.5K).
- There are 40 tracks on a diskette.
- A *single-sided* disk contains 320 or 360 sectors of 512 bytes each, for a total of 163,840 or 184,320 bytes.
- A single-sided disk is known as a 160K or 180K disk.
- A *double-sided* disk contains 640 or 720 sectors of 512 bytes each, for a total of 327,680 or 368,640 bytes.
- A double-sided disk is known as a 320K or 360K disk.

Before we move on to the hard disk information, we need to see how the word *track* has a rather loose meaning. A track is basically one of the concentric circles on a disk on which data can be recorded. When people first started talking about sectors per track, only one side of a disk could be used. When the technology advanced so that both sides could be used for data, the old concept of sectors per track stuck; we still use the sectors-per-track measure as if a track could only have one side. That is why you can say there are 40 tracks on a diskette at nine sectors per track, and come up with a total of 720 sectors on a diskette.

The picture changes when talking about hard disks. Because hard disks often have more than one platter, the track-as-concentric-circle idea gives way to the cylinder concept. A cylinder naturally describes all the same-radius concentric circles on which data can be recorded.

The Sector Layout for the Hard Disk

The IBM-supplied, 10-megabyte fixed disk [2.0] has two rotating disks (platters) within it. Data is recorded on both sides of each platter, giving four tracks (heads) per cylinder. The heads are numbered from zero to three.

Note that the information that follows is for the 10MB hard disk. Let's look at some facts:

- A sector is 512 bytes; it is the same size on a diskette as on a fixed disk.
- The 10MB fixed disk has 17 sectors per track.
- A track on a hard disk contains (17 × 512 =) 8704 bytes (8.5K).
- There are four tracks per cylinder.
- The 10MB hard disk has 306 cylinders, giving a total of 1224 tracks.
- Each of the cylinders has 68 sectors (34,816 bytes per cylinder), for a total of 10,653,696 bytes.

This total space available figure can be misleading. *First,* a fixed disk can be divided into four partitions, so that four separate and independent operating systems can coexist on a disk. The sizes of these partitions, in terms of number of cylinders, are defined by the user via the FDISK program. On a fixed disk you have control over the amount of space available to PC-DOS. *Second,* one whole cylinder and four sectors of each of the other cylinders are reserved, so the capacity is reduced to 305 cylinders of 64 sectors each, for a total of 9,994,240 bytes available for your programs and data. That is still a lot of space for data.

DISK SECTOR NUMBERING

PC-DOS has several numbering schemes—all using the name *sector*. There is one for all the sectors on a disk (logical or absolute); one for those sectors after the sixth sector on a diskette (relative), and one for just those sectors within a track.

Let's now look at the numbering scheme that covers all the sectors on a disk. PC-DOS calls this form of addressing the *logical sector number* or *absolute sector number*.

Logical Sector Numbering

This numbering scheme allocates addresses to sectors beginning at the very first sector on a disk. The sequence in which the sectors are numbered is not the same in versions 1 as it is in version 2.0. Let's first see how logical sector numbers are applied in versions 1.

Logical Sector Numbering in Versions 1

In PC-DOS versions 1, we have to give addresses to a total of 640 sectors. The first 320 sectors are on the first side of the disk and have the same addresses for both single- and double-sided disks. The first side's sector addresses are 0 to 319 (0H to 13FH) on both single- and double-sided disks. The second side of a double-sided disk has addresses 320 to 639 (140H to 27FH).

(By the way, the DOS version 1.1 manual, in its description of the interrupt 25H and 26H absolute disk read and write routines, uses the name *logical record number* in place of *logical sector number;* but they mean the same thing.)

Let's now look at the logical sector numbering scheme in version 2.0.

Logical Sector Numbering in Version 2.0

In version 2.0, the logical sector numbering scheme has changed. All the sectors on a track (or cylinder) are assigned numbers before moving on to the next track.

To get a clear picture of this, we will compare the logical sector numbering between versions 1 and version 2.0 on a double-sided diskette formatted for eight sectors per track.

Track zero, head zero has logical sector numbers 0–7. In versions 1, the sectors accessed by the second head on that track (track zero, head one) are numbered 320– 327. In version 2.0 they are numbered 8– 15. The consequences of this difference in logical sector numbering are usually hidden from the user, but sometimes you need to know that the difference exists.

Fixed Disk Logical Sector Numbering

Logical sector numbering on a hard disk follows the pattern established with version 2.0. All the tracks on one cylinder are numbered before moving on to the next cylinder. The sectors read by head zero are numbered 0– 16, those read by head one are numbered 17– 33, those read by head two are numbered 34– 50, and those read by head three are numbered 51– 67. The second cylinder begins at logical sector 68.

Relative Sector Numbering—One of PC-DOS's Failures

This numbering scheme is associated with the allocation of space to files. The sectors are numbered starting with the sixth sector on the disk. (The first five sectors don't have sector numbers in this scheme.) I suspect this anti-intuitive numbering scheme was adopted by a programmer for the purpose of saving three (or maybe eight) whole bytes of code, and a little execution time, in the file allocation routines. I resent the thousands of hours that this approach must be costing system-level users of DOS.

To compound the failure, the name *relative sector* is not applied with uniformity throughout the manuals. If you get used to what relative sector means in versions 1, you will have to readjust your thinking when you upgrade to 2.0. Relative sector is used in the version 2.0 manual (in DEBUG's Load command description) to describe what was called the logical sector in the versions 1 manuals.

Sectors within a Track

Now on to numbering the sectors within a track. If you need to compute addresses to find a location (a not-unusual requirement in computer programming), it makes life simpler to have those addresses start at zero instead of one. Following this principle, the sectors within a track would be numbered from 0 to 7 for each track. PC-DOS, however, numbers the sectors from 1 to 8. The ROM BIOS disk routines also use 1 to 8; perhaps someone at Microsoft followed an offbeat but historical precedent in adopting this odd way of numbering sectors within a track.

This use of 1 to 8 shows up in the absolute disk access routines provided by the interrupt 25H and 26H vectors, and in the diskette maps on pages C-9 to C-19 of the versions 1 DOS manual.

DISK MAPS, OR
WHAT'S WHERE ON A PC-DOS DISKETTE

The first few tracks of a diskette have a highly predictable content. This section is devoted to showing you that content. After the first few tracks, we know the rest of the disk will be either unused or populated here and there with bits and pieces (clusters) of the files listed in the directories. To find out how files are mapped into diskette sectors, read the "Allocation of Disk Space" section found at the end of Chapter 2.

Four maps are provided: two for single-sided (SS) and two for double-sided (DS) diskettes. The first two maps apply to eight-sector versions 1 diskettes.

For all versions of PC-DOS (1.0 through 2.0), the first few files are in the same sequence; they occur in the order shown in Figure 3.1.

File	Lengths:	SS,8	DS,8	SS,9	DS,9
Bootstrap sector		1	1	1	1
File Allocation Table—first copy		1	1	2	2
File Allocation Table—second copy		1	1	2	2
Directory		4	7	4	7

If the diskette was formatted with the /S option (which adds the system files to the diskette), the sequence continues:

File	Lengths:	SS,8	DS,8	SS,9	DS,9
IBMBIO.COM		4	4	10	10
IBMDOS.COM		13	13	34	34
COMMAND.COM		—	—	—	—

Figure 3.1: The First Few Files on a Formatted Diskette

The first four items in Figure 3.1—the bootstrap, two file allocation tables, and the directory—are not files addressable via the PC-DOS directory.

COMMAND.COM grows longer as the version number increases, to accommodate the improved commands. In version 1.0 it occupies 7 sectors, in version 1.1 it occupies 10 sectors, and in version 2.0 it occupies 36(!) sectors.

Figures 3.2 and 3.3 show the locations of the fixed-position files on single- (Figure 3.2) and double-sided (Figure 3.3) versions 1 disks. Following are the explanations of abbreviations of file names used in Figures 3.2 and 3.3:

Boot   = Bootstrap program
FAT   = One copy of the file allocation table

FAT   = Another copy of the same file allocation table
DIR   = Directory
BIO   = IBMBIO.COM
DOS   = IBMDOS.COM
COM   = COMMAND.COM
COM1   = Extra COMMAND.COM sectors in version 1.1
?   = Sectors belonging to files of your choice

In looking at these two figures, remember that the BIO, DOS, COM, and COM1 files will only exist on the diskette if it was formatted using the /S option.

(Track 0)	Sector #:	0	1	2	3	4	5	6	7
	Content:	Boot	FAT	FAT	DIR	DIR	DIR	DIR	BIO
(Track 1)	Sector #:	8	9	10	11	12	13	14	15
	Content:	BIO	BIO	BIO	DOS	DOS	DOS	DOS	DOS
(Track 3)	Sector #:	16	17	18	19	20	21	22	23
	Content:	DOS	DOS	DOS	DOS	DOS	DOS	DOS	DOS
(Track 4)	Sector #:	24	25	26	27	28	29	30	31
	Content:	COM	COM	COM	COM	COM	COM	COM	COM1
(Track 5)	Sector #:	32	33	34	35	36	37	38	39
	Content:	COM1	COM1	?	?	?	?	?	?

Figure 3.2: File Positions on an Eight-Sector-per-Track, Single-Sided Diskette

(Track 0 Side 0)	Sector #:	0	1	2	3	4	5	6	7
	Content:	Boot	FAT	FAT	DIR	DIR	DIR	DIR	DIR
(Track 0 Side 1)	Sector #:	320	321	322	323	324	325	326	327
	Content:	DIR	DIR	BIO	BIO	BIO	BIO	DOS	DOS
(Track 1 Side 0)	Sector #:	8	9	10	11	12	13	14	15
	Content:	DOS	DOS	DOS	DOS	DOS	DOS	DOS	DOS
(Track 1 Side 1)	Sector #:	328	329	330	331	332	333	334	335
	Content:	DOS	DOS	DOS	COM	COM	COM	COM	COM
(Track 2 Side 0)	Sector #:	16	17	18	19	20	21	22	23
	Content:	COM	COM	COM1	COM1	COM1	?	?	?
(Track 2 Side 1)	Sector #:	336	337	338	339	340	341	342	343
	Content:	?	?	?	?	?	?	?	?

Figure 3.3: File Positions on an Eight-Sector-per-Track, Double-Sided Diskette

It may be that you have seen enough of these tables by now. They are presented mostly for reference, so you might wish to skip careful scrutiny of Figures 3.4 and 3.5, which show slightly less extensive maps for version 2.0 disks. Notice how the logical sector numbers are different.

You may be reading this with a view to understanding the allocation of diskette space (sectors) to files. The process is straightforward and goes as

(Track 0)	Sector #:	0	1	2	3	4	5	6	7	8
	Content:	Boot	FAT	FAT	FAT	FAT	DIR	DIR	DIR	DIR
(Track 1)	Sector #:	9	10	11	12	13	14	15	16	17
	Content:	BIO	BIO	BIO	BIO	BIO	BIO	BIO	BIO	BIO
(Track 3)	Sector #:	18	19	20	21	22	23	24	25	26
	Content:	BIO	DOS	DOS	DOS	DOS	DOS	DOS	DOS	DOS
(Track 4)	Sector #:	27	28	29	30	31	32	33	34	35
	Content:	DOS	DOS	DOS	DOS	DOS	DOS	DOS	DOS	DOS
(Track 5)	Sector #:	36	37	38	39	40	41	42	43	44
	Content:	DOS	DOS	DOS	DOS	DOS	DOS	DOS	DOS	DOS
(Track 6)	Sector #:	45	46	47	48	49	50	51	52	53
	Content:	DOS	DOS	DOS	DOS	DOS	DOS	DOS	DOS	COM

Figure 3.4: File Positions on a Nine-Sector-per-Track, Single-Sided Diskette

(Track 0 Side 0)	Sector #:	0	1	2	3	4	5	6	7	8
	Content:	Boot	FAT	FAT	FAT	FAT	DIR	DIR	DIR	DIR
(Track 0 Side 1)	Sector #:	9	10	12	13	14	15	16	17	18
	Content:	DIR	DIR	DIR	BIO	BIO	BIO	BIO	BIO	BIO
(Track 1 Side 0)	Sector #:	19	20	21	22	23	24	25	26	27
	Content:	BIO	BIO	BIO	BIO	DOS	DOS	DOS	DOS	DOS
(Track 1 Side 1)	Sector #:	28	29	30	31	32	33	34	35	36
	Content:	DOS	DOS	DOS	DOS	DOS	DOS	DOS	DOS	DOS
(Track 2 Side 0)	Sector #:	37	38	39	40	41	42	43	44	45
	Content:	DOS	DOS	DOS	DOS	DOS	DOS	DOS	DOS	DOS
(Track 2 Side 1)	Sector #:	46	47	48	49	50	51	52	53	54
	Content:	DOS	DOS	DOS	DOS	DOS	DOS	DOS	DOS	DOS
(Track 3 Side 0)	Sector #:	55	56	57	58	59	60	61	62	63
	Content:	DOS	DOS	COM	COM	COM	COM	(COM continues)		

Figure 3.5: File Positions on a Nine-Sector-per-Track, Double-Sided Diskette

follows: On single-sided disks, sectors are allocated sequentially (if available) to a file. On double-sided disks, space is first allocated from one side of a track, then from the other side of the same track.

The different logical sector numbering schemes for versions 1 and version 2.0 can cause confusion. In versions 1, the second side of a track has logical sector numbers 320 greater than those on the first side. In version 2.0 the logical sector numbers for the second side of a track start at one greater than the last logical sector number on the first side of that track. This potential for confusion is perhaps one reason why the concept of *clusters* came into being.

What's Where on a Fixed Disk

Fixed disks are supported by version 2.0. As we have already seen, the 10MB fixed disk can be divided into four partitions, so that four different operating systems and their files can exist on the same disk. This means that the start of the PC-DOS partition may not be at the beginning of the hard disk. However, the arrangement of the files at the beginning of the PC-DOS partition is the same as for the diskettes.

DISKETTE CAPACITIES

Using 160K as a descriptor of the capacity of an eight-sector-per-track diskette is not exactly accurate, but it is reasonable. It matches the use of 64K for 65,536 bytes of memory. There is overhead associated with storing data on a diskette (the directory, file allocation table, etc.), so the whole 163,840 bytes of a 160K disk are never all available for your data. When referring to disk capacities, you have the choice of being accurate (which is not often necessary) or being approximate (using 160K) and remembering that you are being approximate. For those who are interested in accurate information, here it is. (Note: Figure 3.6 summarizes the capacities derived in the next few paragraphs. You are encouraged to skip the detail and go straight to it.)

Single-Sided Diskette Capacity—Versions 1

On a 160K, single-sided disk, there is room for a total of 163,840 bytes of data. The first seven sectors are always occupied by the disk bootstrap, two copies of the file allocation table (FAT), and four sectors of directory entries. These files take up 7 × 512 = 3584 bytes. So the maximum available space on a single-sided, eight-sector-per-track diskette is 160,256 bytes.

If the diskette was formatted with the /S option, the next 4 sectors are always occupied by IBMBIO.COM, the next 13 by IBMDOS.COM, and the next 7 (version 1.0) or 10 (version 1.1) by COMMAND.COM. This is the bare minimum overhead for a functional PC-DOS disk. This /S option overhead is a further reduction of 24 (version 1.0) or 27 (version 1.1) sectors, or 12,228 or 13,824 bytes, thereby leaving 147,968 or 146,432 bytes for data and programs.

If the single-sided disk is to be used purely for files of data (no programs), you will lose just under 2% of the space to overhead (under both versions 1.0 and 1.1) and end up with 160,256 bytes available for data. If the disk contains PC-DOS, about 10% (9.7% in version 1.0, 10.6% in 1.1) is consumed by overhead, thereby leaving 147,968 (version 1.0) or 146,432 bytes (version 1.1) for programs and data.

Single-Sided, Nine-Sector Diskette Capacity—Version 2.0

The following figures are for a diskette that has been formatted for nine sectors per track:

- A nine-sector-per-track diskette has room for 184,320 bytes of information. The boot record, the two file allocation tables (each FAT is two sectors long in nine-sector diskettes), and the directory occupy 4608 bytes (nine sectors). The available remaining space is 179,712 bytes, which is the figure you see when you run CHKDSK.

- If the diskette was formatted with the /S option, the system files (IBMBIO.COM, IBMDOS.COM, and COMMAND.COM) occupy another 80 tracks, or 40,960 bytes.

- If the single-sided disk is to be used purely for files of data (no programs), in version 2.0 you lose 2.5% of the space to overhead and end up with 179,712 bytes available for data. If the nine-sector diskette contains PC-DOS version 2.0, almost 25% is consumed by overhead, leaving 138,752 bytes for programs and data. One quarter of the disk may seem like a large amount of space to lose, but if you are using version 2.0, you will probably be operating with a PC that has two double-sided drives, if not a fixed disk.

Double-Sided Diskette Capacity—Versions 1

The only difference in overhead between single- and double-sided disks is three extra sectors allocated to the directory to give it capacity for 112 files instead of 64.

On a 320K double-sided disk, formatted without the /S option, there are 322,560 bytes of available space for your data. A double-sided diskette containing PC-DOS (i.e., formatted with the /S option) has space for 308,736 bytes (version 1.1) of program and data files.

Double-Sided Diskette Capacity—Version 2.0

The following figures are for a double-sided diskette that has been formatted for nine sectors per track:

- A nine-sector, double-sided diskette has room for 368,640 bytes of information. The boot record, the two file allocation tables (each FAT is two sectors long on nine-sector diskettes), and the seven-sector directory occupy 6144 bytes (twelve sectors). The available remaining space is 362,496 bytes, which is the figure you see when you run CHKDSK.

- As with the single-sided diskette, if the diskette was formatted with the /S option, the system files (IBMBIO.COM, IBMDOS.COM, and COMMAND.COM) occupy another 80 tracks, or 40,960 bytes.

- If the double-sided disk is to be used purely for files of data (no programs), in version 2.0 you lose about 1.5% of the space (6144 bytes) to overhead and end up with 362,496 bytes for data.

- If the diskette contains PC-DOS version 2.0, just under 13% of the space (47,104 bytes) is consumed by overhead, leaving 321,536 bytes for programs and data.

Double-Sided, Eight-Sector Diskette Capacity—Version 2.0

If a double-sided diskette has been formatted for eight sectors per track under version 2.0, and if no system files are added to the diskette, the capacity figures are the same (322,560 bytes for data and programs) as for versions 1.

A version 2.0 eight-sector, double-sided diskette formatted with the /S option will have 282,000 bytes for programs and data. Just under 24% of the space goes to overhead. A summary of these capacity figures appears in Figure 3.6.

DISK ACCESS MECHANISMS

PC-DOS has available absolute disk access routines in addition to those related to file structure access (described in Chapter 2). This disk access

Single Sided/ Double Sided	Sectors per track	Version	Bytes Available (Disk formatted without /S option)	Bytes Available (Disk formatted with /S option)
SS	8	1.0	160,256	147,968
SS	8	1.1	160,256	146,432
SS	8	2.0	160,256	119,296
SS	9	2.0	179,712	138,752
DS	8	1.1	322,560	308,736
DS	8	2.0	322,560	282,600
DS	9	2.0	362,496	321,536

Figure 3.6: A Summary of Diskette Capacities

capability provides, within PC-DOS, alternatives to the ROM BIOS diskette I/O routines. As usual, to enhance the portability of your PC-DOS programs, instead of using the disk access routines in ROM BIOS, we recommend that you use the PC-DOS disk routines.

The relevant interrupts are as follows:

    25H   Absolute disk read
    26H   Absolute disk write

These routines read or write any number (specified by CX) of consecutive 512-byte sectors, starting at the sector number found in DX. (DOS documentation calls this the "beginning logical record number," which is the same as the absolute sector number.)

The buffer into which the data is read or from which it is to be written is specified in DS:BX; the drive number (0 = A, 1 = B, etc.) is specified in AL.

On return, the carry flag (CF) will be zero if the transfer was successful. If CF is 1, AL will contain at least one of the following error codes:

    80H   Attachment failed to respond
    40H   Seek operation failure
    20H   Controller failure
    10H   Bad CRC on diskette read
    08H   DMA overrun on operation
    04H   Requested sector not found
    03H   Write attempt on write-protected diskette
    02H   Address mark not found
    00H   Error other than those above

Note that whether or not the transfer was successful, on return the stack will have grown by one word, because the interrupt call saved the original flags before executing your disk operation. Be sure to use a pop instruction to remove that word from the stack whether or not you want its contents. All the registers, except the segment register, are destroyed by this call.

PROGRAMMING FOR NONSTANDARD DISK DRIVES

You may want to add nonstandard diskette drives or hard disks to your PC. It can be done; the amount of work it takes to add a drive or drives varies according to how unlike the standard drives your drives are. I have not yet seen a PC where the first diskette drive, from which the system is booted, has been replaced with a drive that is not hardware-compatible with IBM's diskette drives (some of which have been manufactured by Tandon Inc. and by Control Data Corporation).

Programming for your own drives can become quite complex. What follows will serve as the barest minimum groundwork required to understand the task.

Alternate Diskette Drives

ROM BIOS contains a set of parameters specific to the IBM 5¼-inch disk drives. The ROM BIOS parameters (at F000:EFC7) are found in a table pointed to by interrupt vector 1EH. This vector may be pointed at another, similarly structured table to accommodate a (not very) different diskette drive.

The diskette I/O interrupt vector 13H also points into ROM BIOS, to the diskette I/O routines at F000:EC59. If you are willing to go to the extent of writing your own diskette I/O routines, you can add other drives. Your I/O routines will have to be calling-sequence and result compatible with the ROM BIOS routines if they are to be used by PC-DOS.

Alternate Fixed Disk Drives

If you have an IBM fixed disk, the controlling software resides in ROM on the fixed disk adaptor card. The fixed disk BIOS is a little more generous in the variety of drives it can handle, probably because IBM may later offer hard disks with different configurations. Interrupt vector 13H (normally for diskette I/O) points to this code if a fixed disk is installed.

Interrupt 41H is a vector to the fixed disk parameter table. System initialization sets the vector to point to one of the entries in the table of the four different drive types found in fixed disk BIOS ROM. This vector can be changed to point to a table of parameters for other disk drives. If a fixed disk is installed, interrupt 40H becomes a vector to the diskette I/O routines.

SUMMARY

We have seen how all kinds of diskettes, as well as the PC-DOS partition in the fixed disk, contain the same first few files: the boot sector, two copies of the file allocation table, and the directory. We have seen how the capacity of diskettes varies according to the number of sectors per track, the version of PC-DOS used to format them, and whether the /S option was used to transfer the system files when they were formatted. The different sector numbering schemes, and the functions for reading and writing sectors, have been reviewed.

The next chapter is devoted to the set of functions that PC-DOS provides for accessing the keyboard.

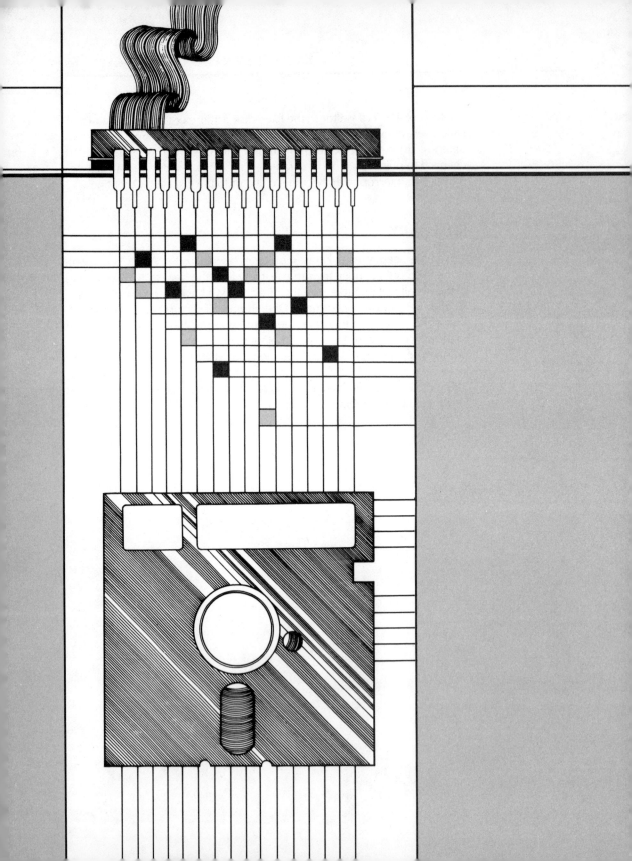

PC-DOS and the Keyboard

INTRODUCTION

PC-DOS provides a rich set of functions that a program can use to access characters entered at the keyboard. These functions permit the construction of a flexible and friendly interface with the user of your program. The somewhat formidable task of creating your own command processor (COMMAND.COM) is made simpler by the variety of PC-DOS keyboard input functions available.

Following are the issues to consider when getting characters from the keyboard:

- Control break handling
- Keyboard status sampling
- To echo or not to echo
- To wait or not to wait
- Buffered input of character strings
- Dumping of unwanted keystrokes
- Standard interpretation of nontext keystrokes
- Changing the meaning of the keys

PC-DOS provides a set of keyboard access functions, from which you can choose one or more to meet your needs. All the keyboard functions exist under interrupt 21H.

Features of the relevant keyboard functions are included in the following discussions of each issue. The keyboard status sampling and buffered input functions (numbers B and A, respectively) are described in the so-titled sections. Function number C, which clears the keyboard buffer and invokes another keyboard function, is described in the section "Dumping Unwanted Keystrokes." The remaining keyboard functions, numbers 1, 6, 7, and 8, are presented in the section "Single-Character Input Functions." The chapter closes with a summary of the keyboard access functions.

CTRL BREAK PROCESSING

The standard action for PC-DOS to take when Ctrl Break is entered at the keyboard is to execute interrupt 23H. Interrupt 23H is part of PC-DOS; it points to the code for processing the "stop everything right now" command—Ctrl Break.

However, your program may not want to lose control when a Ctrl Break is encountered. It has two options for preventing this—it can trap the Ctrl Break interrupt, or it can use keyboard input functions that don't check for the Ctrl Break key combination. The keyboard input functions that don't check for Ctrl Break are the single-character input functions 6 and 7; all others check.

KEYBOARD STATUS SAMPLING

A program frequently has to know if there is a character pending. The function that checks keyboard status (function B, interrupt 21H) tells you this. On return, AL = FF if a character is pending; AL = 0 if not. The character is not returned by this function—only the status is returned.

TO ECHO OR NOT TO ECHO

There are times when it is inappropriate to echo to the screen the character entered at the keyboard. PC-DOS provides for these times when it is operating in single-character mode; it gives you three function calls (6, 7, and 8) that do not echo the character entered at the keyboard.

Functions 7 and 8 are the same, except for their handling of Ctrl Break. They both wait for a character to be typed at the keyboard. When one is ready, they return the character in AL without echoing it to the screen. A character is ready when it has been typed but not retrieved via function calls. When functions 7 and 8 are called and a character is ready, they return it immediately in AL .

Function 6 also does not echo a character entered at the keyboard. This function is described at the end of this chapter.

TO WAIT OR NOT TO WAIT

The question is whether your program, when accessing the keyboard, is willing to be suspended (to wait) until a character is entered at the keyboard.

Let's consider two different programs. At a certain stage of operation, the first program has nothing else to do apart from wait for the next character to be entered at the keyboard. A more complex program may always have work to do, errands to run, while waiting for the rather long-intervaled input from the human being, who relies on the relatively slow mechanical activation of several pounds of flesh to communicate. All right, a finger only weighs a few ounces. The first program can afford to wait; the more complex program cannot.

The choice of waiting or not waiting applies only to single-character input, functions 1, 6, 7, and 8. The program using buffered keyboard input (function A) always waits.

To Wait

The first program is prepared to wait for the next character, and uses functions 1, 7, or 8 for single-character input. These functions wait for keyboard input (unless the character is ready, in which case they have no reason to wait). Functions 7 and 8 do not echo the character to the screen, and function 7 does not check the character for Ctrl Break.

Set AH to 1, 7, or 8, and execute interrupt 21H to wait for single-character input. If a character is pending, the functions return the character immediately in AL. If no character is pending, the functions wait until one is entered at the keyboard, then return it in AL.

Not to Wait

The more complex program needs to know whether a character is pending. To read the keyboard it can use either function 6, direct console I/O (with DL set equal to FF), or function B, keyboard status check, in combination with other keyboard input functions.

Function 6 returns immediately—with a character if one was ready, or without one if not. The more complex program can check the zero flag on return from function 6 to see whether it has time to do other nonkeyboard work. (See the end of this chapter for the full description of function 6.)

Function B, keyboard status check, tells the program when a character is pending. After that, one of functions 1, 6, 7, and 8 can be called to get the character. It can be seen that the author of the more complex program has quite a variety of options to choose from.

In summary, if you want a function that will return with at least one character, use functions 1, 7, 8, or A. If your program has better things to do than wait for keyboard input, use function 6 alone, or the combination of function B (for status checking) and then your choice of functions 1, 6, 7, and 8.

BUFFERED INPUT OF CHARACTER STRINGS

Buffered keyboard input is provided by function A under interrupt 21H. This function is the heart of the software used to support the PC-DOS editing keys and the editing of single lines in EDLIN. Keyboard access via this function lets the user play with all the PC-DOS in-line editing capabilities before the Enter key is used.

To receive an input string terminated by a carriage return, your program will correctly set up an input buffer, then call function A. This function accepts characters until the Enter key is pressed by the user. (A correctly set-up input buffer is one where the first byte contains N and the buffer is of length N + 2.)

The user types characters, correcting (editing) as necessary, then finally types a carriage return, or as it is known in the PC-DOS world, the Enter key. The function returns to your program with the second byte of the buffer indicating the number of characters entered, excluding the carriage return. The last of the N (or less) characters is always 0DH, the carriage return.

As when the user is entering or editing a line within EDLIN, if there is no more room in the buffer for any character other than the carriage return, a bell sounds when another character is typed, and that character is ignored.

To call the buffered keyboard input function, point DS:DX to the prepared buffer, set AH equal to A, and execute interrupt 21H.

DUMPING UNWANTED KEYSTROKES

It is sometimes desirable in a program to accept input from the keyboard only after disposing of characters that might be in the input stream for other reasons. Function C (clear the keyboard input buffer and execute an input function) has been provided for this purpose. Function C is an envelope function to the other keyboard functions 1, 6, 7, 8, and A; your choice of one of them is called by function C after the input buffer has been cleared.

To clear the keyboard input buffer and invoke a keyboard input function, set the desired input function number in AL, then set AH to C; set DS:DX if you are calling function A; set DL if you are calling function 6; and execute interrupt 21H.

For example, if your program is to be used by children who are new to computers, there is a chance they will be typing on the keyboard long before your program is ready to read what they type. If the program asks for the user's name, the sequence of operations should be as follows:

1. Display the "What is your name?" question.
2. Clear the keyboard input buffer.
3. Call the buffered input function.

Your program would probably use function 9 (string output) to display the question, then take the shortcut offered by function C, calling it with A (the buffered input function's number) in the AH register.

STANDARD INTERPRETATION OF NONTEXT KEYSTROKES

This is a plea for uniformity in the interpretation of keystroke combinations and individual keystrokes that we, as users, use.

Software users often get stuck with a program that uses nonstandard and unique interpretations of one or more keystroke control functions. For instance, the WordStar word processing program is odd about its interpretation of the Del key. For most sane software, striking the Del key deletes the character at the cursor. The WordStar program (for the IBM PC) backspaces before deleting a character!

Programmers, and other people (such as philosophers) who are trained to consider all the different options, tend not to reach the most obvious solution to a problem. A programmer may produce splendid trains of logic to support his or her oddball choice of keystroke interpretation. The person in charge of the overall coherence of a project may yield, knowing that decent programmers are hard to find. So we get the odd and inconvenient, and sometimes, but almost never, a stroke of genius.

IBM has recognized the tendency of software package developers to come up with odd keystroke interpretations. For the benefit of us all, and of IBM's reputation, IBM has supplied in Table 27 in the Technical Reference manual (page 3-17), a piece entitled Keyboard—Commonly Used Functions. This table shows a set of (suggested) standard interpretations for the common key and key combinations available on the PC keyboard. Unlike the keyboard itself, the table has no awkward or odd features. The key interpretations can be recommended for their practicality. The full-screen editor that comes with QNX (a UNIX-like operating system for the PC) follows the conventions given in table 27, and it's the best editor I've seen by far.

Table 27 is where you can find what the Scroll Lock key is for. (It changes the functions of the cursor movement keys from cursor movement to whole screen (scrolling) movement.) It is instructive to review that table; we would all benefit if software for the PC adopted the standards suggested. Now let's return from the plea for standards to look at the flexibility we have in assigning meanings to nontext keystrokes.

CHANGING THE MEANING OF THE KEYS

This section gives an overview of the processing that occurs during the time that your finger depresses a key on the keyboard and a character (or characters) appears on the display. If you are new to computers, this may take a little time to absorb. Even if you are not new to computers, at the end of this section you may find that you know more about the IBM PC keyboard and character translation than you ever thought you wanted to know.

Before examining a map of our journey, please note that if you plan to use the keyboard key reassignment feature in version 2.0, you need only read that particular section and learn the difference between scan codes, ASCII, and IBM Extended ASCII.

In our discussion we will first examine how the keys are arranged on the keyboard, how the keys are numbered, and what scan codes are. While on the subject of codes, we will look at the difference between scan codes, ASCII codes, and IBM Extended ASCII codes. Next we will examine the different software components that are brought into play when a key is depressed.

To see where we might make changes in order to alter the meaning of a key, we will follow the path taken by the keystroke codes when the F1 key is pressed, noting where diversions and reconstruction might affect changes in the meaning of the F1 key along the way. After that, we will show how version 2.0 makes it a simple task to change the meaning of a key. Let's begin with the keyboard and its scan codes.

The Keyboard Layout

A glance at the IBM PC keyboard reveals three major groups of keys: (1) the (almost standard) typewriter keyboard (in the middle); (2) the ten function keys (on the left); and (3) (on the right) a group of keys serving two purposes, numeric data input and cursor control.

The keys are numbered (starting at 1, not 0) from left to right and top to bottom, within the three key groups (typewriter, function, and numeric/cursor). This number, which corresponds to the position of the key on the keyboard, is called the *scan code*.

The Keyboard's Scan Codes

Appendix K of the version 2.0 BASIC manual includes a diagram of the keyboard, which shows the scan code for each key. In case you do not have that diagram, here are the scan codes for each keyboard group.

The Typewriter Group's Scan Codes

The typewriter group of keys is the rectangle formed by the Esc key at top left, the backspace key at top right, the Alt key at bottom left, and the CapsLock key at bottom right. The rectangle includes the PrtSc key, but its perfection is marred by the intrusion of the left half of the Ins key, which belongs in the third key group.

The Esc key has a scan code of 1. The left-to-right, top-to-bottom numbering scheme gives the backspace key a scan code of 14, the Tab key a scan code of 15, the return (Enter) key a scan code of 28, the Ctrl key a code of 29, and so on, up to the CapsLock key's scan code, which is 58.

The Function Keys' Scan Codes

The function keys are numbered next, again from left to right and top to bottom. The F1 key's scan code is 59, F2 is 60, and F10 is 68.

These are the keys whose meaning we most likely will want to change. The ten function keys can mean anything the currently running program chooses. Their presence permits software developers to provide users with single keystrokes that can save a lot of time and confusion. You probably have seen how BASIC uses the F1, F2, and F3 keys to mean LIST, RUN, and LOAD, and how EDLIN and PC-DOS at the prompt level use those same keys for in-line editing functions.

The Numeric/Cursor-Control Group's Scan Codes

Finally, the remaining right-hand keys are numbered. The NumLock key's scan code is 69, the + key's code is 78, and the scan code for the Del key (the last code on the keyboard) is 83.

Now that we know that the scan code is just a key position, let's see how the scan code, or something like it, is used in extended ASCII codes.

ASCII and Extended ASCII Codes

Several keystrokes and keystroke combinations, such as the function keys, the Home key, and the PgUp and PgDn keys, are not represented in the full ASCII 256-character set that the IBM PC supports. To resolve the problem of how to tell a calling program that those keys have been pressed, IBM has devised another way of passing nonstandard keystrokes to the application programs. They have introduced "Extended ASCII" codes to represent nonstandard keystroke and keystroke combinations.

Extended ASCII codes are two-byte codes, where the first byte is null (zero). The second byte has, despite the name, no connection with ASCII. It is usually the scan code of the primary key pressed. Table 26 in the Technical Reference manual (page 3-14) and page G-6 of your BASIC manual provide a match between the second byte of an extended code and the key or key combinations that it represents.

This arrangement is a little strange, but it works reasonably well for some of the extended codes. It is fairly convenient to represent the F1 key as 0,59 and the Home key as 0,71.

Let's look at the software components that work for us when our program gets a character from the keyboard.

From Fingertip to Application Program

When you strike a key, the keyboard sends a scan code to the PC; the scan code is received by the PC's ROM BIOS keyboard interrupt routine. The ROM BIOS keyboard I/O routines convert the scan code (or codes) into ASCII or Extended ASCII, and hand them out in a single word to software that seeks input from the keyboard via interrupt 16H. Often, it is PC-DOS that has called interrupt 16H. Let's review that process.

When characters are returned to an application program that uses the PC-DOS keyboard input functions, the keystroke information has traveled from the keyboard to ROM BIOS via interrupt 9H, from ROM BIOS to PC-DOS via interrupt 16H, and from PC-DOS to the applications program via interrupt 21H. (Note: We are not seeing the full complexity here, just the essentials. For more detail, consult the Keyboard sections of the Technical Reference manual, pages 2-14 to 2-17, pages 3-11 to 3-19, and the ROM BIOS listings.)

Before we look at how we can change the meanings of keys, we need to look a little more closely at the path taken by information from the keyboard before it reaches our program, and how that information gets translated along the way. Once we know the path, we will see that there are several points at which changes can be made. Let's follow the path of the F1 keystroke from keyboard to applications program.

The Path That F1 Takes

When the F1 key is pressed, scan code 59 is sent to the PC, generating a keyboard interrupt. Interrupt 9H points to the keyboard interrupt service routine in ROM BIOS. This routine translates the F1 key's scan code (59) into a two-byte extended ASCII code (0,59).

System-level programs (such as PC-DOS) that want to get the next character from the keyboard use interrupt 16H, which points to the keyboard I/O routines in ROM BIOS. The keyboard I/O routines return the F1 keystroke as an extended code in the AX register, with AL = 0 and AH = 59. When the applications-level programs (the type that you and I usually write) want a character from the keyboard, they call the PC-DOS keyboard input function (number 1, 6, 7, or 8) to get a character.

The PC-DOS routines return characters one at a time. One call to the function gets the character code, unless PC-DOS has an extended code to give out. PC-DOS tells its caller that it has an extended code to return to the caller by returning with AL = 0. When the applications program sees the zero code, it must call the keyboard input function one more time to get the extended code.

Changing the Meaning of F1

We will now look at three approaches for changing the meaning of F1. The first takes much work; the second avoids tinkering with the system; the third does what we want most economically. Let's look at the "rewrite everything" approach.

The Big Rewrite

This approach involves the most work. Your applications program takes over all the functions supplied by the ROM BIOS interrupt routines, the ROM BIOS character translation routines, and the PC-DOS keyboard input function calls. To use this approach, you must

1. write the substitute keyboard interrupt routine and point vector 9H to it;
2. write the substitute character-translation-and-fetch routine and point interrupt vector 16H to it; and
3. write a filtering routine that catches all keyboard input functions within interrupt 21H, passing on other function calls untouched, and point interrupt 21H to it.

All this work is not recommended unless you have a lot of time on your hands and are desperate to produce the quickest response possible to each character entered at the keyboard. Reviewing this wholesale rewrite approach has, however, revealed a few less laborious possibilities.

The Minimal Intervention Approach

One approach that totally avoids tinkering within the system is to have your applications program do the character translation. For example, your applications program could have a central routine that

1. gets characters from the keyboard using the (usual) PC-DOS interrupt 21H keyboard input function calls;
2. compares those characters (and extended codes) against your table holding the characters or extended codes to be translated (the table also holds their translation); and
3. on finding a match, translates the character before passing it to the rest of the applications program.

This approach does not involve changes to any interrupt vectors.

If the translations between scan codes and ASCII or extended codes that ROM BIOS performs do not conflict with your needs, the cleanest and most economical way to provide the (additional) translation you need is to trap the calls to ROM BIOS that are made via interrupt 16H.

The Economical Approach

The most economical approach is to point interrupt vector 16H to your own routine, which would

1. accept the calls that normally go to the ROM BIOS keyboard I/O routines via interrupt 16H;
2. pass those calls on, unchanged, to the address in ROM BIOS that vector 16H normally points to (i.e., the value normally found in locations 58H – 5BH);
3. look at, and where necessary translate, the characters or extended codes that the ROM BIOS routines return; and
4. pass those characters to whichever routine it was that thought it was calling the ROM BIOS I/O routines directly.

If your translation requirements involve substituting several characters for a single character or extended code, your routines would also have to be smart enough to pass the multiple character strings out to the caller, one by one.

Note that under this method any software that uses vector 16H (not just PC-DOS) will have characters translated by your routine.

Under any of these methods, be sure that when your software terminates, it resets all the interrupt vectors it changed!

Adding routines and substituting interrupt vector contents is not prohibitively difficult, but buying and using version 2.0 may be a better approach for your needs.

Keyboard Key Reassignment in Version 2.0

Version 2.0 makes it fairly easy to change the meanings of various keystrokes and keystroke combinations. The reassignment capability costs a few bytes of memory (about 1.5K), but that is its only disadvantage. Let's now discuss what to do to make key reassignments happen in version 2.0, then go through an example where we change the meaning of the F10 key so that a single keystroke at the PC-DOS prompt level produces a directory listing.

Changing the Meaning of a Key in Version 2.0

The meaning of a key is reassigned when a unique sequence of characters, known as a control sequence, is seen by keyboard functions 1, 2, 6, and 9 within interrupt 21H. Key reassignment only operates if the ANSI.SYS software is incorporated in PC-DOS. ANSI.SYS is a device driver for keyboard control. To incorporate it into PC-DOS, add the command

    DEVICE = ANSI.SYS

to your configuration file. If you don't yet have that file, you can create it using COPY, as follows. Type

    COPY CON CONFIG.SYS
    DEVICE = ANSI.SYS
    <F6>

< F6>means the F6 key. If you are going to use COPY to create the configuration file, be careful that CONFIG.SYS does not exist, or that you don't mind destroying it if it does. If in doubt, use EDLIN instead of COPY.

Once the CONFIG.SYS file exists, reboot PC-DOS to get the device driver included in the resident portion of PC-DOS.

To reassign the meaning of an ASCII or extended code, write a small routine that sends out, via DOS function calls 1, 2, 6, or 9, the correct stream of control characters to effect the change in meaning desired. Sending a string to the display (function 9) is simplest. The stream of control characters is as follows:

1. The Esc code, a byte value 1BH
2. The [character
3. A string of ASCII characters that express in decimal the ASCII code for the character being mapped
4. The ; character
5. The decimal ASCII value of the character that replaces the one being translated
6. The p character

Chapter Thirteen of the version 2.0 DOS manual gives examples and more information.

If you are reassigning the meaning of an extended code, or replacing an ASCII-representable character with an extended code, items 3 and 5 above use a string of characters that expresses in decimal the extended code. The two extended code values are separated by a semicolon.

Giving It a Whirl

You can experimentally change F10 to mean DIR by using DEBUG. Here's how:

Call DEBUG. Use the assemble command to enter the code that sends a control sequence to the display. Type the following lines (exactly):

```
a 100
mov ah,9
mov dx,200
int 21
<return>
e 200 1b'[0;68;"dir";13p$'
g=100 107
q
```

Now you are back at the prompt. Press the F10 key.

What Happened in the Whirl

The three-instruction program at CS:100 calls function 9 within interrupt 21H. It sends to the display the string at DS:200 (DEBUG has been kind enough to set the segment registers for us; CS = DS).

The enter instruction creates, at DS:200, the control sequence that reassigns the meaning of the F10 key. Let's examine that control sequence:

- 1b is the code for Esc.
- ′ tells the Enter command to treat the following characters as a string.
- 0;68 is the extended code for F10.
- ; separates the code from its new meaning.
- ″ tells the control sequence processor that the next characters will replace the keystroke(s) being translated.
- dir is part of the translation.
- ;13 adds a carriage return to "dir".
- p is always the last character of the control sequence.
- $ terminates the string that function 9 puts out.
- ′ terminates the string for the Enter command.

We have now seen how version 2.0 can reassign the meanings of keys. It was a long journey. The rest of the chapter describes the single-character input functions, ending with a summary of all the keyboard access functions.

SINGLE-CHARACTER INPUT FUNCTIONS

We have mentioned the four PC-DOS single-character input functions here and there, but we haven't provided in one place a description of all their features. We'll do that now. Three of the input functions always get a single character from the keyboard (assuming there is no Ctrl Break intervention); the other, function 6, returns immediately, even if no character is available. The functions differ in their Ctrl Break detection and whether or not the character is echoed to the screen.

Functions 1 and 8—
Single-Character Input with Ctrl Break Detection

These two functions are the same, except that function 8 does not echo the input character to the display. These functions wait for a character to be typed at the keyboard (unless one is ready), then return it in AL.

To implement this function, set AH equal to 1 or 8 and execute interrupt 21H. On return the character will be in AL.

If keys or key combinations are pressed that cannot be represented by a standard ASCII code, an extended code is returned. When this happens AL will contain 00, and another call has to be made to the function to get the extended code.

Function 7—
Single-Character Input without Ctrl Break Detection

Function 7 is a single-character input function with no echo. It is the same as function 8, except that no check is made for Ctrl Break. The function waits for a character (unless one is ready), then returns it in AL.

To call the function, set AH to 7, and execute interrupt 21H. On return, the character is in AL; it has not been echoed to the screen.

Function 6—
Single-Character Input
without Wait, Alias Direct Console I/O

Function 6 is used either for input from the keyboard or for output to the screen, but not both at the same time. If on entry DL = FF, it is a keyboard function; otherwise, it is an output function, where the character in DL is output to the screen and no keyboard interaction takes place.

This is the one keyboard input function that, if there is no ready character, does not wait for a character to be typed. On return, the zero flag is a status indicator. If the zero flag is set, there was no character ready. If a character was ready, the zero flag is clear and the character is in AL. Remember that for function 6 to act as a keyboard input function, DL must be set to FF.

SUMMARY OF THE KEYBOARD ACCESS FUNCTIONS

The seven keyboard access functions can be separated into the following groups: the five different keyboard input functions, one of which returns status information; a separate keyboard status checking function; and an envelope function that calls one of five input functions after clearing the input buffer.

To invoke one of these functions, put the function number in register AH, set the arguments (if any) as necessary, and execute interrupt 21H. In the summary in Figure 4.1, a function that "waits for" a character will return immediately if one is ready.

Function Number	Purpose and Arguments
1	Waits for and echoes a character, which is returned in AL; Ctrl Break is detected.
6	If DL = FF, returns with character in AL if one was ready, zero flag is set if none ready. No echo is performed, and Ctrl Break is not detected.
7	Waits for a character, which is returned in AL. No echo is performed, and Ctrl Break is not detected.
8	Waits for a character, which is returned in AL. Same as function 1, except the character is not echoed. Ctrl Break is detected.
A	Waits for a string (which may be empty), terminated by the Enter key. Full PC-DOS in-line editing features are supported. String is echoed; Ctrl Break is detected. On entry, DS:DX points to an input buffer.
B	Checks keyboard status. Does not return a character. If one is available, AL = FF; if no characters are ready, AL = 00.
C	Clears keyboard input buffer and invokes keyboard input function. On entry, AL specifies which of functions 1, 6, 7, 8, and A is to be invoked after clearing the buffer.

Figure 4.1: Keyboard Access Function Summary

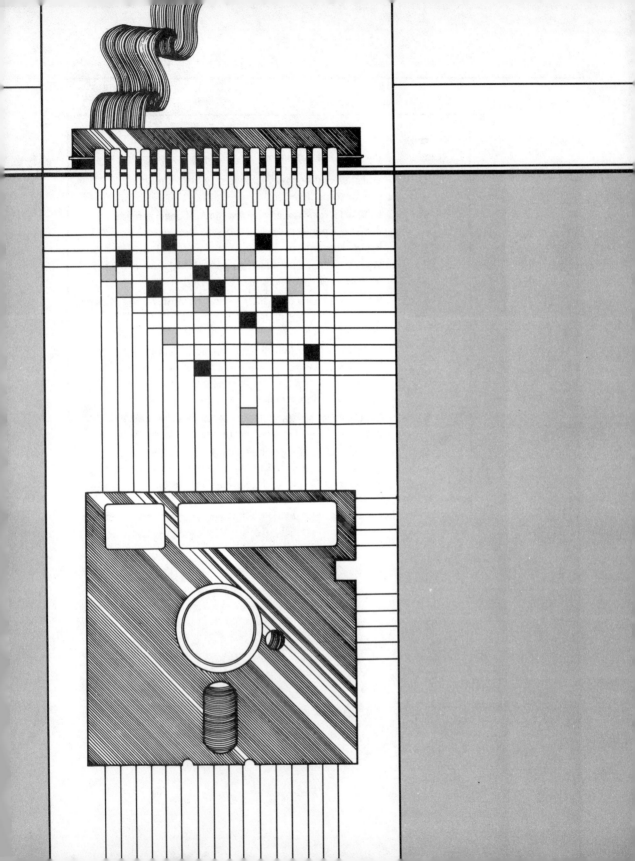

Output to the Monochrome and Color/Graphics Monitors

INTRODUCTION

This chapter is about using PC-DOS and ROM BIOS functions to output characters and graphic images to the screens. To make sense of the functions that are offered, we need to be aware of the two video display options offered by IBM. They are (1) the IBM monochrome display driven by the monochrome and parallel printer adaptor board, and (2) any monitor (or television) driven by the color/graphics adaptor board.

We will first examine the PC-DOS function calls that get characters out to the main display unit. This unit can be monochrome or color/graphics, depending on the switch settings on the system board. Next we will discuss those attributes of a character that are important in controlling the appearance of the character on the screen. We will describe the values that are useful for monochrome and those that are useful for color character displays. We will then look at the cursor control, color specification, and other features that are included in PC-DOS version 2.0. We will then discuss the ROM BIOS video I/O capabilities.

There is sad news about the versions 1 PC-DOS output capabilities: neither color specification nor graphics output tools are available. With PC-DOS function calls you can only output to "the display" (type not defined). A fixed attribute byte of value 07H is used for all characters. This value gives you what you normally see on your monochrome screen—a white-on-black character. There is slightly improved news if you have version 2.0. It gives you (1) the ability to specify a character's color, (2) cursor control operations, (3) simple erasure commands, and (4) mode setting capabilities. It does not, however, give you graphics output tools.

The good news is that if you write your own routines or use ROM BIOS function calls, you have access to both color and graphics capabilities. Easy access to these capabilities is also provided by IBM/Microsoft's Advanced BASIC, which has good facilities for making use of color and some facilities (more in version 2.0) for making use of graphics.

Since you probably want to know more about how to control easily the placement of characters and images on the screens, and about scrolling parts of, or the whole, screen, much of this chapter is devoted to the ROM BIOS facilities for programming character output to the screens.

If you have a PC with both the monochrome and the color/graphics adaptor boards, you will want to know how to switch between the two screens. We will show you which location to patch to redirect output to the other screen and how version 2.0 supplies a better way of doing this.

The last part of the chapter covers two other programming issues that pertain to character output to the screen:

1. The question of whether difficulties arise because there are two different display options that need to be programmed

2. The locations of characters and attributes, for those who wish to address directly the screen image in the adaptor boards' memories

Finally, if you are not yet ready for the material in this chapter, a description of the monochrome and color/graphics adaptor board options and their features is provided in Chapter 13. You may wish to read about the differences between these two devices before continuing.

THE PC-DOS FUNCTION CALLS THAT AFFECT THE SCREEN

PC-DOS provides character output routines that operate on characters or strings of characters. There are, however, no facilities provided in versions 1 for setting character attributes or cursor positions. We will look at what version 2.0 can do after we have learned about character attributes.

The three function calls that output to the screen, numbers 2, 6, and 9, exist within interrupt 21H. They are described below. One other PC-DOS function that affects the screen is the keyboard input function (number 1, also within interrupt 21H), which echoes the character entered at the keyboard to the screen.

No return status is indicated in the descriptions of routines below, since none is made available. Not much can go wrong (said the optimist) with sending a character to the screen.

Sending a Character to the Display (with Backspace Translation)—Function 2

When you output a backspace, this function acts in a civilized manner—it blanks the preceding character and leaves the cursor at that blanked character.

To output a character, set AH equal to 2 and execute interrupt 21H. The character in DL is output to the screen.

When you use this routine there is a chance that control will be whipped away from you if a Ctrl Break is detected in the input stream. If you wish to retain control in this eventuality, before using this function you will need to redirect interrupt 23H to your own Ctrl Break routine. To do this you can use function call 25H, in interrupt 21H, to point interrupt vector 23H to your own code.

Sending a Character to the Display—Function 6

IBM calls this the *Direct Console I/O* function. The single character in DL is output to the screen. No translation of the backspace or any other character takes place. Since this function becomes a keyboard input function if DL = FF, the FF character cannot be sent to the screen using this routine. The other significant difference between this and function number 2 described above is that a Ctrl Break in the input stream will remain undetected.

To output the character, set AH to 6, set the character you want to output in DL (not FF), and execute interrupt 21H.

Sending a String to the Display—Function 9

This function will save you a little time when you have a string of characters to output to the display. There is, however, one restriction—you cannot output a dollar sign. To use this function, point DS:DX to the beginning of a character string that is terminated by a dollar sign (24H), set AH to 9, and execute interrupt 21H.

CHARACTER ATTRIBUTES

Each character on the monochrome display can have one of several attributes. An *attribute* is a modifier to the basic character, controlling how it appears on the screen. Each bit in the attribute byte controls a feature of the character.

We will see the useful values for monochrome attribute bytes. The effect of each of the eight bit positions in the attribute byte is described for the color/graphics adaptor. The attribute byte can have a slightly different effect on the character, depending on whether it is directed to a display via a monochrome display adaptor or via a color/graphics adaptor operating in alphanumeric mode. However, two features of the attribute byte, blinking and high intensity, which are each represented by a single bit, remain consistent between monochrome and color displays.

When the color/graphics adaptor is operated in the APA (all points addressable, i.e. graphics) mode, the meaning of the attribute byte, in terms of being the byte following the character byte in the display memory of the adaptor board, evaporates. If, however, you use the ROM BIOS function calls to output characters via the color/graphics adaptor while it is in the graphics mode, an attribute-byte argument is recognized by the routines. This byte controls the color of the character.

Let's now look at how the value of the attribute byte affects the appearance of characters on the IBM monochrome display.

The Effect of Character Attributes on IBM's Monochrome Display

The attributes that are available on the IBM monochrome display are as follows:

- Normal—white character on black ground
- Reverse video—black character on white ground
- Underline (for white character only)
- Blinking character
- High-intensity character

	7	6	5	4	3	2	1	0
	FG	Background			Foreground			
Normal character	b	0	0	0	i	1	1	1
Reverse video	b	1	1	1	i	0	0	0
Underlined character	b	0	0	0	i	0	0	1
No display, black on black	b	0	0	0	i	0	0	0
No display, white on white	b	1	1	1	i	1	1	1

Bit 7 when set makes the character blink
Bit 3 when set makes the character high intensity

Figure 5.1: Attribute Bytes Recognized by the Monochrome Adaptor

As you will see, not all attribute combinations are available. For example, underlined reverse video cannot be obtained.

Figure 5.1 shows the purpose of the bits in the attribute byte as they are recognized by the monochrome adaptor board. Blinking and high intensity are each caused by a specific bit in the attribute byte: bit 7 for blinking and bit 3 for high intensity. (The blinking bit is interpreted by the monochrome and color/graphics boards in the same way.) The other six bits have a limited range of effective values.

Figure 5.2 shows a table of useful attribute values and the effects they create. From this figure it can be seen that the adaptor boards assign a higher priority to the underline request than the reverse video request; it is for this reason that underlined reverse video is not available.

Attribute Value (Hex)	Effect
00	No display, black on black
01	Underlined character
07	Normal character, white on black (this effect is also obtained with attribute values 02 through 06)
08	No display
09	Underlined, high-intensity character
70	Reverse video
71	Underline only, not reverse video
78	Reverse video, high intensity, the character appears thinner, more finely drawn
79	High intensity, underlined, not reverse video
81	Blinking underlined character
87	Blinking normal character
89	Blinking, underlined, high-intensity character
F0	Blinking, reverse video
F8	Blinking, reverse video, high intensity, the character appears thinner

Figure 5.2: Useful Monochrome Attribute Byte Values

Character Attributes with the Color/Graphics Adaptor Board

The color/graphics board operates in two modes: *text* (alias alphanumeric or A/N), and *graphics* (alias all points addressable or APA). The attribute byte gives full control of the character's foreground and background colors when the board is operating in the text mode. (Note: For a description of color control in the medium-resolution graphics mode, see Chapter 13.)

The attribute byte for colored characters is perhaps the easiest to understand. The colors are made from combinations of red, green, and blue. The eight bits and their functions appear in Figure 5.3.

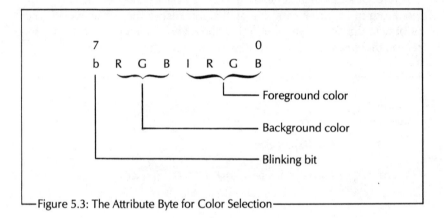

Figure 5.3: The Attribute Byte for Color Selection

Each character can have one of sixteen (defined by bits 0 to 3) foreground colors and any of eight (defined by bits 4 to 6) background colors. Each character can be made to blink by setting bit 7.

Now let's briefly look at the video options available with the IBM PC. Chapter 13 gives a fairly thorough view of the video options. We recommend you read it if you have unanswered questions at the end of this chapter.

Video Options

IBM supplies two adaptor boards through which output to a display can be directed. You can have either one or both of the boards installed. If you have both installed (and the system board switches are correctly set), the character that is output will go to the monochrome screen, unless specifically directed otherwise.

One video option is all IBM—it consists of a high-quality display (monitor) and the monochrome (and parallel printer) adaptor board. This operates in one mode only: 80 × 25 characters, black and white. It has buffer space for a single page of display.

The other option is IBM's color/graphics adaptor board, with a suitable monitor or television of your choice (you can't use IBM's monochrome display). This adaptor board allows you to output both characters and single dots to the screen (a character is made from a matrix of 5 × 7 dots within an 8 × 8 box) and, as the name implies, allows you to control the colors of the characters and the dots.

The color/graphics board operates in several modes; it offers four text and two graphics modes. You have a choice of a 40 × 25 or an 80 × 25 character display (a 40 × 25 mode is required for most televisions and lower-resolution monitors, since it doubles the width of the character). Color is available in both of these character widths. In graphics, the choice is between two resolutions: 320 × 200 or 640 × 200. Color is available in the 320 × 200 mode; the 640 × 200 mode is black and white only.

When the color/graphics adaptor is in the high-resolution graphics mode, it requires enough memory to address 128,000 (640 × 200) points (i.e., 16,000 bytes). When the board is in text mode, that memory is made available in the form of additional pages of text. Four pages of 80 × 25 characters, and eight pages of 40 × 25 characters, are available. A call to the video I/O routines will set the "active" page (the page that the controller currently displays).

VERSION 2.0'S EXTENDED SCREEN CONTROL

The authors of versions 1 PC-DOS must have experienced washes of guilt every now and again, until they were able to produce and release version 2.0. The color/graphics feature of the IBM PC existed, but no software had been created in PC-DOS to run it. Version 2.0 relieves a little of that guilt by providing extended screen control. Let's examine it by first looking at what extended screen control gives us. Then we will see what we have to do to make it work for us.

The Benefits of Extended Screen Control

Version 2.0's extended screen control gives us the following capabilities:

- The use of color
- The use of the underline, reverse video, high-intensity, and blinking character attributes
- Extensive cursor control
- Partial and whole screen erasure
- Mode setting capabilities

Roughly, these capabilities let us write block-character game and business graphics in living color. We still don't have medium- and high-resolution graphics capabilities, but graphics package standards have not yet been solidly established. Besides that impediment, flashy graphics software for the PC might not benefit from (i.e., it might be slowed down by) having PC-DOS between it and the screen.

Working with Extended Screen Control

The extended screen control features can be exercised by (1) including the ANSI.SYS extended screen control device driver in the PC-DOS configuration, and then (2) sending unique control sequences through the display output functions within interrupt 21H. The control sequences set colors, move the cursor, erase pieces of the screen, set foreground and background colors, and select text and graphics modes. We will briefly go over how to include the ANSI.SYS device driver before we look at control sequences and how to use them.

Configuring PC-DOS to Include ANSI.SYS

ANSI.SYS is the device driver that includes the extended screen control software. The device driver needs to be part of PC-DOS for the extended screen control features to be effective.

Adding a device driver (once it is written and debugged) is easy in PC-DOS. To add this one, the line

```
DEVICE=ANSI.SYS
```

must be included in the CONFIG.SYS file. Refer to Chapter 4 to see how to add a line to the CONFIG.SYS file. Don't forget to reboot the system once the configuration file has been altered. Resident PC-DOS increases by about 1.5K bytes when this device driver is added.

Control Sequences

A control sequence is a unique string of characters that the display functions respond to. The action depends on the content of the string. Only the display functions within interrupt 21H (2, 6, and 9) will respond correctly to an extended screen control sequence.

The first two characters of a control sequence are always Esc [. You can see what all the control sequence options are by looking at Chapter Thirteen of the DOS manual. We will now review these options.

Cursor Control   The cursor control sequences are identified by three-character mnemonics. The sequences themselves are highly unmnemonic.

The CUU, CUD, CUF, and CUB sequences move the cursor from its current position one or more steps in the four cursor directions: up, down, forward (to the right), and backward (to the left). The sequences are Esc [# A, Esc [# B, Esc [# C, and Esc [# D. (Spaces are included for readability; they do not belong in the control sequences.) The # sign represents an optionally included decimal number of steps (default is one) specified in ASCII characters. For example, the sequence to move the cursor right two columns is

Esc[2C

The sequence to move it left one column is

Esc[D

Note that Esc stands for the single-byte ASCII code for escape, which is 1BH. Also note that there are no spaces in the examples.

CUP and HVP are two control sequences that move the cursor to Cartesian coordinates. They both have the same action: the cursor moves to the line and column specified. The sequences are Esc [# ; # H and Esc [# ; # f. The first # stands for row (line number), the second one stands for column. For example:

Esc[13;40H

moves the cursor to about the middle of the (80-column) screen. (Why there are two different sequences for the same action is a mystery.)

The current position of the cursor can be found by issuing the DSR (device status report) sequence, which is Esc [6 n. By the way, the case of the command letter in all these control sequences is important; if the last character in this sequence is N, no cursor position is reported.

Once the DSR sequence is issued, the cursor position is reported in the form Esc [# ; # R. You can read it into a buffer using function A, buffered keyboard input. Alternatively, you can read the CPR (cursor position report) sequence by looping on function 1, keyboard input. The control sequence is conveniently terminated by 0DH, the carriage return character.

As an example, let's say you issued the DSR sequence after our cursor positioning command above. Then you used function A to read the CPR into a buffer. If you then used DEBUG to look at the buffer at location 930:200, you would see

        0930:200 1B 5B 31 33 3B 34 30 52 0D ...   .[13;40R.....

SCP and RCP save and restore the current cursor position. Those sequences are Esc [s and Esc [u.

Erasure Sequences   Two erasure sequences are supported. ED erases the whole screen; EL erases to the end of the line. The sequences are Esc [2 j and Esc [k.

Mode Setting Sequences   The same mode setting capabilities are available via control sequences as can be achieved using the ROM BIOS mode setting function (function 0 within interrupt 10H).

The same limitation applies. These mode setting sequences cannot be used to switch output between monochrome and color/graphics adaptors without a little trickery. They are quite satisfactory for switching between the seven modes available on the color/graphics board. The trickery is explained a little later in this chapter.

The mode setting sequence is Esc [= # h, where the # sign is an ASCII digit from 0 to 7. The correspondence between digits and modes appears in Figure 5.4 of this chapter. Mode 7 does not switch to monochrome. It controls whether characters typed (or output to the display by a program) after the right-hand edge of the screen is reached are moved to the next line or thrown away. If they are thrown away, any additional characters replace the last character in the line, until you stop typing (or the input buffer fills) or until the program stops sending out characters to the display.

Finally, we have reached the control sequences that make this all worthwhile—attribute byte control.

Set Graphics Rendition   These SGR (set graphics rendition) sequences set an attribute byte, which is applied to all characters output thereafter. Another SGR sequence is required to change the attribute byte again. This control makes it easy to output everything in reverse video, or with high-intensity blinking if you dislike whoever is going to be reading the display.

The SGR sequences permit attribute byte selection for foreground and background colors, reverse video, blinking, high intensity, underlined, and invisible characters. The codes for these attributes are shown on page 13-8 of the version 2.0 DOS manual. The SGR sequence is Esc [# ; # ;....; m. For example, to make all subsequent characters appear in reverse video, output the SGR sequence

Esc[7m

To make all subsequent characters appear in reverse video and blinking, use the sequence

Esc[7;5m

Version 2.0 does not provide all we need. It does not support either medium- or high-resolution graphics, nor does it support some of the extensive video I/O capabilities offered by the ROM BIOS function call, interrupt 10H. Let's look at those ROM BIOS capabilities.

VIDEO I/O USING THE ROM BIOS FUNCTION CALLS

With ROM BIOS you have almost complete control of video I/O. You can only go further by directly programming the 6845 CRT controller chips found on the adaptor boards.

The ROM BIOS function call allows you to specify (and read) the mode in which the adaptor board is to operate. Assuming you have the required adaptor board(s), this gives you the choice of operating in either the text or graphics modes—already a vast improvement over what PC-DOS versions 1 offer. With ROM BIOS you can also control the appearance of the cursor, set and read the cursor position, read and write characters with their attributes, and read and write dots (and their colors) in the graphics modes.

The fancier things that ROM BIOS allows you to do include scrolling parts of (or the whole) screen and interacting with the light pen. The ROM BIOS function is not all powerful; it won't draw lines or shade areas for you in the graphics mode.

Pages A-43 to A-45 of the Technical Reference manual show you what interrupt 10H can do for you. If you plan to write your own low-level character or graphics output routines, or if you plan to program the 6845 directly, the ROM BIOS listings from pages A-45 through A-67 can be informative. Pages 2-45 to 2-46 and 2-59 to 2-64 of the same manual will show you the flexibility built into the 6845 controller chip.

Let's look at how to get things done using interrupt 10H.

The Format of ROM BIOS Video I/O Function Calls

ROM BIOS video capabilities are split into sixteen different functions. The choice of function is dictated by the value of the AH register on entry to interrupt 10H. To invoke a video I/O function, set the arguments appropriate to the specific function call, set the AH register to the number of the function required, and execute interrupt 10H.

Let's begin by looking at the mode setting capability within ROM BIOS interrupt 10H. Remember, version 2.0 can be configured to include another way (extended screen control) of setting the mode.

Setting the Video I/O Mode

ROM BIOS identifies seven different modes, numbered from 0 to 6. To set the mode, set AH to zero, set AL to the mode required, and execute interrupt 10H. The modes are shown in Figure 5.4.

AL	Mode
0	Text, 40 × 25, black and white
1	Text, 40 × 25, color
2	Text, 80 × 25, black and white
3	Text, 80 × 25, color
4	Graphics, 320 × 200, black and white
5	Graphics, 320 × 200, color
6	Graphics, 640 × 200, black and white

Figure 5.4: Display Modes Recognized by ROM BIOS

A value of 7 is used internal to ROM BIOS to indicate the 80 × 25 mono-chrome display. Although the mode *reading* function will return a 7 if the monochrome display is in use, the mode *setting* function in ROM BIOS will not respond usefully to 7 as an argument in AL. This function will not switch back to the monochrome display from the color/graphics display. (There is a way to fool the mode setting function into switching between color/graphics and monochrome. This is explained toward the end of the chapter.)

There may be a time when you wish to know the current display mode—perhaps so that you can restore it later. Function 15 is provided for this purpose.

Reading the Current Mode

To read the current display mode, set AH equal to 15 (0F) and execute interrupt 10H. On return, AL will contain the current mode. AH will con-tain the number of columns of characters on the screen. You can glean this information from the current mode value, but this function saves you the work of doing that. BH contains the number of the currently active display page if the text mode is being used.

Now that we have learned how to set and read the mode, let's look at the next most basic function: character output. You have a choice of two main functions for this purpose: (1) output of character and attribute byte and (2) output of character only. We will look at the simpler of these two functions—output of character only—after a brief intoduction to the "active" page and cursor functions.

The Active Page

The active page is the page currently being displayed. We have seen that in text modes the color/graphics adaptor board contains room for either four or eight pages; only one of these is active (being displayed) at any one time.

Your program can be building other pages while the user is viewing the page that is currently on display. Consequently, each time you write characters, the page must be indicated. The page is one argument to the output character(s) function calls. When you want another page to be displayed, the function to set the active page can be invoked.

Setting the Active Page

The function to select the active page is function AH = 5, within interrupt 10H. The page number is passed in AL; its value is 0 to 7 for 40 $\times$ 25 modes (modes 0 and 1), and 0 to 3 for 80 $\times$ 25 modes (modes 2 and 3).

To set the active page, put the page number in AL, set AH equal to 5, and execute interrupt 10H. The newly selected page is instantly displayed. Of course, this only applies to output controlled by the color/graphics adaptor. The active page for the monochrome adaptor is always 0. The active page is set to 0 when the system is booted.

The Current Cursor Positions

The ROM BIOS functions write characters to the current cursor position. Eight cursor positions are maintained—one for each of the eight possible pages. Once you have set the cursor position (function AH = 2), it is maintained by the routines that write characters to the page.

Before we move on to discuss character ouput, we will look at both setting and reading the cursor position and altering the appearance of the cursor. Remember, if you have PC-DOS version 2.0, it can be configured to accept cursor control commands; you may not need these ROM BIOS alternatives.

Setting the Cursor Position

Function AH = 2 sets the cursor position. The arguments to the function are the row and column (numbered from 0,0 in the top left corner) and the page on which the cursor is to be set. You can set the cursor position while operating in either the text or graphics mode. The function always understands the cursor position arguments in terms of text coordinates (varying from 0 to 25 and 0 to 80), not graphics coordinates. In the graphics mode the page argument must be zero.

To set the cursor, put the page number in BH, the row in DH, and the column in DL; then set AH equal to 2, and execute interrupt 10H.

Reading the Current Cursor Position

This function (AH = 3) reads the current cursor position in the page specified. It also tells you what the cursor looks like. To read the cursor position, set BH to the page number you want to look into, set AH equal to 3, and execute interrupt 10H.

On return, DH and DL are the row and column positions of the cursor. If you have previously changed the appearance of the cursor, CH and CL will show you the start and end line for the cursor. You may be wondering what the "start and end line for the cursor" means. Please read on.

Changing the Appearance of the Cursor

The cursor's appearance can be quite different from the thick underline character that you usually see. Function AH = 1 allows you to control the upper and lower limits of the blob that blinks. You can move it upward, enlarge it, split it into two parts, or shrink it so that it looks like the underline character.

To understand what "start and end line" means, we need to explain what horizontal scan lines are. If you already know about horizontal scan lines, you can skip the next paragraph.

Images on monitors are made by zipping a narrow electron beam across the screen—turning it on when you want the phosphor to glow and leaving it off for dark spots. The beam is thin, so to cover the whole screen it has to trace a path across the screen many times. The beam starts at the top of the screen, moves across (and back), then moves downward a distance slightly greater than its thickness, and then moves across the screen again. The path traced by the beam across the screen is called the *horizontal scan line*.

On the IBM monochrome display there are 14 horizontal scan lines devoted to each line of characters. They are numbered from 0 through 13, starting at the top. The normal monochrome cursor, which is two lines thick, can be produced by starting it at line 12 and ending it at line 13.

A cursor designed to occupy a whole rectangle can be produced by instructing ROM BIOS to start drawing it at line 0 and stop drawing at line 13. A split cursor, where blinking lines appear at both top and bottom of the character rectangle, can be obtained by setting CH, the start line, to 12, and CL, the end line, to 0. Note that these values apply to the monochrome display driven by the monochrome and parallel printer adaptor board. On screens driven by the color/graphics adaptor board, there are 8 lines per character rectangle, numbered from 0 to 7 from the top down.

To change the appearance of the cursor, set CH to the start line for the cursor, CL to the end line, AH equal to 1, and then execute interrupt 10H. The cursor type (shape) is set for all pages at once.

Now let's look at the functions that write characters to a page.

Character I/O Using ROM BIOS

ROM BIOS provides three different functions for sending characters to a page, and one function that reads the character at the current cursor position. We will examine the two major output functions first: character output without attribute and character output with attribute. A note on the limitations of these character output functions when the color/graphics adaptor is operating in either of the two graphics modes (5 or 6) is included.

Character Output, No Attribute

This function is the simpler of the two major character output functions, because it does not require the character's attribute byte to be passed as one of the arguments. With this output function, any attribute byte(s) that exist in the adaptor's memory will be used "as is." Like the other character-writing function call, this one will output the same character more than once if required.

We have now been through enough background information to understand the arguments needed by the character output functions. To output one or more of the same characters, starting at the current cursor position, use the function addressed by AH = 0A. Set BH to the display page you wish to write to, set CX to the count of characters to write, put the character to write in AL, set AH to 0A, and execute interrupt 10H.

Character Output, with Attribute

This output function uses one more argument than the simpler function, and that argument contains the attribute byte. Like the other function, the character, with its attribute byte, is output to the page of choice at the current cursor position. Several copies of the character may be output.

Set AL to the character to write, set CX to the count of characters, set BH to the display page, set BL to the attribute byte, set AH equal to 9, and execute interrupt 10H.

Character I/O in the Graphics Mode

If you wish to output characters to the screen while in the graphics mode, ROM BIOS will do extensive work for you. In the graphics mode the write-character functions use a built-in table of dot patterns and output each character dot by dot. These functions, however, contain the information to do this only for the first 128 ASCII characters. You can point interrupt 1FH (locations 7C through 7F) to your own table of dot positions for the ASCII characters 128 and up.

If you wish to output multiple characters in the graphics mode, the performance of the two major character-write functions is not guaranteed beyond the end of the line on which the output begins.

Read the Character at the Current Cursor Position

It may sometimes be useful to read the character (and attribute) in the display buffer. Function AH = 8 does this for you.

The only argument for this interrupt 10H function is the display page. To read the character and its attribute byte, set BH to the page of interest, set AH = 8 and execute interrupt 10H. On return, the character at the current cursor position for that page will be in AL; the attribute byte will be in BL.

The Third Character Output Routine

We have talked about two "major" character output routines. Well, here is another one, a minor one. It is a simple (considering all the previous sophistication) character-output routine; in fact, it is the equivalent of teletype output. The character is in AL, the page is in BH, and if we are operating in the graphics mode, the foreground color is in BL. You will need to set AH equal to 0E, then execute interrupt 10H. A single character will be output to the current cursor position.

There are yet more capabilities built into the ROM BIOS video I/O function. Scrolling is one of them, and it's fun to play with. Let's look at the scrolling facilities.

Scrolling with ROM BIOS

The tools exist for scrolling whole pages or parts of pages, either up or down. When you call upon function AH = 6 (scroll up) or AH = 7 (scroll down), the window in the active page, defined by the row and column positions of the upper left and lower right corners, scrolls up or down by the number of lines specified. The lines (or partial lines) scrolled "away from" are blanked and have the specified attribute byte added to them.

To scroll, set AL to the number of lines (zero means scroll the whole window, i.e., blank it), set CH and CL to the row and column position of the upper left corner, set DH and DL to the lower right coordinates, and set BH to the attribute byte to put into the blanked lines. When all the arguments are ready, set AH equal to 6 to scroll up, or 7 to scroll down, and execute interrupt 10H. That piece of the screen should then scroll as directed.

Now that we have covered character output, let's look at the graphics capabilities in ROM BIOS.

Graphics Output in ROM BIOS

Three functions are available for graphics output—write dot, read dot, and color control. The write and read functions are almost self-explanatory; the color control function requires a little attention, so we will look at it first.

To set the color palette, function AH = 0B, you need to understand the color control available via the color/graphics card. Color control only applies to medium-resolution graphics (320 × 200). Basically, you have a choice of sixteen colors for the background and two sets of three colors for the foreground.

Setting the Color Palette

Let's learn how to establish your color choices using function 0B. You need to specify color for two different parts of the screen: background and foreground. Register BH is used to specify whether it is background or foreground you wish to set a color (or colors) for. Once you have established which aspect of the screen your color choices apply to, you need to indicate the color choices. This is done via register BL.

To choose one of sixteen colors for the background, set BH to 0 and BL to the color of your choice. To choose one of the two color palettes available for the foreground dots, set BL to 0 to get the green, red, and brown (sort of yellow) group, or set BL to 1 to get the cyan, magenta, and white group. Once you have the BH and BL arguments ready, set AH equal to 0B and execute interrupt 10H.

Write a Dot in Graphics Mode

All you have to do to write a dot is specify the location and, if operating in medium-resolution mode (320 × 200), the color of the dot.

The location is specified in terms of row and column. The row coordinate varies from 0 to 199 in both medium- and high-resolution modes. The column coordinate varies from 0 to 319 in medium resolution, and from 0 to 639 in high resolution. Location 0,0 is the top left corner of the screen; location 319,199 or 639,199 is the lower right corner.

The color of the dot can be any one of four colors: the background color or one of the three foreground colors. If you don't write a dot, it will be the background color.

To write a dot, set DX to the row, set CX to the column, set AL to the color (0, 1, 2, or 3), set AH equal to 0C, and execute interrupt 10H.

Read a Dot in Graphics Mode

Reading a dot gets you the color of the dot at the position you specify. The color is returned in AL. To read a dot, set DX to the row, CX to the column, AH equal to 0D, and execute interrupt 10H.

There is one last capability of the ROM BIOS video functions to be revealed: the light pen function.

Reading the Light Pen Position

If you want to know where the light pen is currently positioned on the screen, set AH equal to 4 and execute interrupt 10H. On return, if AH = 0 the light pen switch is not triggered, so no location is made available.

If AH = 1, you have the light pen position expressed in two forms. The row and column of the character position are in DH and DL. DH will vary from 0 to 25, and DL from 0 to 80. A more refined position is returned in the CH and BX registers. CH contains the horizontal scan line (alias raster scan row), varying from 0 to 199; BX contains the pixel column, varying from 0 to 319 or 639.

SWITCHING OUTPUT BETWEEN MONOCHROME AND COLOR/GRAPHICS

Version 2.0's MODE command includes an option to switch output between monochrome and color/graphics. It is quicker than the method we are about to review. If your system has the memory to permit use of the EXEC command, version 2.0 applications programs can execute the MODE command and remain ignorant of the following information.

Most, but not all, of the software for the PC uses ROM BIOS to output characters to the displays. This includes PC-DOS and a large proportion of application software. ROM BIOS at boot time looks at the system-board switch settings to establish, among other things, the current hardware configuration. The encoded configuration is placed in location 0:410 in memory. Bits 5 and 6 of that location are used to describe the display options.

A value of 20H in the equipment configuration word (0:410) indicates that an IBM monochrome display is the primary output display. A value of 30H indicates that the color/graphics board is the primary character output device. The method for switching between monochrome and color/ graphics involves (1) setting those two bits, then (2) immediately invoking a mode setting function. The mode setting function can be either function 0 in interrupt 10H, or the set-mode control sequence of the extended screen control facility in version 2.0. The actual mode selected is not very important. After you have switched modes, any character output that goes through ROM BIOS will be directed to your chosen display.

To change from monochrome to color/graphics output, mask out bits 5 and 6 (AND 0:410 with CFH) and specify color/graphics (OR 0:410 with 20H). To change the other way (from color/graphics to monochrome), no masking is necessary, just OR 0:410 with 30H. Let's look at two examples.

From Color/Graphics to Monochrome

If the monochrome unit is the current display, the value at location 0:410 might be 7DH (at least, both bits in the 30H mask will be set). To switch from monochrome to color/graphics, first turn off bit 4 in location 0:410 in our example (change the value 7DH to 6DH), then immediately set the color/graphics mode to 3 (80 × 25, color).

From Monochrome to Color/Graphics

If the current display is a color/graphics unit, the value at location 0:410 might be 6DH (at least, only the high-order bit in the 30H mask will be set). To switch from color/graphics to monochrome display, set location 0:410 to 7DH, then immediately set the color/graphics mode to 2 (80 × 25 black and white). If you read the mode after this operation, you will find it set to 7, ROM BIOS' internal value for the monochrome display. BASIC programs to change from one display to the other are shown in Figures 5.5, 5.6, and 5.7.

```
10 'Program to switch to monochrome display
20 KEY OFF: CLS
30 WIDTH 40: DEF SEG = 0
35 A = PEEK(&H410): POKE &H410,A OR &H30
40 WIDTH 80 : LOCATE ,,1,12,13
50 KEY ON
```

Figure 5.5: BASIC Program to Switch to Monochrome Display

```
10 'Program to switch to color/graphics adaptor
20 KEY OFF: CLS
30 WIDTH 80: DEF SEG = 0
35 A = PEEK(&H410): POKE &H410, (A AND &HCF) OR &H20
40 WIDTH 80 : SCREEN 0: LOCATE ,,1,6,7
50 KEY ON
```

Figure 5.6: BASIC Program to Switch to an 80-Column Color/Graphics Display

```
10 'Program to switch to color/graphics adaptor
20 KEY OFF: CLS
30 WIDTH 80: DEF SEG = 0
35 A = PEEK(&H410): POKE &H410, (A AND &HCF) OR &H20
40 WIDTH 40 : SCREEN 0: LOCATE ,,1,6,7
50 KEY ON
```

Figure 5.7: BASIC Program to Switch to a 40-Column Color/Graphics Display

THE DIFFERENT DISPLAY, DIFFERENT SOFTWARE QUESTION

You may already have gathered that there are two different main output devices to consider when programming for a display. If you are working in the text mode, the problem of having to consider which adaptor you are writing software for is not difficult to resolve.

In general, you can ignore the differences in devices. Characters with attributes designed for color/graphics can be sent to the monochrome display, and characters with attributes designed for the monochrome display can be sent via the color/graphics adaptor.

The difference is resolved for you at most levels by these facts:

- Switch settings on the PC system board specify the type of main display unit.
- The software in ROM BIOS relies on a mode setting to determine which display adaptor to address.
- The function calls in PC-DOS address only "the display"; the type of display is unspecified.

The only odd effect is that an underlined character turns into a light blue character when sent via the color/graphics adaptor, and vice versa.

For further information, peruse Table 3 (Monochrome Vs Color/Graphics Attributes) on page 2-55 of the Technical Reference Manual.

LOCATIONS OF THE CHARACTERS AND THEIR ATTRIBUTE BYTES

This section is for those of you who want to directly access the character buffers in the monochrome and color/graphics adaptor boards. Without programming the 6845 CRT controller directly, this approach may be the quickest way to modify an image on the screen.

The attribute byte follows the character byte in the display buffer. An 80 × 25 character display will show 2000 characters. It requires a 4000-byte buffer, however, because each character on the screen is represented in the buffer by a character byte *and* an attribute byte. The character byte is found on an even address—the attribute byte on the following odd address.

The buffer space for both monochrome and color/graphics displays exists on the respective adaptor boards. The address of the beginning of the monochrome display buffer is B0000H. The beginning of the color/graphics display buffer is B8000H. Since the attribute byte follows the character, the address of the first attribute byte is B0001H on the monochrome adaptor, or B8001H on the color/graphics adaptor.

The address of the last character (lower right corner of the screen) on the monochrome board is B000:F9E; the address of the last attribute byte is B000:F9F. The addresses for the four 80 × 25 pages available on the color/graphics adaptor are B800:0, B900:0, BA00:0, and BB00;0.

SUMMARY

In this chapter we have seen how to program output for displays driven by the monochrome and color/graphics adaptors, and how those two adaptors are different. We also examined character attribute bytes and their effect on the character in both monochrome and color/graphics modes. We reviewed the extended screen control that version 2.0 provides, and then explored the ROM BIOS video I/O capabilities in some detail. These capabilities include almost all the functions you may want when programming output to a display.

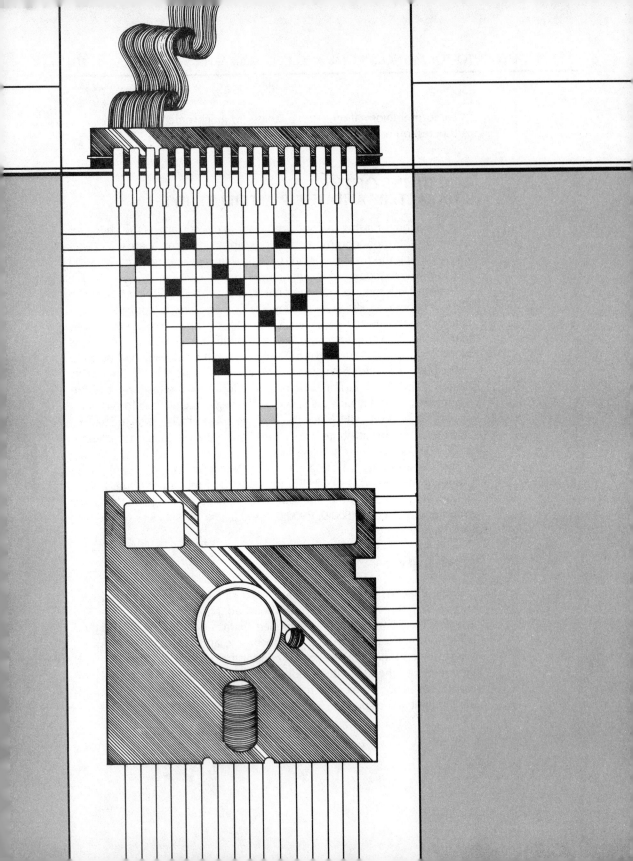

6

The Serial and Parallel Ports

INTRODUCTION

This brief chapter discusses the tools the programmer has for conducting input and output via the serial* and parallel ports that can be attached to the IBM PC. It is brief because PC-DOS versions 1.0 and 1.1 are not strong on data transfer via these two ports at the programmer's level.

If you are familiar with the MODE command in version 1.1, you might expect better tools to be available to programmers. Version 1.1's MODE command allows the user to redirect output originally destined for the parallel port to the serial port. Letter-quality printers, which for some purposes are preferable to the Epson/IBM dot-matrix printer commonly sold with the PC, are often built with serial interfaces. In addition, software exists in the MODE command for communication with other devices and computers, via the serial port. However, the designers of PC-DOS chose not to provide function calls that allow the programmer to call the routines used by the MODE command.

Serious work with the serial port is supported by the PC's ROM BIOS, under interrupt 14H. We recommend you use this approach instead of the PC-DOS facilities, although with version 2.0 you may be able to use combinations of the EXEC function and CTTY and MODE commands to meet the needs of your application.

In this chapter we will first discuss the PC-DOS serial port function calls—more to acknowledge their existence than to provide useful information. This is followed by a description of the ROM BIOS serial port function calls within interrupt 14H, thus giving you something you can work with. We will then move on to a discussion of the version 2.0 possibilities for serial communications, followed by a note on the hazards of programming for RS-232 serial communications. We will also describe the single function call within PC-DOS for output to the parallel port. Finally, we will examine the ROM BIOS printer I/O function calls under interrupt 17H.

---

*IBM calls the serial port an asynchronous communications adaptor.

PC-DOS SERIAL PORT FUNCTION CALLS

The facilities provided by PC-DOS for accessing the serial port from within a PC-DOS program (one not written in BASIC) are minimal, in fact inadequate.

PC-DOS provides two function calls, numbered 3 and 4, within interrupt 21H for single-character, unbuffered, noninterrupt-driven input and output. In versions 1 at the programmer's level, PC-DOS recognizes only one serial port, even though the IBM PC supports at least four. Let's examine these two serial port function calls.

Input from the Serial Port with PC-DOS

To get a character from the serial port, set AH equal to 3 and execute interrupt 21H. The character is returned in AL.

With this function call, the input is unbuffered, so your software had better be there waiting for a character any time one is likely to arrive, or some input characters will be missed. This means that, among other complications inherent in this approach to serial port management, the time your program takes to process a character and do whatever else it has to do, then call function 3 in interrupt 21H (to go wait for the next character), must be less than the interval between characters arriving at the port.

Output to the Serial Port with PC-DOS

To output to the serial port, set AH equal to 4; put the character you wish to output into DL; and execute interrupt 21H. The character in DL is output to the first serial port. No error conditions are returned.

As with the matching PC-DOS input function, you will be better served by using the ROM BIOS facilities for serial port I/O.

ROM BIOS SERIAL I/O FUNCTION CALLS

The PC's ROM BIOS provides under interrupt 14H the following functions for either or both of two serial ports:

AH	Function
00	Initialize baud rate, parity, word length, and number of stop bits
01	Output a character
02	Receive a character
03	Read port status

Descriptions of these functions are found in the ROM BIOS listings in the Technical Reference manual, pages A-20 to A-21. The routines that do the work are listed on pages A-23 to A-24. To call any of these functions, set the DX register to indicate which serial port is being addressed; set the parameter registers (if any); set the function number in AH, and execute INT 14H. Let's look at the four functions, starting with the one that initializes a serial port.

Serial Port Initialization

This function specifies the baud rate, parity, word length, and number of stop bits that the serial port's hardware and software have to handle. These four parameters are all defined within the AL register: the baud rate is defined in the three high-order bits (bits 7–5), the parity in the next two bits (bits 4–3), the number of stop bits is defined by bit 2, and the word length is defined in the last two bits (bits 1–0). Figure 6.1 illustrates this. Figures 6.2 through 6.4 show the meanings of the bit values for the baud rate bits, the parity bits, and the word length bits. For the stop bits parameter, if one stop bit is to be used, bit 2 is zero; if two stop bits are required, bit 2 is set.

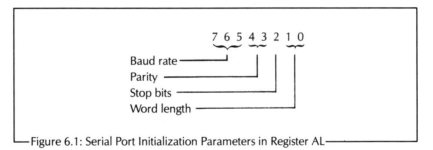

Figure 6.1: Serial Port Initialization Parameters in Register AL

Bits 7–5	Baud Rate
0 0 0	110
0 0 1	150
0 1 0	300
0 1 1	600
1 0 0	1200
1 0 1	2400
1 1 0	4800
1 1 1	9600

Figure 6.2: Baud Rate Bit Definitions for Serial I/O

Bits 4, 3	Parity
0 0	None
0 1	Odd
1 0	None
1 1	Even

Figure 6.3: Parity Bit Definitions for Serial I/O

Bits 1, 0	Word Length
1 0	7 bits
1 1	8 bits

Figure 6.4: Word Length Bit Definitions for Serial I/O

(Note: If you want to communicate at 19,200 baud, you will need a serial port that can be programmed to run that fast (several serial boards support 19,200 baud), and you will need to address the 8250 controller chip directly. The Technical Reference manual's section on the Asynchronous Communications Adaptor (page 2-127 through 2-151) supplies a large amount of not very decipherable information. As usual, the information is all there, it is just that no path has been provided through it all.)

Send a Character

Function 1 within interrupt 14H sends out the character in AL. On return, if there was an error, bit 7 of AH is set and the rest of the bits in AH contain the serial port status, the same status as is returned by the read status function.

Receive a Character

Function 2 within interrupt 14H waits for a character from the serial port. If AH is nonzero on return, an error has occurred, and bits 7, 4, 3, 2, and 1 of AH are set, as described in the read status function. If AH is zero, the character received is in AL.

Read Serial Port Status

Function 3 within interrupt 14H reads the serial port status. Figure 6.5 shows the conditions returned.

AH Bit	Line Control Status
7	Time out
6	Transmitter shift register empty
5	Transmitter holding register empty
4	Break detected
3	Framing error
2	Parity error
1	Overrun error
0	Data is ready

AL Bit	Modem Status
7	Received line signal detect
6	Ring indicator
5	Data set ready
4	Clear to send
3	Receive line signal detect changed since last checked
2	Trailing edge of ring detector
1	Data set ready changed since last checked
0	Clear to send changed since last checked

Figure 6.5: Status Conditions, ROM BIOS Serial I/O Function

Problems Experienced with ROM BIOS Serial I/O

Experience with these interrupt 14H capabilities has remained not completely satisfactory to date. The receive character function (AH = 2) would only work when the output function (AH = 1) had been called immediately preceding the receive function. There has not been time to explore this possible deficiency, nor to find corroborating evidence from other users.

A problem concerning time out reporting exists with an early version of the PC's ROM BIOS. If you have this version (04/24/81), one instruction is not correct. The instruction to set the time out indicator bit appears as

OR AH,80

when it should have been written as

    OR AH,80H

The wrong bits are set by the instruction (bits 6 and 4, not bit 8), with the result that time out conditions are not always reported correctly by the function call that sends characters out over the line. Software that uses function 1 within interrupt 14H will not find out that the device is not ready, and characters will be missing from the output.

It's a shame this flaw exists. IBM has so far not seen fit to offer any means of correcting it, unless you buy a PC hard disk extension chassis. Chapter 15, "The Delights of DEBUG," shows you how to see if your PC has this version of ROM BIOS.

SERIAL I/O WITH VERSION 2.0

In version 2.0, the EXEC function (number 4B of interrupt 21H) permits the MODE command to be called from within a program. It takes a little setup work, but the facility is there to do within your software anything that you can do with the MODE command from the keyboard. The minor disadvantage of this approach is that the EXEC function brings in another copy of the command processor, which is 17K of additional space you have to find room for.

You might think of using version 2.0's I/O redirection capabilities to send and receive data via serial ports. This will work in a limited number of situations. It is not, however, a general-purpose solution. Serial communication is not simply a case of shoveling characters out to the serial port instead of, say, the display. The display does not talk back, nor does it need communications protocol characters inserted in the text to continue operations over any appreciable period of time. The applications need to be fairly simple for 2.0's I/O redirection to provide a communcations solution. Use of the MODE command for redirection and communications is discussed in Chapter 14.

THE HAZARDS OF
PROGRAMMING FOR RS-232 COMMUNICATIONS

Routines capable of handling bidirectional communication over serial ports generally end up being much more extensive in their capabilities, and therefore requiring much more programming effort, than at first expected. The problems with programming such routines are twofold: (1) your program does not control both ends of the transfer, so it has to deal with an unusual variety of logical error conditions; (2) the integrity of the electronic path over which the signals travel is often poor, so the routines have to be able to issue, and honor, retransmission requests after checksum errors have been detected.

Should you now be discouraged from trying to write serial I/O routines, take heart. The examples provided by the ROM BIOS routines are useful, and the Technical Reference manual section on the Asynchronous Communications Adaptor, pages 2-127 through 2-152, is reasonably helpful. For issues concerning the correct cabling of devices using the serial ports, see Chapter 14 of this book. When you write serial I/O routines, remember to use interrupt-driven, buffered I/O instead of character-by-character transmission directly from the noninterrupt levels of your program.

To assist your serial I/O programming efforts, there is a book on RS-232 connections, written by Joe Campbell and published by Sybex. It offers much more insight than can be provided here.

THE PARALLEL PRINTER INTERFACE

PC-DOS does not provide programmers with extensive software tools for handling output to the parallel port. PC-DOS assumes that error conditions can be ignored, and that there is only one printer. ROM BIOS provides better functions for parallel printer control.

IBM's parallel printer adaptor can, in fact, be used to drive parallel devices other than printers. It is not exactly a general-purpose parallel I/O device, but it has some flexibility beyond output to a printer. Neither PC-DOS nor ROM BIOS contains routines to drive the parallel port at this level. The Parallel Printer Adaptor section of the Technical Reference manual (pages 2-69 to 2-73) gives the port addresses and meanings of the information transmitted across the ports. You may need this information if you wish to add to your PC a printer that doesn't have the same characteristics as the Epson/IBM dot-matrix printer.

Let's first examine the PC-DOS function call for output of a character to that one printer. Then let's examine the ROM BIOS function calls, which are far more satisfactory for driving a parallel printer.

Output to the Printer with PC-DOS

A single function call, number 5 in interrupt 21H, is provided for sending a character to the printer. To use this function, set AH to 5; put the character to be output into DL, and execute interrupt 21H. The character in DL is sent to the first printer. No error conditions are reported.

Output to the Printer Using ROM BIOS

The PC's ROM BIOS contains functions under interrupt 17H that are capable of addressing three separate parallel ports as follows:

AH	Function
00	Print the character in AL, with provision for completion checking
01	Initialize the port (one configuration only), status returned
02	Read the printer status

DX is used to specify which printer to use—0, 1, or 2. These ROM BIOS routines are described and listed on pages A-42 to A-43 of the Technical Reference manual. Let's look a little more closely at these three functions.

Print the Character in AL

Function 0 within interrupt 17H prints the character in AL. On return, AH contains the status bits described in the read status function.

Initialize the Printer Port

Function 1 within interrupt 17H initializes the printer port. The printer's response depends on how it interprets the output of this function. The twitch the Epson/IBM dot-matrix printer makes when you boot PC-DOS is caused by this function.

Read the Printer Status

Function 2 within interrupt 17H returns the printer status in AH. The meaning of the status bits is shown in Figure 6.6.

Bit	Meaning
7	Printer busy
6	Acknowledge (not normally set)
5	Out of paper
4	Printer is selected
3	I/O error (e.g., printer off line)
2	Unused
1	Unused
0	Time out

Figure 6.6: Status Conditions, ROM BIOS Parallel Printer Control

SUMMARY

We have seen how PC-DOS offers the programmer only the simplest of facilities for applications that need to address either the serial or parallel ports of the IBM PC. The PC's ROM BIOS offers much better facilities, but with one significant bug in the 04/24/81 version of the serial character output routine. We have reviewed both the PC-DOS and ROM BIOS functions, and have seen how version 2.0 offers more power because of the presence of its EXEC function. We noted that programming at the I/O port level is complex for serial I/O control, and somewhat simpler for parallel printer control.

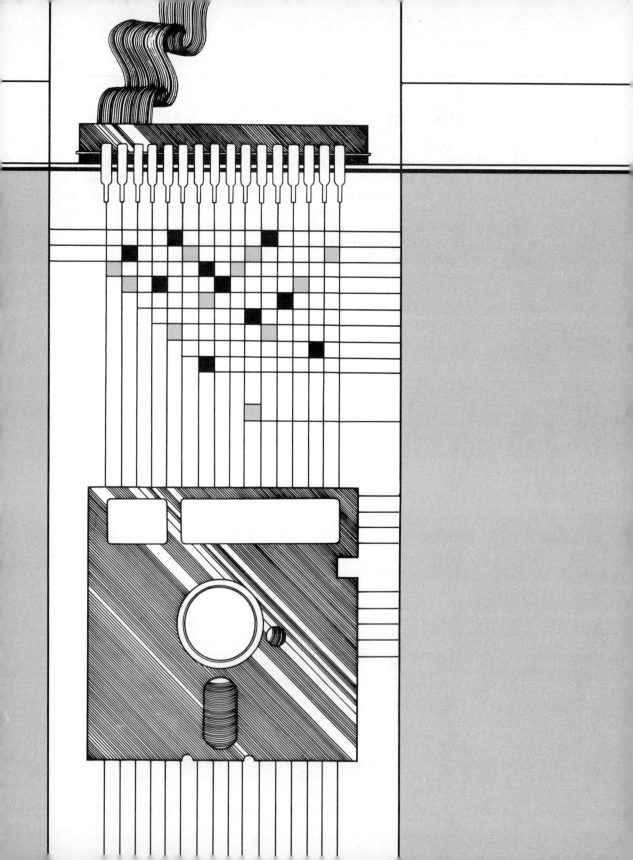

7

Dates and Times in PC-DOS

INTRODUCTION

This chapter gives you the different formats used for representing date and time in PC-DOS. It describes the PC-DOS function calls that exist to read and set the date and time from within a program. In addition, it discusses the ROM BIOS time-of-day function (interrupt 1A) and the interval-timer functions (interrupts 1C and 08). Notes are included on the accuracy that can be expected from the PC time routines. The chapter concludes with a discussion of how your software can be interrupted at every tick of the time, and how you can have total time control, at a price.

DATE FORMATS IN PC-DOS

Two formats for representing the date exist in PC-DOS: (1) the format used in the PC-DOS diskette directory entries, and (2) the format used by the function calls that read and set the system's date. Let's examine these formats.

Date Format in the Directory

The PC-DOS file routines use bytes 24 and 25 of each file's directory entry to indicate when the file was last updated or when it was created. If you write programs that create or alter this field, you will need to know the format. Otherwise, PC-DOS handles it for you.

Figure 7.1 shows the format. The five low-order bits contain the day, 1–31. The next four bits, 5 to 8, contain the month, 1–12. The seven high-order bits contain the year, a value 0–119 (which must be added to 1980 to obtain the correct year).

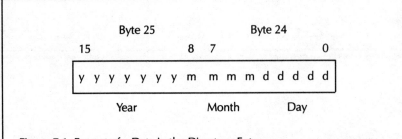

Figure 7.1: Format of a Date in the Directory Entry

If the date is not set on a system restart (power on, or the Ctrl-Alt-Del key combination) and the files are subsequently altered or created, the year field will have a zero value and the month and day fields will be set to one.

Version 2.0 of PC-DOS includes function 57H, which allows you to read or set a file's date and time. The same date format is used, except that when the date is passed between the program and the function in the DX register, the order of the bytes is reversed. DH contains the low-order portion of the date.

Date Format Used in the Read- and Set-System-Date Function Calls

Function calls 2A and 2B within interrupt 21H get and set the date that the system maintains. These routines use the CX and DX registers to pass the date. The year, 1980–2099 in binary, is in CX. DH contains the month, 1–12, and DL contains the day, 1–31. The formats for the date in the CX and DX registers are shown in Figure 7.2.

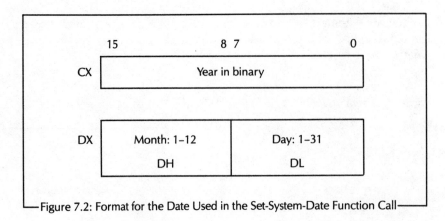

Figure 7.2: Format for the Date Used in the Set-System-Date Function Call

To read the system date, you set AH equal to 2A and execute interrupt 21H. On return, CX will contain the year; DX, the month and day.

To set the system date, use AH = 2B, with CX and DX appropriately set, and execute interrupt 21H. On return, if the PC-DOS routines did not like the value of the date, AH will be FF. Otherwise, it will be 00.

Computing Differences in Dates

Neither of these two date formats is suitable for immediate computation of date differences. They are not Julian-like in their format (where January 1 = 1, February 1 = 32, etc.), so computing date differences has to be done by your own routine on a field-by-field basis—simple but tedious.

Now that we have a familiarity with the date formats, let's discuss the different representations of time.

TIME FORMATS IN PC-DOS

PC-DOS uses two formats for the time, as it does for the date: (1) the format used by the PC-DOS directory entries, and (2) the format used by the function calls that read and set the system time. Yet another format for the time is used by ROM BIOS, but we will learn about that later.

Time Format in the Directory

The PC-DOS file routines maintain bytes 22 and 23 in each directory entry to indicate the time the file was last updated, or when it was created (if it has not been updated). (Note: If you don't intend to manipulate the directory data with your own program, this information may not interest you.) The internal format of each directory entry's time field is shown in Figure 7.3. The five low-order bits, bits 0 to 4, contain the number of two-second increments. That two-second interval is a small concession to having to fit the time of day into sixteen bits. The next six bits, bits 5 to 10, contain the minutes, 0–59; the five high-order bits contain the hours, 0–23.

Version 2 provides function 57H within interrupt 21H to set a file's time (and date). As with the date, when the time argument is passed in the CX register the bytes are reversed, with CH containing the low-order portion of the time.

If you don't set the time on a system restart, any files created or updated soon after that will appear to have been worked on in the early hours of the morning. This is because on system restart the system clock is initialized to 0:0:0.0, which to you and me is a moment after midnight, the beginning of a new day. If you ever need the time information in the directory, and sometimes you do work in the wee hours, the value that the time field has of indicating the latest copy may be lost.

If you share your PC with others, be sure to check the date and time when you take over the PC. Others may lead you down dark paths.

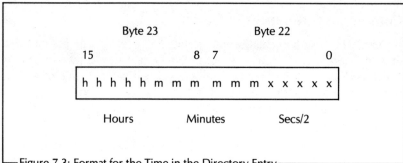

Figure 7.3: Format for the Time in the Directory Entry

Time Format in Read- and Set-System-Time Function Calls

Function calls 2C and 2D within interrupt 21H get and set the system time. As with the system date-setting function calls, CX and DX are used to pass parameters—here the time of day. Four 8-bit binary fields make up the time. CH contains the hours, 0–23; CL contains the minutes, 0–59; DH has the seconds, 0–59; and DL contains the hundredths of seconds, 0–99. Figure 7.4 shows the formats for the CX and DX registers.

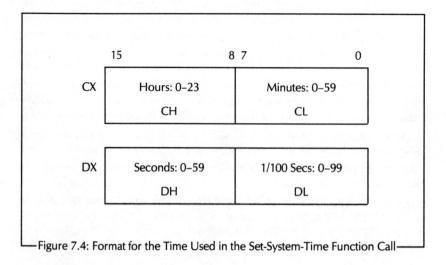

Figure 7.4: Format for the Time Used in the Set-System-Time Function Call

Accuracy in the PC-DOS Time Format

PC-DOS uses the ROM BIOS timekeeping routines, thus it is a little presumptuous when it pretends to an accuracy of 1/100th of a second. The time as expressed by ROM BIOS will be, on average, off by about 1/36th of a second in either direction. Therefore, relying on it to the nearest 1/100th of a second is not appropriate. If you need that kind of accuracy, you will have to build your own timing routines, using carefully timed delay loops.

Computing Time Differences in PC-DOS

Differences in time can be computed, as with dates, by a simple but slightly tedious byte-by-byte subtraction of each of the fields, thereby taking into account borrows from the next higher byte.

If you are interested in timing intervals of less than one hour, and you don't mind working in odd units, perhaps the ROM BIOS function call provides for the easiest time interval computation. Let's now discuss the ROM BIOS timekeeping routines.

ROM BIOS TIME

We now know that ROM BIOS keeps time in the PC. PC-DOS uses interrupt 1A, the time of day interrupt call, to get its time value from ROM BIOS. Let's now examine the time format that ROM BIOS uses and discuss the function call that gets and sets the time. After that we shall cover the subject of time overflow in ROM BIOS.

Time Format in ROM BIOS

ROM BIOS uses a time format unlike those used in PC-DOS or the directory entry. The time is kept in two words. The high-order word, TIMER_HIGH, contains the hours, 0–23 (sometimes higher than 23); the low-order word, TIMER_LOW, contains a count of increments of approximately 5/91 seconds. The sanity of choosing 5/91 seconds as a unit is revealed when you see that 64K (65,536) of these units make up 3600 seconds, or one hour. TIMER_HIGH and TIMER_LOW are the labels of the locations that ROM BIOS uses to store the time.

The ROM BIOS Read- and Set-System-Time Function Call

Interrupt 1A calls the ROM BIOS functions that read and set the time of day. CX and DX are used for passing the arguments: the high-order value is in CX, the low-order value in DX. CX contains the hours; DX contains the number of seconds × 18.206481. Figure 7.5 shows the ROM BIOS time formats.

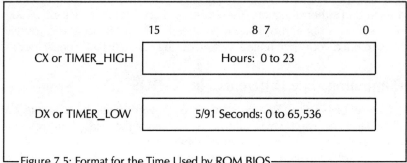

Figure 7.5: Format for the Time Used by ROM BIOS

To read the time, set AH equal to zero and execute interrupt 1AH. On return, CX and DX are set to the high- and low-order time values.

To set the time, set AH equal to 1; set CX and DX to your time values, and execute interrupt 1AH. You may set the time values to whatever you like. ROM BIOS makes no check on the CX or DX values. Therefore, if by mistake you set the hour (CX) to greater than 23 (with a DX of greater than B0H) it will be a long time, about seven and one-half years, before the end of the day (the timer's 24-hour overflow condition) is registered.

It is appropriate to repeat the admonition that if there are even hints of needing to maintain compatibility with further versions of PC-DOS, it is better for your program to use function calls in PC-DOS routines rather than the ROM BIOS function call.

Accuracy of the ROM BIOS Timekeeping

The clock timer in the PC interrupts 18.2 (5/91 = 1/18.2) times per second, when TIMER_LOW is incremented. An overflow from TIMER_LOW increments TIMER_HIGH at almost exactly one-hour intervals. In an attempt to be as accurate as possible, the ROM BIOS routines adjust for exactness at the end of every day by waiting an additional 9.65 seconds before setting the time to zero for the next day. This suggests that the PC clock gains just under 1/2 second every hour, but it corrects for that at the end of each day.

How accurately 18.2 times per second describes the time interval between interrupts can be seen by reviewing the following information: there are 1193180/65536 or 18.206481 interrupts per second; thus each interval is 0.0549254 seconds.

Computing Time Differences in ROM BIOS Times

Finding the difference between two times stored in ROM BIOS format is truly simple: you subtract the smaller from the larger. (Note: If you arrived at this paragraph from the index, see the section "Time Format in ROM BIOS" above for more information).

The Location of the Time Cells

Now that you understand how timekeeping works, you may want to see the two timer locations: TIMER_LOW and TIMER_HIGH. You can use DEBUG to look at locations 0:046C and 0:046E. It appeals to some to look at PC-DOS busily working when it appears to be quiet. Given a highly anthropomorphic, and perhaps maudlin, point of view, 0:046C is evidence of a PC heartbeat.

Time Overflow in ROM BIOS

The ROM BIOS time read function (INT 1AH) tells you whether the time has overflowed to another day since it was last read (or set). On return from the read function, if AL is nonzero, the time has overflowed to another day. If AL is zero, the timer is still on the same day as when it was last read or set. (Note: AL does not contain the number of days it has overflowed.)

We have previously discussed the (approximate) 1/2-second-per-hour "gain" in the ROM BIOS clock. We also showed how this is compensated for once a day (the time-update routines make the transition from one day to another when TIMER_HIGH equals 24 *and* TIMER_LOW is equal to B0H). The time overflow flag is not set until the extra time (9.65 seconds) has elapsed. The next day's time is established by setting both TIMER_HIGH and TIMER_LOW to zero. (Note: This adjustment is visible if your program uses the ROM BIOS time function call; it will not be visible if it uses the PC-DOS function calls.)

This review of date updating points us to a situation that might, once in a while, cause a problem. You might have routines that print the date and time, where the time is based on the ROM BIOS time value and the date is incremented on the basis of the return from the BIOS time call having a nonzero AL value. Because of the 9.65-second wait, immediately after midnight the date will not be updated for the first few seconds of the next day. Your programs may be confused when a date has been saved or printed in the first post-midnight 9.65-second interval. The moral of this is that if you are going to use the ROM BIOS time function, use it for time interval management, not time and date recording.

Let's now move on to see how your program can be interrupted 18.2 times per second.

Catching Ticks with the ROM BIOS Timer

There is a feature in ROM BIOS that will interrupt a program 18.2 times per second. Interrupt 1CH is executed every time the ROM BIOS timer routine is executed. This means that you don't have to use the ROM BIOS time values to measure elapsed time. Your program can keep track of time in its own way.

On system restart, the vector for interrupt 1CH (i.e., bytes 70 to 73H) is initialized to point to an IRET instruction. Your program can redirect the vector to your own timer-tick service routine. With this routine you can keep track of time in a format that is more convenient than that provided by ROM BIOS or PC-DOS. But don't forget that before your program terminates, it must reset the interrupt vector to its original value.

TOTAL TIME CONTROL

Your software can take over the entire management of time by redirecting interrupt 8H, locations 20 to 23H. The ROM BIOS time-update routines will no longer be executed, and all time management functions, such as providing a response to the PC-DOS read- and set-system-time function calls, become your program's responsibility. This may turn out to be a heavy burden with few advantages—power with a price.

SUMMARY

In this chapter, we have learned about the two PC-DOS date formats; the one that is used in directory entries, and the other that is used in the date-access function calls. We also have seen three time formats: one used in directory entries, one used in the PC-DOS time-access function calls, and one used by ROM BIOS. We examined the accuracy of timekeeping in both ROM BIOS and PC-DOS, and looked at how, by redirecting an interrupt vector, a program can keep its own time. PC-DOS's handling of dates and times is quite simple.

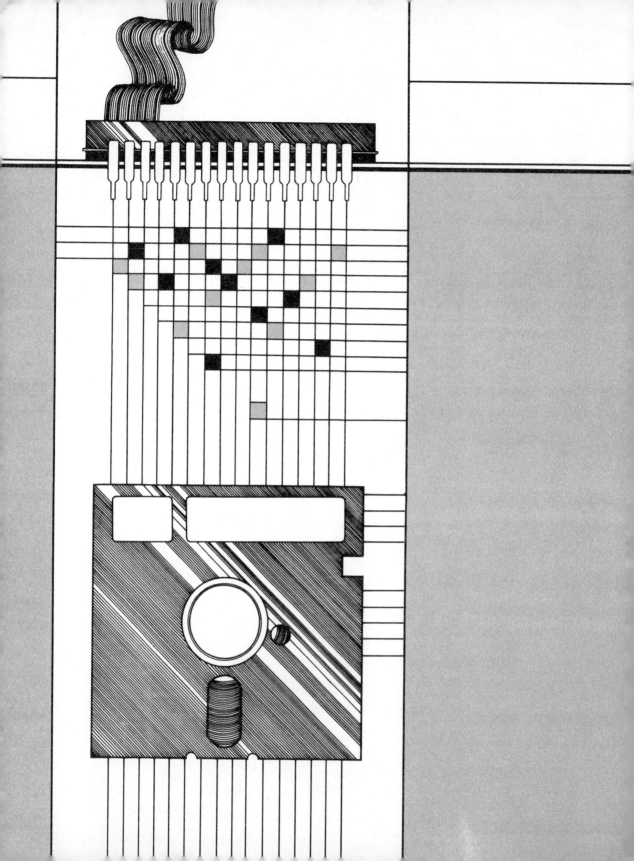

8

Version 2.0 at the Systems Level

INTRODUCTION

The purpose of this chapter is to introduce, from the programmer's point of view, the parts of version 2.0 that have not yet been described or mentioned. The new function calls for accessing the tree-structured filing system have been described in Chapter 2, and the character strings for keyboard key reassignment and extended screen control have been described in Chapters 4 and 5.

We will begin with a summary of the new features in version 2, and briefly review the new file access strategy. We will then cover (1) the new approach to function call error return reporting, (2) the cleanup of version 1's loose ends, and (3) the function that permits control of the level of Ctrl Break checking. Next we will explore the memory management functions in some depth. After that we will examine the execute function, one of the two most important features of version 2 (the other is tree-structured files).

WHAT'S NEW WITH VERSION 2

Version 2 includes pipes, filters, I/O redirection, and a new file access strategy. At the programmer's level, this translates into the ability to call one program from another, memory management functions that allocate and deallocate blocks of memory, a generalized I/O control function that works for both devices and files, and the concept of handles (a 16-bit file or device ID) associated with opened files or devices.

Version 2.0 also brings expanded termination functions (which allow for simpler overlay handling), a more consistent approach to function call error reporting, and a few functions that clear up some of the loose ends of versions 1.

Version 2.0 is a step toward XENIX, the UNIX-derived system offered by Microsoft. Version 2 is still a single-task system, except under some special circumstances, for example, when the PRINT command is in operation.

PC-DOS has been reengineered so that many of the barriers to multitasking existent in versions 1 have been cleared away.

Let's begin with a brief summary of the new file access strategy, for those of you who missed Chapter 2.

NEW FILE ACCESS STRATEGY

An entirely new strategy for file, data, and directory access is included in version 2.0. The file control block concept is gone (although, for compatibility, all the versions 1 FCB-oriented file access function calls are still included). It is replaced by access based on the file's name and the path to the file through a tree structure of directories, and on an address within the file. This new strategy is simpler and more flexible than the FCB-based approach, and it is very welcome.

NEW FUNCTION CALL ERROR RETURN REPORTING

Version 2.0 has adopted (not consistently) a new convention for indicating function call error conditions. The error status is indicated by the carry bit: the carry bit is set if there was an error, clear if there was no error. The error type is returned in AX, and may be interpreted by reference to a common table of errors containing, in version 2.0, seventeen different error possibilities. This "Function Call Error Return Table" can be found in Chapter 17.

SOME LOOSE ENDS CLEARED UP

Version 2.0 supplies a few of the items that are obviously missing from versions 1. For example, functions are provided to read the current DTA (in versions 1 the DTA could only be set), to read the read-after-write verify state, and to get and set an interrupt vector. However, repeating the last versions' mistake of supplying only one-half of a function, version 2.0 contains the ability to read the country-dependent information (currency symbol, date format, etc.), but not to set it. Rumor has it that version 2.01 has corrected this omission.

THE BREAK FUNCTION—FUNCTION 33H

The break function is the internal equivalent of the BREAK command. This function either reads or sets the level of Ctrl Break checking.

Normally, PC-DOS checks for the Ctrl Break character being entered at the keyboard only during PC-DOS functions that access the keyboard, the screen, the printer, or the auxiliary devices. Function 33H (and the BREAK command) allow you to tell PC-DOS to check for the Ctrl Break character every time any PC-DOS function call is used. This expanded level of checking still won't help you abort from a purely computational process, but any disk and file accesses will open up a program to the Ctrl Break character.

To read the current state of Ctrl Break checking, set AL equal to zero, set AH equal to 33H, and execute interrupt 21H. On return, if DL = 0, Ctrl Break checking is off. If DL = 1, Ctrl Break checking is on.

To set the Crtl Break checking status, enter the function with AL = 1. Set DL = 0 to turn Ctrl Break checking off, or DL = 1 to turn it on.

MEMORY MANAGEMENT— FUNCTIONS 48H, 49H, AND 4AH

Version 2.0 provides memory management functions that (1) allocate to the caller a block of memory, (2) deallocate (return to the system pool) previously allocated blocks of memory, and (3) change the size of allocated memory blocks. The allocation takes place from memory that is not currently assigned to other purposes.

Memory is allocated in units of "paragraphs," which are 16-byte chunks. The allocated memory always begins on a paragraph boundary; the low-order hex digit of its address is zero.

The quantity of memory used up by a memory allocation call (assuming it was successful) is one paragraph more than the number of paragraphs requested. PC-DOS uses the extra paragraph to record the size of each allocated block of memory. A program that asks for many small blocks of memory will exhaust the available memory sooner than a program that asks for a few large blocks of memory.

If you ask for two blocks of memory in a row, the blocks will not be contiguous. They will be separated by the record-keeping paragraph that belongs to the second block of allocated memory.

The PC-DOS command processor assigns to most programs the entire memory pool when the programs are loaded, so function 4AH must be called before function 48H. Let's examine the memory allocation functions.

Allocating Memory—Function 48H

This memory allocation function allocates the number of paragraphs specified in BX. It returns in AX the segment address of the allocated memory.

To acquire memory, put the number of paragraphs required in BX, set AH equal to 48H, and execute interrupt 21H. On return, if the memory was available, AX:0 points to the allocated memory. If not enough memory was available, the carry bit will be set and BX will contain the maximum number of paragraphs that could be successfully allocated.

Deallocating Memory—Function 49H

This function returns to the system pool memory that has been previously allocated by a call to function 48H. The function will fail if the memory control block (the extra paragraph) associated with the previously allocated memory has been damaged, or if the deallocation function does not recognize the address of the block being returned.

To return memory to the system pool, put the segment address of the allocated block into ES, set AH equal to 49H, and execute interrupt 21H. If the carry bit is set on return, the function has failed for one of the reasons just mentioned.

Changing the Size of Allocated Memory Segments—Function 4AH

Memory is allocated in blocks of contiguous paragraphs, so it is either happy coincidence or a product of your program's organization that if you wish to expand a previously allocated memory segment, there is free memory following it.

This function will either reduce the size of a previously allocated memory block or, if space allows, expand its size. To change the size of an allocated segment of memory, put the segment address of the memory into ES, put the new number of paragraphs requested in BX, set AH equal to 4AH, and execute interrupt 21H. On return, if the carry bit is set, BX will contain the maximum number of paragraphs available for allocation, as it does when function 48H fails.

Now that we have seen the memory management functions, let's examine a function that is often used along with them, the execute function.

THE EXECUTE FUNCTION

In version 2.0 the execute function has two separate purposes: (1) it will load and execute a program, and (2) it will load an overlay. Using this function requires more preparation than most other functions require. However, once mastered, the execute function is powerful and useful.

Before we see how to use the execute function, let's have a look at some of the implications of its existence.

The Execute Function and Multitasking

Once a program has called the execute function, it can do nothing else until the program it called is complete (this would not be true in a multitasking system). So, typically, the calling program (the one that calls the execute function) will immediately call the wait function. The wait function (4DH) gets the return code supplied by the called program.

If version 2 made multitasking available to us, our programs could keep working (i.e., they would not immediately call the wait function) while the executed program proceeded. We could also start dealing with processes as well as programs, and really keep the PC busy. Version 2 is tantalizingly close to multitasking.

Executing PC-DOS Commands

The program that is loaded by the execute function may be another copy of the command processor. The effect of this is to have all the normal PC-DOS commands at the disposal of any program. Appendix F of the DOS manual outlines the method of calling the command processor to execute a PC-DOS command. An example is given here.

Using the Load and Execute Option of Function 4B

Let's have a look at the steps required to use the load and execute option. They are as follows:

1. Make sure memory space is available.
2. Build a parameter block.
3. Build a drive, path, and program name string.
4. Call the execute function.
5. Call the wait function.

We will examine these steps one by one, presenting an example at the end.

Returning Memory to the Pool

In the current versions of PC-DOS, programs usually have allocated to them the entire installed memory of the PC. Other programs cannot be loaded until some of this memory is returned to the system's pool of available memory. This is accomplished with function 4AH, which takes as an argument the segment address of the allocated memory block.

To return memory to the system pool, you need two pieces of information: (1) the length, in paragraphs, of the currently running program (so you know the new memory block size to give function 4AH), and (2) the segment address of the currently running program.

When the currently running program was loaded, the memory management function was used to get the space to hold it. The segment address of the allocated memory was put into the CS, DS, and ES registers.

Constructing the Parameter Block

Once enough space is available for the program to be executed, a parameter block needs to be constructed so that the called program will have (1) an environment string, (2) a command line (at 80H in the new PSP), and (3) correctly set default file control blocks at 5C and 6C in the new program segment prefix. The format of the parameter block is included in the description of the execute function in Appendix D of the DOS manual.

The Environment String   You can create your own, or you can use the environment string belonging to the currently running process (the program calling the execute function). Creating your own requires an understanding of the contents of the CONFIG.SYS file. To use the existing environment string, set the first two bytes of the parameter block to zero.

Creating a Command Line   Your program needs to create the command line that will be moved to 80H of the called program. The format of the command line is

        L string CR

where L is the number of bytes in (the command text) string, string is the text of the command, and CR is 0DH. Note that the command text does not contain the name of the program being called, just the characters that would follow the command, including the space and slash characters as appropriate.

The Default File Control Blocks   If your program is using only version 2 file access functions, it does not matter what the default FCBs contain. Bytes 7–14 of the parameter table may be 0. For versions 1 file access, if the command line's first and second arguments are file names, then bytes 7–10 and bytes 11–14 of the parameter block should point to default file control blocks.

The default file control block is 16 bytes long and consists of (1) a one byte drive designator (00 for default drive, 01 for drive A, 02 for drive B, etc.), followed by (2) the filename of the first or second argument, in uppercase, padded out with spaces on the right to make it eight characters long, and (3) the filename extension in uppercase, padded with spaces on the right, if necessary, to make it three characters long, and (4) four undefined bytes.

Bytes 7–10 of the parameter block should point to the default FCB constructed from the first file name argument.

Building a Drive, Path, and Command Name String

Your program needs to contain a string of the form

d:\path\file name

terminated by a zero byte. This is the string that tells the execute function which program to execute.

Calling the Execute Function

To execute another program, point DS:DX to the ASCII drive, path, and file name string (which is terminated by a zero byte, as always), point ES:BX to the constructed parameter block, set AL equal to 0 and AH equal to 4BH, save the registers that your program cares about on the stack, save the SS and SP registers other than on the stack, and execute interrupt 21H.

On return from the executed function, most of the registers have been changed, including SS and SP. At this point, SS and SP must be restored from where they were saved, and the registers your program cares about restored from the stack.

Calling the Wait Function

In version 2.0 of PC-DOS, the caller program stops executing until the called program runs to completion (or is terminated early for some reason). (In future versions that include multitasking, the caller program could continue to run until it needs to know that the called program has concluded.) The caller program uses the wait function to wait for the completion of the called program, and to collect whatever error or completion code is returned as the called program.

The executed program uses function 4CH to return its error or completion code. This code is available to the calling program when it calls the wait function, 4DH. A program can only call the wait function once for each program it executes. A second wait call would risk waiting for the completion of a never-executed program.

An Example

This example shows how a program can execute any of the regular PC-DOS commands. The difference between this example and one where a program of your own creation is called will occur in the name of the program called and the command line passed. Let's assume that you want a program to run CHKDSK on the disk in drive B. We will assume that the system's memory pool is adequate to hold a copy of the command processor (COMMAND.COM), which is the program we are going to execute.

Parameter Block Construction   We will pass on the existing environment, so word zero (the first two bytes) of the parameter block is zero.
The command line to be placed at 81H in the called program's PSP will look like this:

     /C CHKDSK B:

At 80H will be the count of characters in the string (0CH). The character following the string (the terminator) will be 0DH. So words one and two will point to an area whose first byte is 0CH, whose following bytes contain /C CHKDSK B:, and whose last byte contains 0DH. Word one is the low-order (offset) part of the address, word two is the high-order (segment) part of the address.
The command processor does not use the formatted file control blocks at 5C and 6C to run the CHKDSK command, so we can set the next two pairs of words to point to a character string of eleven spaces.

Drive, Path, and Command Name String   The program we wish to execute is COMMAND.COM. It resides on drive A in the primary directory, so the string that DS:DX will point to is

     a:command.com

terminated by a zero byte. We have now set up the parameters that the execute function will use. It is time to call it.
We might think that CHKDSK.COM could be directly executed. This is not so simple, because the command processor (COMMAND.COM) and CHKDSK.COM know about one another and have their own method of communicating arguments.

SUMMARY

We have reviewed the new features that version 2.0 of PC-DOS supplies, and we have examined the memory management and execute function calls. The chapter ended with an example of how to use the execute function to call the command processor program from within your program.

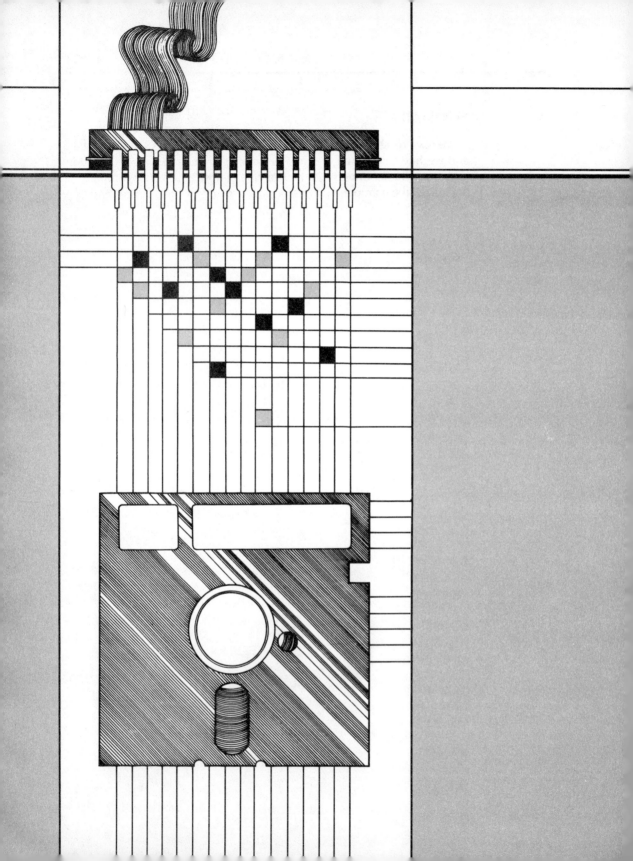

9

A User-Level
Introduction to PC-DOS

INTRODUCTION

Welcome to PC-DOS. This chapter begins the second half of the book, which is devoted to describing PC-DOS at the user's, instead of programmer's, level.

User-level subjects that need to be covered in detail have a chapter to themselves, after this one. This chapter is a place to put information that does not deserve a whole chapter, but nonetheless needs to be presented so that you can use PC-DOS efficiently and productively.

PC-DOS does not take long to learn. It has been written to be friendly to the user, and its commands are not obscure. The DOS manual is a good source of information about each command, so we do not describe each command in detail. We recommend you read through the command descriptions once, so you get to know the selection of available commands. Then experiment with each command to learn more about it.

By including the DEBUG chapter toward the end of this part of the book, we hope that we will draw you into perhaps a more interesting part of the system, which is described in the first half of the book.

We will begin the chapter with a brief description of PC-DOS from the user's point of view, showing how it meets the criteria for a useful, well-organized operating system. We will compare PC-DOS with CP/M, which may be useful for those of you who have had experience with CP/M. We will learn about the keyboard and how PC-DOS takes advantage of some of the features built into it. The keyboard is your main path of communication with PC-DOS; knowing how to use it effectively saves you time and effort. Next we will see what happens when PC-DOS encounters disk errors. After that we point out parts of the DOS manual that have a high degree of information value, relative to the amount you have to read. In the last part of the chapter we will examine a few of the PC-DOS commands, see how to get the most out of them, and how, on occasion, their operation may not immediately be clear.

A BRIEF DESCRIPTION OF PC-DOS CAPACITIES

PC-DOS is an operating system. The task of an operating system is to monitor commands given by the user to a computer, to load and execute programs specified by the user, to manage the devices attached to the computer, to manage the files of data and programs that the computer will work with, and to make available a small host of utility functions that provide the user with the tools and information he needs to be productive and efficient.

For example, an operating system needs to include easily used tools for (1) loading programs, (2) transferring files from one disk to another, (3) preparing a disk to accept files of data or programs, and (4) sending information to a printer. PC-DOS has all these features, and more, including a convenient utility that keeps track of the time of day, and another that, given a date, computes the day of the week.

THE DIFFERENCE BETWEEN PC-DOS AND CP/M

CP/M and PC-DOS are both respectable operating systems. PC-DOS has the major advantage that it was developed later, for 16-bit computers. PC-DOS does not reproduce the weaker areas of CP/M, and it now contains significant improvements in its fundamental design.

Both operating systems are designed for microcomputers, and both have about the same range of functions. Until PC-DOS version 2.0 was released, it could be said that CP/M was a better system for software development, but that is no longer true. The major differences that the user experiences between CP/M and PC-DOS are (1) PC-DOS uses a more natural way of accepting commands, and (2) PC-DOS handles error conditions with more aplomb. (An operating system that handles error conditions poorly gives the user the sudden experience of being thrust back into the dark ages, where, at the whim of some unreachable demon, your whole day's work is lost. PC-DOS is not such a system.)

As an example of the first difference, look at the command to copy a file called FILE.EXT from drive A (the default drive) to drive B in CP/M:

        PIP *B: = FILE.EXT

In PC-DOS the same effect is achieved with the command

        COPY FILE.EXT B:

PC-DOS AND THE PC'S KEYBOARD

In this section we will examine features available at the keyboard that are not regular PC-DOS commands. (Commands are examined in the last section of this chapter.)

PC-DOS has made good use of the first six function keys to provide in-line editing of any command we may type. Before we examine in-line editing and other key features, we must note that some of these keyboard features are not available all of the time. In the section on each key feature, we will mention whether it is applicable over the whole scope of PC-DOS operations, or just at the command level (when you see the prompt). Let's see how to edit a command.

Editing a Command

We make mistakes when we type commands at the keyboard. We also frequently have to issue the same or a similar command more than once. PC-DOS has provisions for helping us correct our typing errors, as well as for resurrecting the last command issued so we don't have to type it again.

Resurrecting the Last Command

The F3 key does this for you. Unless PC-DOS has just finished executing a batch file, when you press the F3 key, you will see the last command reappear. All you have to do to execute it again is press the enter key.

You may want to change the last command a little before entering it again. The PC-DOS in-line editing features will meet just that need.

The In-Line Edit Feature

Function keys F1 through F6, and the Esc, Ins, Del, and cursor control keys can be used to edit a command. Until you press the Enter key you may rearrange, respell, shorten, or lengthen whatever you type at the PC-DOS prompt level.

The use of the in-line editing keys is described in detail in Chapter 10, in the section called "The Edit Command."

The Availability of the Edit Feature

In-line editing is guaranteed to work only at the command level. At this level (when you see the A>prompt), PC-DOS controls the interpretation of the function keys. Once another program has been called, it can alter the effect of the function (and other) keys, and so block out some, or all, of the in-line edit capability. For example, BASIC uses different interpretations for the function keys; BASIC also allows you to redefine them once again.

EDLIN and DEBUG do not change the effect of the function keys, so they retain the in-line editing capability. It is worth your while to learn how to use this feature of PC-DOS.

Now that we have seen how to resurrect a command, and learned that until you press the Enter key you can play around with the text of a command all you like, let's consider long lines.

Entry of Long Lines

A long line is one that runs off the edge of the screen. At the command level, if you keep typing until characters reach the right-hand edge of the screen, the extra characters will wrap around to the beginning of the next line. You can cause wrapping to occur before the edge of the screen by typing Ctrl Enter. This helps make what you type more legible. It may seem to you that this feature is not going to change your experience of any one day from average to exquisite, and you are probably right. However, I have found it useful once or twice.

Unlike most word processing programs, when you use the Ctrl Enter key combination to move to the next line, no space will magically appear at the boundary; you need to supply one if you press Ctrl Enter at the end of a word, so that the long command you are entering has the correct format. There are circumstances when characters entered after the right margin is reached do not wrap to the next line. See the section "Mode Setting Sequences" in Chapter 5.

Hard Copy Generation

PC-DOS supports two keyboard features for generating printed output of what you type and what appears on the screen. The first, Shift PrtSc, is the snapshot mode. The second, Ctrl PrtSc, is the "keep copying everything" mode.

Shift PrtSc

When you press these two keys, an image of the screen is sent to the printer. The keyboard interrupt routines keep alert for this key combination. When the combination is pressed, everything else stops and a copy of the whole screen is sent to the printer.

Ctrl PrtSc

This key combination toggles on or off the echoing of characters from the screen to the keyboard. When you first press the two keys together, everything you type that appears on the screen will be echoed to the printer. The characters are echoed when you press the Enter key at the end of a line, not one by one. To stop this echoing to the printer, press Ctrl PrtSc again.

The Availability of the Shift and Ctrl PrtSc Features

These features operate at a very deep level of the operating system, and are always available at the command level.

Few applications (programs) have any need to interpret the meanings of the Shift and Ctrl PrtSc key combinations in any other way, so one might expect them to be active all the time. For most applications, the Shift PrtSc feature is always available.

However, the Ctrl PrtSc feature involves accessing the printer at the end of every typed line. This can slow the operations of programs intolerably. In this situation, and where the printer is being used by the program currently running, either the program turns off the Ctrl and/or Shift PrtSc features, or when you use them, the resulting printed page is a mess.

Stopping the Rushing Text

When a program puts out many lines of data in rapid succession, you need a way to stop the flow so you can read it before it rolls off the screen. Ctrl NumLock will do this. Ctrl NumLock is not a toggle—after you have stopped the flow of text, you start it again by pressing a different key.

Ctrl NumLock is a two-handed operation. You can't drink a cup of coffee and review screens very easily using this feature. If you are lucky, the program displaying all that data will respond to the xon/xoff commands or a similar protocol. A program that recognizes the xon/xoff (transmission on/transmission off) protocol will stop transmitting characters when the receiving device, in this case the console, sends a message (xoff) saying it is not ready for more characters. This means that Ctrl S and Ctrl Q often stop and restart the flow of data. Sometimes just the Ctrl S combination will both stop and restart the flow. Experiment—you may free a hand!

Keyboard Key Reassignment

Version 2.0 allows you to redefine the meaning of keystrokes and keystroke combinations. You can use this feature to make character strings appear at the touch of a key. The character strings can be whole commands or just words that you use frequently, such as anthropomorphic or PC-DOS.

If you choose to reassign the meaning of the first six function keys, you will lose the in-line edit capability. You might want to consider using combinations of function keys with either the Shift, the Ctrl, or the Alt key, rather than reassign the meaning of the function keys alone.

PC-DOS AND DISK ERRORS

When PC-DOS cannot successfully perform a disk access that a program has asked it to do, it prints a message. In the middle of whatever program is running, a deep-level disk-error handling routine displays the message

Abort, Retry, or Ignore?

A correct response is one of the three characters A, R, or I (lowercase or uppercase). No carriage return (Enter key) is required. Choose your response carefully—the error routine responds immediately to the first key pressed.

If you respond to this message by pressing the A key, the deep-level routine believes you wish to abort the currently running program, not just the disk transfer. When you type A, you will suddenly be back at the command (PC-DOS prompt) level. The program that was running won't be any more. Any data that it had accumulated will be lost, including, for example, the whole (unsaved) text file you were creating. So avoid responding with an A if you can.

Each program may be different in the way it responds to disk errors. PC-DOS won't lie to a program about disk errors, so if you select the Ignore response (I), it is up to the program that is running to decide what to do about the error.

WHAT'S WHERE IN THE DOS MANUAL

We recommend that you read the DOS manual and keep it handy, with this book, for reference. However, there are parts of the manual that you are more likely to need than others, and parts that give information with such a wide range of applicability that if you don't read them with close attention, joys that you might otherwise experience while using your PC will be lost.

Introductory Information

The versions 1 DOS manuals tend to jump right into showing you how to execute commands without much of an introduction. This is fine for people who have some experience with microcomputers and operating systems. However, many others will need a more thorough introduction, some of which is presented in the Guide to Operations manual that comes with the PC. By contrast, the version 2.0 manual provides, in Chapter One and the first half of Chapter Two, a thorough grounding for people new to microcomputers.

Command Syntax

The DOS manuals compress much useful information into the sections entitled Format Notation and DOS Command Parameters. Read these with care. They appear toward the beginning of Chapter Three of the versions 1 manuals, and in Chapter Six of the 2.0 manual.

Skipping, for the moment, the Reserved Device Names and Global Filename Characters sections, we come to Information Common to All Commands. This section is probably the richest in the manuals. Once the information in this section has become part of you, you will learn new commands with ease, and you will know how to get the most out of familiar commands.

Reserved Device Names

The Reserved Device Names section presents the device names that can be used in place of file names. This minor form of I/O redirection adds power to your commands. For example, the command

    COPY FILE.EXT PRN

is a print utility that operates on files composed of lines of text. The command

    COPY CON: PRN

sends to the printer (one line at a time) whatever you type at the keyboard. (Note: COPY stops operating when it sees an end-of-file character. To enter an end-of-file character at the keyboard, use the F6 key or type Ctrl Z.)

If you keep the list of reserved file names in mind, your experience of the power of PC-DOS commands will be enhanced.

Wild-Card Characters

The Global Filename Characters section shows how ? and * (the wild-card characters) can be used to find files that you don't know how to spell exactly, as well as groups of files having the same filename but different extensions.

Some commands, such as COPY, will accept global file name characters and operate on all the files that match, instead of just a single file.

Command Descriptions

This is where you learn what a command can do. You probably will often refer to this section of the manual. Don't be afraid to reread the description of even a common command. The last time you read it, you may not have had an immediate need for some of its less obvious applications.

If you have experience working with computers, you may be tempted to skim over these command descriptions. Some of the commands are complex and have valuable features that are easily overlooked. It is a little tedious to preach, but if you take the time to read these descriptions all the way through before you rush off to do something with the commands, your work will be more productive and more entertaining.

Here are examples of features of common commands that casual users may have missed.

The DIR Command

The DIR command has a built-in Ctrl NumLock feature—the /P option. The command

    DIR B:/P

will display the names of the files on the diskette in drive B, pausing every screenful so you have time to examine the list.

You probably know about the /W option, which shows only the names of files, five to a line. This option provides a compact display, making it easier to look over a directory for groups of files.

The COPY Command

COPY will concatenate files for you, as well as copy them from one place to another. COPY will also accept CON: as the input or output, allowing you to display a file's contents using

    COPY FILE.EXT CON:

or to create a file from the keyboard using

    COPY CON: FILE.EXT

The DISKCOPY Command

You can copy to an unformatted disk with this command. DISKCOPY formats the target diskette to be identical to the format of the source diskette. This has a sometimes confusing side effect: if you copy a single-sided disk to a previously formatted double-sided disk, after the DISKCOPY operation the target disk will be single sided.

The CHKDSK Command

The CHKDSK command does not check the surface of the whole disk. It will not find unreadable sectors, except in the directory and file allocation tables. What it does do is check that the chains of clusters in the file allocation table are intact.

CHKDSK's report includes, in the last two lines, a report on the amount of memory installed in the PC. If you have 320K memory, it is easy to confuse the memory size report with the disk capacity.

THE EXPANDED CAPABILITIES OF VERSION 2.0

If you have version 2.0 of PC-DOS, do learn how to use pipes and filters. They are explained in Chapter 16. The filter programs provided with version 2.0 (SORT, MORE, and FIND) are not stunningly powerful, but they are useful. Commercial software vendors probably will be offering other filter programs from which you may build inexpensive, tailor-made applications that do just what you want.

SUMMARY

In this chapter, we have briefly examined the purpose of an operating system, and we have noted that PC-DOS is a user-friendly system that provides us with a powerful set of useful commands. We have reviewed some of the PC-DOS features that are available at the keyboard: in-line editing, hard copy production, and stopping the rushing text. We have seen how selecting the abort option in response to a disk error may have dramatic unwanted effects. We have pointed out the sections of the DOS manual that are particularly valuable to study, and we have reviewed a few commands to show you some of their not immediately obvious features. Let's move on to the next chapter to examine EDLIN, a tool you will be using often.

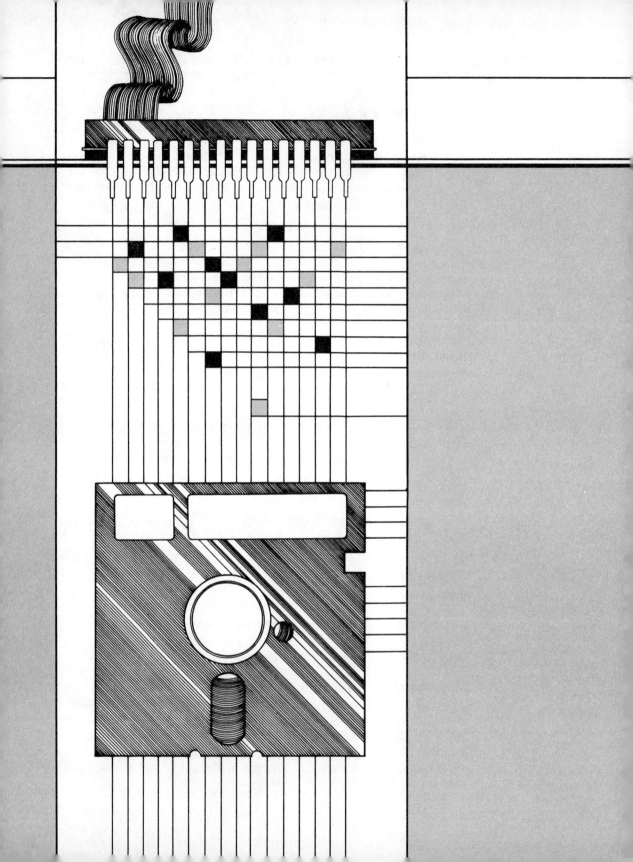

10

A Quick Look at Edlin

INTRODUCTION

EDLIN is a funny little editor, but it's free. You probably will be using it, so we should learn something about it. In version 2.0 EDLIN is more powerful than in the preceding versions, but it is still only a line editor. This chapter is an outline of EDLIN's capabilities and limitations.

EDLIN can understand simple one-character commands; each command is usually preceded by a line number or a pair of line numbers indicating the line or lines of the file on which EDLIN should operate.

We will start the chapter with a description of line numbers in EDLIN, and follow that with a brief introduction to the EDLIN commands. Next we will look at the actions required to create and edit a new file. In the course of this guided tour, all of EDLIN's features will be brought to light; you will see that EDLIN is not a complex editor. Then we will look at the extra facilities provided by version 2.0. The chapter ends with a quick reference command summary, which is repeated in Chapter 17.

Once you have read this chapter, the best path to familiarity and comfort with EDLIN is to use it to write a small program or poem "on the fly"—as you sit at the terminal. This is not a recommended programming practice for any but the simplest of programs (it's essential to think through the problem and possible solutions first), but it suits our purpose here. You will probably make enough mistakes to need most of the features of EDLIN versions 1, except perhaps the R (replace text) command, and you can invent a need for that.

Let's first look at line numbers in EDLIN.

LINE NUMBERS IN EDLIN

EDLIN is a line editor. It is designed to work on one line at a time; you have to specify line numbers to get anything done. An EDLIN command is usually preceded by one or two line numbers. For example:

6,10D

This command deletes lines 6 through 10.

Line Numbers as Butterflies

Line numbers are transient things. They are only part of your program when it is in memory; they are not part of your program when it is saved on the disk. During an editing session a line number's location in the text is not necessarily fixed. One line number may flit from line to line as the session progresses. This is because EDLIN renumbers lines immediately after every insertion and deletion (and after every Append or Write command).

If you want to make several changes to a file, you may find yourself resorting to frequent use of the List and Page [2.0] commands. With these commands you can keep track of what number belongs to which line at each stage of the edit. After you have gained some proficiency in using EDLIN, you may be able to recompute line numbers in your head after each command.

Note: To minimize changes in line numbers, make your editing changes first at the end of the file, working backwards; that way the early line numbers will remain unaltered until you need them.

EDLIN maintains the number of the current line; it will use the current line if you don't give it a line number to work with. EDLIN's choice of the line number to make current is not always what you would expect. In version 2 it's easier to appreciate EDLIN's choice for current line, because logic seems to have played a good part in its selection. EDLIN's interpretation of current line number is like the many odd things one gets used to and eventually finds useful.

EDLIN provides several shortcuts to expressing line numbers, which are described in the paragraphs on the List command.

Let's now look at the groups of commands in EDLIN.

THE EDLIN COMMANDS

The EDLIN commands will modify text, display the results, and perform housekeeping activities, such as saving the text when the work is completed. For a table summary of the commands and their formats, see

Figure 10.1 at the end of the chapter. These are the simple text modification commands:

> Insert line(s)
> Edit a single line
> Delete line(s)

The fancier editing commands are as follows:

> Copy line(s) [2.0]
> Move line(s) [2.0]
> Search for text
> Replace text
> Transfer a disk file into the current file [2.0]

These commands show you the text:

> List line(s)
> Page through the text [2.0]

The last group consists of the housekeeping commands:

> End or Exit EDLIN, saving your work
> Quit without saving
> Append more lines from the rest of the file on the disk
> Write some lines to the disk to make room for more in memory

EDLIN takes the first letter of each of these commands as its cue for action, with the exception of the command to edit a single line, which takes a line number only.

Command Format

The format for EDLIN's editing and display commands is

line number (, line number) command

where both line number values are optional. The Copy [2.0] and Move [2.0] commands have additional arguments. The Append and Write commands take a quantity of lines as an argument. The Transfer [2.0] command includes a file name as an argument. The End and Quit commands take no arguments.

The command E means "write the file to disk and quit to PC-DOS." To edit a line, just type the line number.

You will find examples of the commands in the descriptions that follow. Now that you have seen the available commands and know about line numbers, let's look at the steps that are necessary to create a file.

CREATING A FILE USING EDLIN

If you have used line editors before and want a little practice with this one, you could type along inventively as you read this section.

To create a file, the first thing you need is a file name and a disk on which to store it. This is necessary because before EDLIN will let you enter any text, it creates a temporary file, called MYFILE.$$$, on the disk (where MYFILE is the filename for your file). Note that the temporary file's extension is always .$$$, regardless of any extension you choose for your file.

Let's assume you have chosen MYFILE and you want it to reside on the diskette in drive B. To invoke the editor and create the file, type

    EDLIN B:MYFILE

At the asterisk (*) prompt, use I (Insert) to get going, then enter your text until you are finished or until you make a mistake that you wish to correct immediately. Use Ctrl Break to leave the Insert mode.

Now that you have your file, albeit not yet correct, let's see how to use EDLIN's List and Page [2.0] commands to look at it. After that you might wish to experiment with the Insert and Edit commands to make a few changes.

THE LIST COMMAND

The List command is the letter L. Typed without any arguments, this command lists up to a screenful of lines, centered around the current line. If you are typing along with this example, type L and see the result.

Specifying a Range of Lines

To be more specific about the lines you wish to see, use n,mL. This command will list line numbers n through m, or less if m is beyond the last line in memory. You now know the full power of the List command.

Shortcuts You Can Use When Specifying Line Numbers

The number sign character, #, can be used to indicate the line number one greater than the last line in memory. For example, n,#L will list from line n to the end of text in memory. (Note: See the Append and Write command descriptions for explanations on why the last line in memory is used here instead of the last line in the file.)

When you list your text, an asterisk appears to the right of the line number of the current line. To save you some of the trouble of remembering line numbers, EDLIN will accept a period to denote the current line in case you can't remember (or find) it.

Relative Line Numbers [2.0]

Version 2.0 of EDLIN understands line numbers relative to the current line, as well as absolute line numbers, the # sign, and the period. Examples of relative line numbers are − 2 and + 6. The command − 2I means "insert text prior to two lines before the current line." The command − 5, + 10L means "display from five lines before to ten lines after the current line."

THE PAGE COMMAND [2.0]

The Page command, which is available in version 2.0, gives you a single-keystroke command for paging through your file quickly. If you don't specify any line numbers, each Page command will display the next screenful of lines in your file.

The Page command differs from the List command in two ways: (1) it adjusts the current line number to be the last line displayed each time the command is used, and (2) the default value for the first argument is the current line plus one, unlike the List command's default value of current line minus eleven. This is why the Page command can page through your file for you if you use the default arguments. If you supply both arguments, Page works like the List command.

If you have been typing along here, you have now seen the text you entered. If not, at least you now know how to look at text, so let's go on to look at the Insert command. Then we'll see what EDLIN offers for making changes to text that already exists (i.e., the Edit command).

THE INSERT COMMAND

The Insert command inserts additional lines into your text. It will not insert extra characters within a line; see the Edit command for that. (The Insert command is also the first command you use on an empty file.)

Imagine a two-line program that for some reason you find deficient. The program is in need of additional code between lines 1 and 2. Use the command 2I. The lines that you type will be inserted *before* line 2, and will be numbered starting at 2. Your original line 2 will be renumbered.

When you have finished inserting text, you will want to have the other EDLIN commands available again. To exit the insert mode, use Ctrl Break on a new line.

Argumentless Inserts

If you do not specify an argument with the Insert command, text will be added before the current line. If you want text to be added after the last line in memory, use I or a very large line number. EDLIN won't allow gaps in its line numbers, so very large numbers are interpreted as if you had specified a line number one greater than the last line.

THE EDIT COMMAND

If you have been typing along with this guide to text creation, you will probably need to use the Edit command (remember, not E—just specify the line number) to alter the contents of a line or two.

You may already be familiar with these line editing conventions; the EDLIN Edit commands are consistent with the use of the PC-DOS editing keys, which are described on pages 2-17 through 2-19 of the version 1.1 DOS manual. Extensive but not very gripping examples of these commands can be found on the succeeding pages of that manual, up to page 2-30.

EDLIN's in-line editing keys are F1 through F5, Del, Ins, cursor left, cursor right, backspace, and Esc. These keys operate as edit keys by controlling the reproduction of a line that already exists. For example, the F1 key will copy one character from the existing line onto a new line. The new line will replace the old when editing is complete.

The functions of the keys are noted below, but this is not an area where it is just as easy to learn by concept as it is by experience. If you have never used these capabilities, it is worth taking the time to practice a little. Here are the in-line editing keys and their effects:

- F1 copies a single character onto the new line.
- F3 copies the rest of the characters onto the new line.
- F2 copies all characters up to a specified character.
- F4 skips all characters up to a specified character.
- Del skips over one character when copying characters onto the new line.
- Ins allows insertion of new characters.
- Cursor right has the same effect as the F1 key.
- Cursor left and backspace undo the effect of the F1 key.
- F5 is useful when you are content with how the line looks now, but don't want to hit Enter yet. F5 replaces the old line with the new and allows further editing.
- Esc allows you to abandon the line and start over.

For editing short lines, the most useful keys are F1, F2, F3, Del, and Ins. If you wish to change one character in a line (perhaps to correct a mistyped command), press F2, then the character you wish to change, then the replacement character, and then F3. In lines where the character you wish to change appears in several other places, you can hold down F1 (or the cursor-right key) until you reach the character just before the one you wish to change. Then type the character of your choice, and press F3 to finish out the line.

The Ins key toggles the insert mode within a line. As you begin editing each new line, the insert mode will be off. It needs to be toggled on if you wish to add more characters to the line. For example, to change SEGMNT to SEGMENT in a line, select the line, press F2, then N (or F1 until SEGM appears), press Ins, type E, and press F3.

The action of the Del key is a little odd. You use it to say that you don't want the next character that would show up if you pressed F1.

F2 and F4 are the "search for" keys. They are less useful for long lines than for short ones. They lose their usefulness when there are multiple appearances of characters within a line. For instance, in the above insertion example, you might find yourself inserting Es in places you don't want if there is more than one N in the line.

To learn the use of these keys, I recommend trial and error, followed by the enlightenment that the DOS manual may have to offer on pages 2-16 through 2-19. I also recommend that you find a decent full-screen editor and not tolerate the limitations of any version of EDLIN.

Now that you have seen the action of the editing keys within a single line, we will look at the other commands EDLIN provides.

THE SEARCH AND REPLACE COMMANDS

The Search and Replace commands can both be used to find text strings. They both have a question mark option that allows you to make a choice of action at each occurrence of the string found, and both allow line range specification. The question mark, if desired, is inserted between the line numbers (if any) and the command. When the question mark option is used, the Search command will ask if you want to continue the search for others after one matching string has been found. When the question mark is used in the Replace command, you have the choice of replacing each matching string as it is found. The Replace command's search for a matching string continues until the end of the file or until you type Ctrl Break.

The format of the Search command is

(n)(,m)(?)Sstring

The format of the Replace command is

    (n)(,m)(?)Rstring1<F6>string2

The items in parentheses are optional. In both the Search and Replace commands, the string searched for follows the command letter. If you wish to replace the found text, the string searched for is terminated by the F6 keystroke (or Ctrl Z) and followed by the replacement text.

Search and Replace in Version 2.0

In version 2.0, the action of the Search and Replace commands has been changed to make stepping through the file a little quicker. First, the default value for n, the first argument, is the current line plus one, instead of line one. This means that you will have to specify line numbers less often and use fewer keystrokes to step through the file. Second, the commands remember the search string and replace string last used, so you don't have to retype them.

EDLIN in version 2.0 will edit binary files successfully. The technique to use to search for control characters is the same as that used for entering control characters. See the section "Editing Binary Files."

The Search and Replace commands are powerful components of EDLIN. We now look at two housekeeping commands that are used to edit files larger than EDLIN's estimate of available memory.

THE APPEND AND WRITE COMMANDS

The Append and Write commands are used when working on large files. EDLIN considers a file large when it occupies more than about 75 percent of the available memory. EDLIN needs the other 25 percent for work space. When a large file is being edited, not all of it will be in memory at once; some of it, either the beginning, the end, or both, will be on disk. EDLIN's editable window moves sequentially across the file from beginning to end.

The Append command gets more lines to work on. They come from the unedited part of the file that still resides on disk. The Write command moves to the disk a number of lines, making room for more in memory. The format for these commands is simple. It is the count of the number of lines to transfer, followed by the single character A or W.

You can only append from and write to the one file that is currently being edited. The existence of the Append and Write commands may at first lead you to believe that EDLIN provides a facility for merging text existing in two or more files, or that there is a facility for splitting a file into two or more parts. Unfortunately, this is not so, unless you have version 2.0, where the Transfer command will at least merge files for you.

PC-DOS version 2.0 provides four more editing commands than the previous versions. We have already discussed one of them, the Page command. Let's look at the other three. If you don't have version 2.0, you may want to skip this 2.0-specific information and move on to "Ending an Editing Session."

THE COPY COMMAND [2.0]

This command copies blocks of lines from one place to another in the file being edited. Copy will produce multiple copies of a single block of lines if so requested. The format of the Copy command is

(n),(m),dest(,count)C

The items in parentheses are optional.

Lines n through m are copied to the place immediately before the line specified as the destination (dest). If the count field is included in the command, that number of copies of the block of lines is created before the destination line.

To move the current line to appear before line 10, type

,,10C

Note that this has the same effect as typing

.,.,10C

Note, however, that it is not possible use the Copy command to create interesting interleaved patterns by overlapping the range of lines and the destination line.

After the command is complete, the current line is the first line of all the copies that were made.

Let's look at a similar command, where blocks of lines are moved instead of copied.

THE MOVE COMMAND [2.0]

The Move command moves groups of lines around in your file. The lines are moved to the place before the specified line, consistent with other

EDLIN commands. The format of the command is

    (n),(m),destM

The items in parentheses are optional and default to the current line. The command to move the current line to appear before line 10 is

    ,,10M

The destination line must not be included in the range of lines that are to be moved.

The last additional command provided by version 2.0 is Transfer. Let's examine it.

THE TRANSFER COMMAND [2.0]

The Transfer command could equally well be called merge files or read a file, but M and R are already used by the Move and Replace commands.

The Transfer command will add to the file being edited, before the current (or specified) line, the entire contents of the file named in the command. Thus Transfer allows you to merge several files into one, and to concatenate files. Standard pieces of text or code can be kept in individual files, then included in your programs as you need them by using the Transfer command.

The Transfer command has one characteristic that makes it fit right into the EDLIN family. It works, but its reach is short. The Transfer command does not understand path names, just a file name, which can be preceded by a drive identifier. Transfer can reach as many directories as there are disk (including electronic) drives. To make full use of the Transfer command, you need to have your source files well organized before you begin your editing sessions.

The Transfer command redeems itself in a small way by accepting file names (i.e., a filename plus an extension). The DOS manual's description of Transfer suggests it accepts only filenames, but that is not correct.

The format of the Transfer command is

    (n)T(d:)filename(.extension)

EDLIN VERSION 2.0 FEATURES

With version 2.0 you get the following new features:

- The new commands Copy, Move, Page, and Transfer

- Improvements to the Search and Replace commands
- Relative line numbers
- The ability to edit binary files
- Multiple commands per line
- Slightly better .BAK file handling

We have already discussed the four new commands, the changes to Search and Replace, and relative line numbers (current line plus or minus some number).We will look at the last three features in the list in turn.

Editing Binary Files

EDLIN usually works on ASCII files, but in version 2.0 you can use the /B option after the file name to tell EDLIN that the file being edited is in binary format. The difference between binary and ASCII files is that some of the bytes in the file are interpreted differently by the software that processes them. In a binary file you can have any of the 256 possible characters that can be made from eight bits. In an ASCII file, control characters (the ones that are permitted) are interpreted by the software that processes the file and often do not show up in the text that we read. The key example of this is the end-of-file character, Ctrl Z (1AH). Versions 1 of EDLIN will process a file no further than a Ctrl Z character. That character can occur in a binary file long before the end of the file. (Note: PC-DOS maintains a file length indicator in the directory. That is where programs can find out how long a file is if they don't want to rely on spotting the Ctrl Z as they process it.)

The question you may be asking, now that you know binary files can be edited, is how do you get the control characters into the file, past all the software that usually screens them out. The answer is Ctrl V. If EDLIN sees a Ctrl V, it will wait for the next character that you type (it must be uppercase) and make that the control character. For instance, entering Ctrl V followed by Z will tell EDLIN that the character to enter or search for is Ctrl Z. EDLIN will accept some control characters without your having to use the Ctrl V method to enter them, but this is not a recommended approach.

Multiple Commands per Line

In version 2.0 you can string several EDLIN commands together on a single line. The commands do not have to have separators between them (except after the Edit command); EDLIN can figure out what you mean when it sees the command letter. The Edit command, which is just the line number (no letter) must be followed by a semicolon. This prevents it from being confused with an optional line number argument to the next command.

Better .BAK File Handling

During an editing session in version 2.0, the .BAK file is not deleted until the end of the session or until the disk space it is occupying is needed for the file being edited. In versions 1 the .BAK file is deleted as soon as EDLIN is called, so that if the power goes out or another accident aborts EDLIN, the .BAK file, as well as the file being edited, is lost.

We've reviewed all of EDLIN's commands, so it might be time to leave the editor. Let's see how to do that.

ENDING AN EDITING SESSION

When you have finished making changes, type E to exit. EDLIN will save your text on disk. If you want to abort a practice session, type Q. Your changes will not be saved.

EDLIN'S TREATMENT OF .$$$ AND .BAK FILES

It might be useful to know what EDLIN does with .$$$ and .BAK files. In the unlikely event of your system crashing during an edit, the information here will help you reconstruct your file from the wreckage, or, more likely, lead you quickly to the conclusion that the work done during the crashed session is lost. This section is also relevant if you edit files with the same filename but different extensions. Let's look at that first.

EDLIN deletes .BAK files. It also creates them, but it deletes them first. What this means is that if you have a .BAK file with the same filename as the file you are about to edit, and you want to keep that .BAK file unchanged, you need to change its name before you begin the edit. It also means that you cannot successfully call upon EDLIN to edit any file with the extension .BAK. I will explain.

You know that a PC-DOS file name consists of an eight-character filename, optionally followed by a period and a three-character filename extension. When EDLIN is operating, it assumes the rights to three file names:

1. the file name of the file entered at the time EDLIN was called;
2. the filename part (file name without extension) of the entered file name, with the extension .BAK; and
3. the same filename with the extension .$$$.

Command	Format	Explanation
Display commands		
List	n,mL	Lists lines n through m
Page [2.0]	n,mP	Pages through the file
Text modification commands		
Insert line(s)	nL	Inserts line(s) before line n
Edit a single line	n	Line number only
Delete line(s)	n,mD	Deletes lines n through m
Copy line(s) [2.0]	n,m,d,cC	Copies lines n through m to appear before line d, c times
Move line(s) [2.0]	n,m,dM	Moves lines n through m to appear before line d
Transfer (merge) a file [2.0]	nTfilespec	Copies all of filespec to appear before line n
Search and replace commands		
Search for text	n,m?Sstring	Searches for 'string' in lines n through m. If a ? is included, pauses each time it finds 'string'.
Replace text	n,m?Rstring1 <F6>string2	Searches for 'string1', replaces it with 'string2'. '<F6>string2' may be omitted. If a ? is included, pauses each time it finds 'string1'.
Housekeeping commands		
End or Exit EDLIN	E	Exits, saving your work
Quit	Q	Exits without saving
Append	nA	Appends n lines from the rest of the file on disk
Write	nW	Writes n lines to disk to make room for more lines in memory

Figure 10.1: EDLIN Command Summary

When you first call EDLIN, filename.$$$ is created. In versions 1, filename.BAK, if it exists, is immediately deleted. In version 2.0 the .BAK file is not deleted until either the End edit command is given or the disk space occupied by the .BAK file is needed by the .$$$ file. Filename.$$$ is where the editing takes place, although its disk space isn't used until either available memory is about 75 percent full or the End edit command is given.

At the end of the editing session, the file whose name you specified in the EDLIN call, if it was there, is renamed filename.BAK (it loses the distinguishing extension, if it had one). Filename.$$$ is given the file name you specified when calling EDLIN. By this process of deleting and renaming files, the user ends up with the usual two files at the end of an editing session: one named filename and the other named filename.BAK.

Figure 10.1, on the previous page, is a summary of the EDLIN commands.

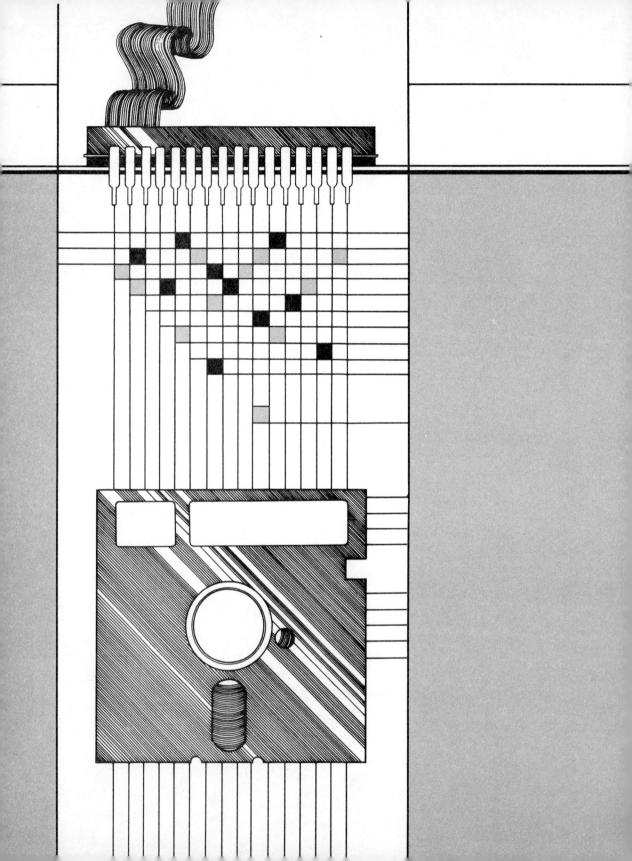

11

Your PC-DOS Files

INTRODUCTION

This chapter shows you what you can expect of the two filing systems offered with PC-DOS. Versions 1.0 and 1.1 offer a simple system of managing files on diskettes. Version 2.0, in recognition of its capacity to use fixed disk drives, with their considerably larger capacity when compared with diskettes, offers tree-structured files and the tools to manage them.

We devote the major portion of this chapter to the filing system supplied with PC-DOS versions 1.0 and 1.1. The last part of the chapter is devoted to the tree-structured filing system made available in version 2.0.

FILES IN PC-DOS VERSIONS 1.0 AND 1.1

This first half of the chapter shows you what to expect of the system of managing files on diskettes in versions 1, and how to make best use of that system. By the end of this section, you will have seen that PC-DOS versions 1 offer few options for creating filing systems at the user level. There are not very many tools at your disposal, but what few there are do have some useful applications. You also will have learned enough about filing systems to help you plan for file structures managed by purchased (or your own) database management software.

We will start with a brief review of how versions 1 organize their files and then move on to file capacities. We will discuss the capacities of the files offered in versions 1 and you will learn how to estimate what you might need by way of space for your own files. The limitation of 64 or 112 files per diskette is noted. This section will give you a feel for the amount of data that can or should be stored in one or several files.

If you are not using file management software and are working only at the user level, we assume that you enter data into your files by way of EDLIN or the COPY CON: FILENAME method, and that you review it with the TYPE command or with EDLIN.

When setting up your own user-level filing system, PC-DOS file capacities can handle almost anything that you would want to enter manually.

After file capacities, file names are the next factor to consider. Careful choice of file names can be important in a filing system, so we will provide some suggestions on how to make best use of the file naming rules and conventions that apply under PC-DOS, and how to stay away from those names that bring you trouble.

The physical placement of files on the disk can make a difference in the performance of frequently repeated jobs, so we will talk about organizing the placement of files on a diskette for best performance.

You may want to set up one or several of your own filing systems under versions 1, so we have provided an example that sets up a personal reminder filing system. This example applies the ideas put forward in this chapter and brings to light other points to consider when creating file structures.

The Organization of Files in PC-DOS Versions 1.0 and 1.1

A file is simply an organized collection of bytes (characters) that the PC-DOS operating system knows how to find, copy from, and make changes in.

Files in versions 1 reside on a diskette. A single-sided diskette can contain up to 64 different files, a double-sided diskette up to 112 files. Each diskette contains, in a predefined location at the beginning of the diskette, a directory of the files to be found on the diskette. The directory contains information on the size of the file, the date and time of the last time the contents changed, and the location on the diskette of the first block, or "cluster," of the file. (Note: the term *cluster* will be explained a little later. For the moment we will use cluster and block interchangeably.)

A file grows and shrinks as the data in it expands and contracts. PC-DOS maintains lists (more accurately, chains) of the blocks that belong to each file, and the lists, which are found in the file allocation table, grow longer and shorter as the file grows and shrinks.

The maintenance of the directory and file allocation table and the insertion and extraction of data take place at a level invisible to the user, except that assorted whirring and clicking occurs as the files are updated. If you want more detail on how the operating system accesses the files and the directory on each diskette, please refer to Chapters 2 and 3 of this book, which talk about programming for file creation and access and the diskette layout in PC-DOS.

If you have had experience with filing systems provided by other operating systems, you may have had hopes that PC-DOS would provide tools for organizing groups of files—terms like tree structuring and hierarchy may come to mind. Sad to say, versions 1 of this operating system provide no such tools. Versions 1 provide no organized way of connecting groups of files. The best they have to offer is the file name, where similar names can be used to indicate some connection in purpose.

What matters to anyone planning a filing system to operate under versions 1 is the 64 (or 112) limit on the number of files that can be put on one diskette, and the likely maximum sizes of the files that are to be stored. Let's look more closely at diskette capacities and what you have to do to estimate the maximum capacity requirements of your particular filing systems.

File Capacities

Each file can contain a very large number of bytes (for the moment we will use bytes and characters interchangeably); in theory, one file can hold more than four billion bytes. A full file containing text can hold about a million and a quarter average-sized pages. In practice, the maximum number of characters is limited by (1) the diskette capacity (about 320K characters for a double-sided diskette, half that for a single-sided diskette), and (2) the ability of the programs that construct and reference the file to tolerate large (say, greater than 64K bytes) files. Because most file access is by way of records within the file, which themselves are almost always of a manageable size, the upper limit for most files should be whatever will fit on one diskette.

You can see that file size is limited more by diskette capacities than by the capacity of an individual file. The problems to be dealt with in planning a filing system exist around how large you want your files to be and how many files you want to fit on one diskette.

Planning Your Own Filing System

To create a filing system that won't come crashing about your ears (fingers?) when more is asked of it than you at first expected, a little forethought is necessary. It isn't difficult, just a bit of work, and the reward is longer life for your filing system(s) and less repetitive work for you.

To plan for your own filing system, some of the issues you might consider are how much data is there going to be in each file, how many files are there going to be, and over how many diskettes would it be convenient for the files to be distributed. The issues relevant to these three basic questions can be arranged as yet more questions: How much data are you going to accumulate over the life of the filing system? How much data do you need around at any one time? Can you organize the data so that what you need at any one time is compacted into one place? What if the data you need comes in small quantities? Will you have to group it into files, then have a way to extract one set of data from many in a single file? Can you afford to allocate a single file to each small quantity of data? Lastly, how often will files be used, and can they be deleted by any automatic method, such as date triggering, so that your overall capacity is kept down?

You can see from these questions that you have quite a choice in how to go about organizing your file. Let's start by answering the first question.

Estimating capacities can be done by counting characters in an average entry, multiplying that number by the number of entries, and multiplying that by the lifespan of the entries. It is vital that you try to think of all the possible items of data you might wish to include. Once you have done this you are not quite finished. You must double your final result and use that as your guide to total requirements. Once you look at this (probably) large figure, you may be stimulated into putting forth inventive efforts toward making such a quantity of data manageable.

When you estimate expected capacities, think of how long the filing system may be expected to last. It could be that it will grow hugely over time, perhaps to such an extent that you should consider another format for storing the data.

Don't forget to consider the extremes, and be clear that your filing system will not necessarily be able to handle every extreme that may occur. Ensure that the response of your system when it comes across one of these extreme situations is reasonable and predictable.

You may want to think of dividing your data among several files. Except for the 64 or 112 maximum number of files per single diskette, having additional files is relatively cheap, and it entails not much in the way of overhead, as long as you don't want to switch frequently between them.

Once you have that doubled capacity estimate, stick with it. Don't be tempted to disregard it when it is not convenient to deal with the difficulties it incurs. There is a tendency not to believe in the need for it when the going gets awkward because of it.

Curtail your urge to be clever and fit everything into a small space. If you give in to that urge, you will be stepping back a generation in computers— back to the 6502 computer, where programmers are for the most part constrained to work within a 64K address space. The PC offers one whole megabyte to work with. You will have to spend much less of your time trying to cram too much into a small space if you don't succumb to the temptation to think small in the first place. Rewrites caused by lack of space are wasted life.

The big message of this section is that you need to estimate file capacity requirements with as much clarity and honesty as you can muster, then double the estimate and stick with the result. A little pain now can save a lot later; in fact, it may save total failure when you discover how large a rewrite you have to do to meet your "unexpected" capacity needs. By the time you have done the rewrite, the whole project may have missed its deadline and been superseded.

Here are two final notes before we go on to choosing file names. The first recommends frequent use of the CHKDSK command; the second is on minimum file sizes and the risk of wasting space.

Use CHKDSK Often

There is a useful PC-DOS command, CHKDSK, that tells you the space available on a diskette. Keep an eye on diskettes that you use at all frequently. Too many application programs don't handle a lack of diskette space with any aplomb at all. Some are downright brutal in that they don't give you the chance to change diskettes. They may waste hours of your work when they can't immediately do what you want by way of storing data on a diskette.

A Note on Minimum File Sizes

Each time a file expands, more space is allocated to it from the diskette (assuming any is available). This space is allocated in fixed amounts, not just the quantity currently needed. The amount of space allocated depends on the type of the diskette. On single-sided diskettes the space is allocated in units of 512 bytes, one sector. On double-sided diskettes the space is allocated in units of 1024 bytes, two sectors. (Both these units are called clusters by the file allocation routines.) You need to keep these quantities in mind when planning your filing system. It may be that each of your files will need 520 bytes to store the required data. That means that each file will be about twice as large as it needs to be, and that you will run out of disk space sooner than expected. As you can see, the situation could be worse on a double-sided diskette, where space is allocated in 1024-byte chunks.

You will want to make sure that as your files grow, there will be sufficient free space on the diskette to accommodate your expanding files. Remember, other files on the same diskette may also be expanding. Instead of putting all potentially large files on one diskette, consider mixing in a few small files. This way, if your capacity estimates are not perfect, more files will have a chance of reaching their expected capacities.

Choosing File Names

One of the few tools you have to work with in creating files under versions 1 is the file name. PC-DOS uses an eight-character filename with a three-character filename extension. Judicious assignment of meaning within those two fields can lead to names of files that are easy to remember and use, and that show, with very little need for interpretation, what the contents of the file might be.

Let's look at file names in a little more detail before we talk about careful choice of file names. First we'll explain the difference between file name and filename, then see how long the file names are in a directory entry, then show the character set from which file names can be made. The last part of this diversion into detail is about PC-DOS's reserved file names.

Distinction between File Name and Filename

The name of a file in PC-DOS terminology consists of a "filename" of one to eight characters, followed immediately by a period and a "filename extension" of one to three characters. The period and filename extension may be omitted.

In this book, *file name* means the name of a file, *filename* refers to the characters before the period, and *filename extension* refers to the period and the characters following it. This may seem pedantic, but the distinction is useful. Also, you often will see "extension" used instead of "filename extension."

Number of Characters in a File Name

We've said that a filename can be made up of one to eight characters. That may be true when you type it, but a filename in a directory entry will always contain eight characters; a filename extension will contain three. If you don't supply all eight (or three) characters, the field will be padded out to the right with spaces to make up the correct number of characters.

Permissible Characters in PC-DOS File Names

PC-DOS provides a broad set of characters that can be used in file names. They are as follows:

- The letters A – Z (if you specify lowercase, the character will be converted to uppercase)
- The digits 0 – 9
- The special characters (left to right, top row of the PC keyboard first):

  ! @ # $ % ^ & ( ) _ –

  { } ~ ˋ ' ¦ < > \

The last four characters listed, ¦, <, >, and \, cannot be used in version 2.0 file names, so their use is not recommended in version 1.0 or 1.1.

You can see that some characters cannot be used. Following are the characters on the PC keyboard, mostly mathematical and common punctuation symbols, that cannot be used in file names:

> * + = [ ] : ; " , . ? /
> Space, tab, and any control characters

Now that we have seen the fiddly details of what goes into a PC-DOS file name, we can look at how PC-DOS reserves some file names for special purposes.

Reserved File Names in PC-DOS

PC-DOS reserves for its own use some specific file names. It is not compulsory that you avoid the use of these names at all times, but using them without understanding their purpose is risky. Files could disappear without trace, replaced by something quite unexpected. However, once you understand what a reserved name is about, you can sometimes use it to advantage. Some commercial application software adopts certain file names or extensions for its own purposes. For instance, if you were editing a large file with the WordStar program and your work was terminated by a power failure, you would later see a file with an extension of .$$$. Like EDLIN, WordStar uses XXX.$$$ for the name of a temporary file, where XXX is your filename for the file. Independent software writers usually stick with PC-DOS conventions, though they sometimes branch out into their own inventions. If you're lucky, that information is available in their documentation.

A table of the PC-DOS reserved file names is provided in Figure 11.1. Now let's finally get to some suggestions for choosing file names.

Choosing Names with Care

There aren't too many brilliant ideas here, just a few common-sense approaches to selecting file names that are clear and unambiguous, and notes on some temptations to avoid.

Assigning names to files becomes simpler when you choose to limit your options by adopting file naming conventions. The conventions must not be unacceptably restrictive; they can be chosen so that the gains they offer far outweigh the disadvantages. People have adopted the convention of driving on the right-hand side of the road (in this country). It is a restrictive convention, but driving is a considerably less messy experience because of it. So it is with file names. And here you can make up your own set of rules, not have others' imposed on you.

When you choose file names for a set of files with a common purpose, varying the extension systematically can be enough to provide distinction between members of the set. For instance, you can use the Julian date for the extension. That fits into three digits, varying from 1 to 365 (or 366 on leap years). The Julian date can be a little hard to decipher, which makes it not the best choice for file names that will be interpreted by people; a program, however, would make sense of it with no trouble.

If you need a file that is specific to a single date, using that date for the filename is an option. It is hard to mistake the meaning of the filename 9-15-83. You need to be consistent in your inclusion of leading zeros, and you could omit the separator characters, thus leaving the other two characters of the filename available for indicating the type of file of that date. More flexibility is gained if you know that files of different years are on different diskettes, where the year is indicated on the diskette label. Here you can use four characters for the type of file on that date. This shifting of indentification from filename to diskette label can be stretched too far—a program can't

---

Reserved Filenames

Filename	Purpose
@ . . .	Any filename beginning with the character @. Used by the autoresponse file in the linker.
BADTRACK	Created by version 1.0 to hold addresses of unreadable clusters.
NUL	Directs the file to the bit bucket, i.e., to nowhere retrievable.
VM.TMP	Created by the linker when there is not enough room in memory for the load module.

Reserved Filename Extensions

Extension	Purpose
.$$$	EDLIN temporary file
.ASM	Assembler source file
.BAK	Deleted and created by EDLIN
.BAT	Batch files
.COM	Command file
.EXE	Executable file, produced by linker
.HEX	DEBUG assumes this is a hex ASCII file and converts it to binary on loading
.LST	Listing file from assembler
.MAP	Linker's map
.OBJ	Assembled object file

Figure 11.1: PC-DOS Reserved File Names

read the diskette label; nor can a person when it is in the drive. (Note: Version 2.0 diskettes have volume names, which can be read by a program.)

For groups of files with a common purpose, in addition to varying the extension, sometimes you may also need to vary one or two characters of the eight-character filename to get enough variety. It is better to vary the "low-order" characters than the leading characters. The wild-card (* and ?) options that PC-DOS makes available for selecting file names are a little easier to apply that way.

Ambiguity in file names creeps in because at the time the name (or set of names) is chosen, whoever is making the choices is deeply involved in his or her project. It is easy to forget to step outside for a fresh look at what you are doing, and so miss the ambiguity of a name like "vest." In an inventory context vest means an article of clothing; in an employee pensions context it may refer to the amount vested. You may be justly unimpressed by the aptness of this example; in your experience ambiguous names will occur with more facility.

Choose meaningful names—not just names that are meaningful to you, but to your grandmother as well if she wanted to run a PC. Don't abbreviate file names, except for those of a few, very frequently used files. Abbreviated names seem to be clarity itself when they are invented, but they often turn out to be thoroughly confusing when viewed in another context. The choice of meaningful names applies to more than just short names. Even long names can be seen by another to mean something quite different.

Mnemonic names can be useful, but not a unique and inconsistent extraction of certain "unnecessary" characters. A phonetic approach is usually doomed. The variety of pronunciation in this country is too great.

Simple truncation is often adequate. Exercise your powers of language, even a dictionary of synonyms to come up with alternatives to ambiguous names. This can also be entertaining for whoever works with your filing system.

Then there is the secret approach. This involves making all names totally indecipherable. This is not infrequently achieved by accident, occasionally by design. You need enthusiasm and a good memory for this approach to work. Don't forget that a year from now you may need the data in your files, and that you may have become absorbed in an entirely unrelated field.

Optimum Placement of Files on the Diskette

You might need the quickest possible execution time in some filing system applications. If you don't have enough memory for an *electronic disk* (a section of memory that software makes look like another disk drive), small improvements in performance can be gained by optimum placement of the files on the diskette.

Keep small files that are to be accessed alternately next to one another and close to the directory. To do that, remember that the directory and file allocation tables are found on the first few sectors of the disk. Use the COPY command (not DISKCOPY), to shuffle files to the right places on the disk. Consider keeping data that belongs in two large files on two separate diskettes, one being in each drive (if you have a two-drive system) for quicker alternate access.

Placement of clusters within files on the diskette is controlled by a disk space allocation mechanism. When a PC-DOS file expands, the file allocation routines step through the file allocation table looking for the first free block (or cluster) to allocate to the file.

When a file shrinks, any extra clusters are returned to the pool of free blocks on the diskette. Over time, as files on a diskette expand and contract, the clusters within a file will occupy indeterminate positions on the diskette. To clean up these files and put them in order, such that each file occupies consecutive blocks on the diskette (and thus is open for the best rate of access), use the COPY command. Make up a fresh disk by using FORMAT, with or without the /S option as desired, then use COPY *.* B: (where the newly formatted disk is in drive B:). This will reorder the clusters within your files. The COPY command can be used with files one at a time to relocate those files that need to be together.

A Simple Reminder Filing System

The purpose of this system is to be a reminder package. Every time you turn on your PC, you will be reminded of what appointments you have arranged for that day and receive any messages previously set aside for that day.

Let's consider the file name. If we choose the date to be the file name, we can skip considering the filename extension. We have eight characters to play with in the filename; that is enough to conveniently represent any date. The only snag in the works is that the character / (which is often used to separate months, days and years) is not acceptable in a PC-DOS file name. Either we leave the separator out altogether and use a six-digit date, or we use another character, such as the dash. The dash is the obvious choice, since that is what the PC-DOS date function uses.

Now that we have a handy set of file names, let's consider capacities. These paragraphs on estimating capacities are a bit plodding, but sometimes plodding pays.

We can estimate that whatever goes into the file for a single day will not take up more than, say, eight full lines. The estimate of eight full lines comes from an assumption of five appointments in a day, each being described by the name (30 characters), company (30 characters), subject (50 characters) and time (6 characters), for a total of about 600 characters. Double that gives a need for one date file of about 1200 characters; 1200 characters will fit into three 512-byte sectors. We need to see how many of these files will fit on a diskette. A diskette has room for about 300 clusters, a cluster being one sector on a single-sided diskette, two sectors on a double-sided diskette. We need only consider a single-sided diskette's capacity; it is more restrictive than that of a double-sided diskette. A total of 64 files can be put on a diskette; we need 3 sectors for each, for a total of 192 clusters.

The estimation process has shown us that it is reasonable to expect to fit two months' worth of date files on one diskette. If you wanted a retrievable record for the whole year, six diskettes a year would be enough (four if you were using double-sided diskettes).

The remaining problems to overcome are (1) how to get the file automatically printed out at each day's beginning, and (2) how to delete the old files when they are of no use.

Making some changes to the AUTOEXEC.BAT file is almost enough to solve the first problem. (For more information about the AUTOEXEC.BAT file, see Chapter 12.) Remove the DATE call from the AUTOEXEC file and add the following at the end of the file:

```
REM    Please enter the following command to set the date and
REM    get your messages for the day:
REM    d mm-dd-yy
```

Then create the file D.BAT with the COPY command:

```
COPY CON: D.BAT
date %1
type %1
< F6>
```

That saves you from having to type the date twice, and it almost ensures that you will see your messages and set the system date. Also, if you get in the habit of using D instead of DATE, you will get your messages each time you set the date.

Deleting the old files is only a problem if you don't want to archive your appointments. You would archive appointments by setting the whole diskette aside, noting on its label the months' appointments it contained. If you keep on using the same diskette, you will need to delete the older files to make room for more. Deleting them in bulk by use of the FORMAT command may be preferable to deleting each date file in turn.

The file for a particular day should be created using EDLIN (or another editor), not the COPY command. After a few date files have been created, it becomes difficult to remember whether the file for a particular day already exists. COPY always creates files anew, so if you re-create an existing file with COPY, whatever did exist is lost. At any time you can use EDLIN to make additional entries.

You probably noticed that in estimating file capacities we forgot to include space for the messages. Unless you are a prolific message sender, the generous allowance for each field and the doubling will probably ensure the survival of this reminder filing system.

Now that we have learned about filing systems in general, and the filing system supplied by versions 1.0 and 1.1 of PC-DOS in particular, let's examine the expanded filing system offered by version 2.0 of PC-DOS.

FILES IN PC-DOS VERSION 2.0

Version 2.0 of PC-DOS introduces a tree-structured, or hierarchical, filing system. In a tree-structured filing system many directories can exist, where each directory is applicable to a set of files that can be grouped conveniently together. This ability to organize files into independently accessible groups gives us much flexibility in the management of files in PC-DOS.

This section will show you how PC-DOS manages a tree-structured filing system. We will introduce the concepts of root directory, subdirectory, and path. We will introduce the five user-level commands related to managing tree-structured systems, show you an example of a set of files that form part of a tree, and, while examining the example, see how these five commands can be used.

A Tree-Structured Filing System

A tree-structured filing system is one where directories not only contain entries for files, but also entries for other directories. The first, or root, directory will contain some entries that point to files and some entries that point to other directories. In turn, these other directories can point to a mixture of files and yet other directories. The usefulness of such a structure becomes clear when you have many files to manage. An example showing a typical tree-structured set of files would have to be very large. Here, to demonstrate how to work with trees, we will use as an example only a small portion of a set of tree-structured files.

The Root Directory

The root directory is the prime directory on the disk or diskette. It is the root of the tree organization for the whole disk.

The root directory is used in two ways: (1) to create major distinctions between the functions of the groups of files in the tree, and (2) to store programs that can be used to operate on files in all areas of the tree.

The root directory is the only directory that is limited in the number of entries it can hold. (The number of entries is limited to 64 or 112 on a diskette; on a hard disk, the upper limit varies according to the portion of the disk devoted to PC-DOS.) It is also the only directory that cannot be deleted.

The entries in the root directory are of three types. Entries for files (the only option in versions 1), entries for subdirectories, and one entry for the volume label. We will ignore the volume label entry (it is not essential to tree structures), and we already are familiar with directory entries for files. Let's look at what a subdirectory entry points to. (By the way, the attribute byte in the directory entry declares the type of the directory entry.)

Subdirectories

A subdirectory is merely a directory that is not the root directory. Frequently the prefix *sub* is omitted. We will often use the word *directory* to refer to both the root directory and subdirectories.

Subdirectories are files with a number of directory entries in them. In practice, there is no limit to the number of entries for files or other subdirectories that a subdirectory can hold.

You can see that when the root directory points to a subdirectory that points to a subdirectory that points to the file of data you happen to be interested in, the operating system and the user will need a path through the forest of directories to find the file.

Paths

A path leads either to a file or to an area of the tree that contains files and more directories. The path is the list of the names of the directories, starting with the primary or root directory, continuing through all the directories that lead you through the right areas of the tree, ending with the directory containing the entry for the file of interest. The directory names in a path are separated by the backslash character.

Now it is time to introduce the five user-level commands for managing tree structures in version 2.0.

Tree-Structure Management Commands

Figure 11.2 shows the five user-level commands that version 2.0 provides for working with a tree-structured filing system.

Command	Function
CHDIR	Change directory
MKDIR	Make a directory
PATH	Define the default path(s)
RMDIR	Remove a directory
TREE	Display the tree structure

Figure 11.2: Tree-Structured File Management Commands

Let's look at an example of the tree structure in use, where we will see some examples of paths and how these commands are used.

A Sample Tree-Structured Set of Files

We will assume that you have a filing system on drive C that contains several tree sections, each of which serves a separate purpose. If you have organized your files well, the data that is associated with one activity is not spread out all over the tree, but is isolated to one directory and its subdirectories.

We will examine two areas of the tree: one area devoted to personal budget files, the other devoted to the source language files of the new game project you are working on. Those two groups of files will never be used at the same time, so they belong in different parts of the tree.

There are several files associated with each of those two activities. The budget files include the data files for each category within the budget. The game project files include the source language and compiled programs, the compiler, and some test results.

The CHDIR (or CD) Command

When you are working on budgets, your programs will be using the budget directory (and its subdirectories, if any) almost all the time. It would be efficient for the operating system to know that you are mostly going to be operating in one area of the tree, and start its search for the relevant files at the prime directory for that area of the tree.

We have now established the purpose for one of version 2.0's new commands, CHDIR—change directory. You would use this command to set as your base (current) directory the part of your tree structure where you and the operating system will be most efficient. This base directory becomes the current directory. At this part of the tree, the operating system will have to make the fewest disk accesses to get to the files you request, and you will have to type the least amount of characters to identify the files you want to work with.

The CHDIR command (which may be abbreviated to CD) to set the current directory takes a path as an argument. Remember that there is a current directory for each disk drive.

The path from the root directory of drive B to your budget files may be

B:\MARY\PERSONAL\BUDGETS

The path to your game project may be

B:\MARY\BUSINESS\DEVELOP\GAMES

That last example demonstrates four levels of directories. To change your directory to the budgets part of the tree, you would type

CHDIR B:\MARY\PERSONAL\BUDGETS

If you do not remember at which part of the tree you are operating, the CD command can be used without any arguments to show you the current directory. For example, if you had just started to work on the monthly budget, which you had been putting off all day, and your desperately hungry husband suddenly opened the door and said, "Hey, you have to look after the kid while I eat," and you left the computer to play with your son, then answered a few phone calls, then saw that it was a nice day and mowed the front lawn, by the time you get back to the computer you may not remember the current directory. That is the time to type

CD B:

You would see

\MARY\PERSONAL\BUDGETS

and remember that indeed you had just begun work on the monthly budget.

The MKDIR (or MD) Command

While you are working on the monthly budget, you may decide to split out into a separate category all the expenses incurred in getting the local wild cat population fixed so their progeny would not overrun the neighborhood. For this, you want a separate group of files, one file per cat. To make the directory, you would type

MKDIR B:\MARY\PERSONAL\BUDGETS\CATS

or

MKDIR B:CATS

In the second example, the lack of the backslash following the drive designator tells PC-DOS to make an entry for the subdirectory in the current
directory, not in the root directory.

Removing a Directory—The RMDIR (or RM) Command

Some time later, you may decide that having a separate filing system for
the cats is not a good idea. You would incorporate the data from the cat files
into existing budget files, and delete the cats directory by typing

RMDIR B:CATS

or

RMDIR B:\MARY\PERSONAL\BUDGETS\CATS

The Current Directory and the DIR Command

When working within a tree-structured filing system for the first time, it is
possible to become confused about which directory you see when you use
the DIR command. We will attempt to straighten that out here. The knowledge gained here applies to using all the directory-related commands. Each
drive has a root directory and a current directory. (Note: If you do not specify a drive, the default drive (the one you see in the prompt) is used. Also
note: The current directory may be the root directory, but since the object
of this section is to reduce the confusion brought about by the current and
root directories not being the same, we will ignore the situation of them
being the same.)

If you wish to see the current directory, type

DIR d:

where d: is the drive designator. You may omit the d: if you want a directory
from the default drive.

If you wish to see the root directory, type

DIR d:\

When the drive designator is immediately followed by a backslash, this
instructs the command to ignore the current directory and revert to the
root directory. If you type more characters following the backslash, then

you are specifying a path to somewhere else in the tree.

Now let's apply this to the MKDIR command. If you wish to extend the directory path beyond the current directory, type

MKDIR B:NEWDIR

If you wish to add a new subdirectory at the root level, type

MKDIR B:\NEWDIR

The TREE Command

Here we return from our diversion into the difference between a drive's current and root directories, and consider an example where you might need the TREE command.

Some years from now, you may come across a diskette with the label "DOS 2.0—Special Files," and have no memory of the contents. To find out what is on the disk, you would boot PC-DOS version 2.0, put the mystery disk in the second floppy drive, and examine its directory. The fact that some of the directory entries would contain the characters < DIR> would prompt you to type

TREE B:

The tree of directories on the mystery disk would show on the screen. You perhaps would see that there were only a couple of subdirectories, and so use the TREE command again, this time with the /F option, to display the files in the directories as well as the directories.

The PATH Command

The purpose of the PATH command is to instruct PC-DOS where it might find the programs and batch files it is asked to execute. If the PATH command has not been executed, PC-DOS expects to find programs it is asked to execute in the current directory of the default drive. If you have programs elsewhere in the tree, to execute them you would have to precede the program name with the appropriate path string. To save you repeatedly typing path strings, the PATH command exists. (The CD command also exists for this purpose, but it only specifies a path that leads to a single directory of the tree.)

The PATH command establishes a set of directories where PC-DOS might find programs it is asked to execute. Several paths, separated by semi-colons, may be specified in the PATH command. The directory at the end of each path is examined in turn when the program is not found in the current directory.

Let's look at an example of how the PATH command can be used. In our previous example, we had two important parts of the tree: the budget section and the game project section. The path to the game project area of the tree is

B:\MARY\BUSINESS\DEVELOP\GAMES

Mary has developed a special set of tools to make game software development more productive. These programs are at

B:\MARY\TOOLS\GAMEDEV

Before beginning work on game development, Mary would type

PATH B:\MARY\TOOLS\GAMEDEV

If older versions of the game development tools, which were occasionally needed, were on drive A at

A:\TOOLS

Mary would type instead

PATH B:\MARY\TOOLS\GAMEDEV;\TOOLS

PC-DOS will look first in the current directory of the drive specified (or the default drive if no drive was specified), then it will look in the GAMEDEV subdirectory on drive B, then in the TOOLS subdirectory on the default drive, which in this case is drive A.

When Mary begins an intense session of work on the game project, and knows that during checkout the system will often crash, she adds the PATH command to the CONFIG.SYS file, so it will be executed every time the system is rebooted.

Summary of Version 2.0
Tree-Structure and Access Commands

We have seen how version 2.0 has introduced a tree-structured filing system, and we have learned the meaning of root directories, subdirectories, and paths. We have seen examples of the five user-level commands provided for managing a tree-structured filing system.

SUMMARY OF USER-LEVEL
FILE MANAGEMENT IN PC-DOS

We have seen how to make best use of the file management system PC-DOS supplies. We have seen that the filing system in versions 1 is limited to a single directory per diskette, permitting at most 112 files per floppy disk. We have seen that version 2.0 expands the file handling capacity of PC-DOS by an order of magnitude, by introducing a tree-structured filing system that is easy to manage and limited only by the capacity of the disks or diskettes containing it.

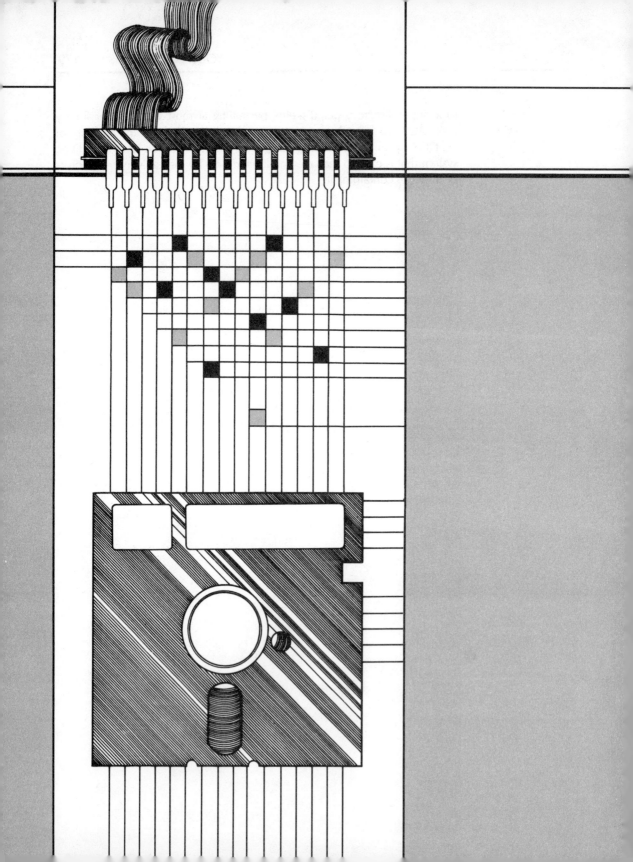

12

Batch Operations, or Bye Bye Repetition

INTRODUCTION

This chapter will win you familiarity with using batch files. It will show you what they are, what they can do for you, and how they work in PC-DOS. In addition, it presents examples showing you how to create batch files.

A batch file contains the commands for a sequence of operations. Once you have created such a file, PC-DOS will work away at those commands while you get coffee, call your broker, or get ready for bed at 2 A.M. (when you want to back up your night's work so you can sleep in peace).

PC-DOS will execute a sequence of commands in a batch file, instead of waiting for you to type them in one by one. If you don't like repetition, the batch file facility is just what you need.

Batch files, by the way, are not the path to background processing or multitasking in PC-DOS—that capability is not available currently. Multitasking allows you to have more than one task running at the same time. Attractive though that is, PC-DOS does not yet offer it, with the exception that in version 2.0 files may be printed concurrently with other activities.

APPLICATIONS FOR BATCH FILES

Batch files have two major areas of application: (1) they give you freedom to walk away from the computer while it performs a sequence of operations unattended, and (2) they serve as a place for storing a (perhaps) complex sequence of commands that you want performed without any being missed.

Batch files can be used for establishing consistent startup procedures and for defining sequences of operations for backup at the end of a day. They are also useful for issuing the sequence of commands that redirect output to a (letter-quality) printer that has a serial interface, or for establishing connection via a modem with The Source or some other on-line information service. It is worthwhile to enter any sequence of often repeated commands into a batch file.

In addition, if your typing skills are not the best and/or you are repulsed by the effort involved in typing the names of certain commands (e.g., CHKDSK B:), you can use batch files to alleviate your pain by abbreviating such commands (e.g., CHKDSK B: to CKB).

Batch files can contain messages and prompts, to guide you through nontrivial operations and thereby ensure that your performance is flawless.

The canonical batch file is AUTOEXEC.BAT. If it exists, AUTOEXEC.BAT supplies a set of commands that are executed any time the system is booted. By the way, if you create your own AUTOEXEC.BAT, do remember to include the DATE and TIME commands.

HOW BATCH FILES WORK

In brief, the command processor calls the batch file processor when it sees a command which is a file name that ends with the letters .BAT. Let's expand on that a little.

PC-DOS contains a set of routines for recognizing commands. This set is called the command processor. It also contains a set of routines for processing batch files. This group of routines is called the batch file processor.

The command processor looks at the characters that are typed in response to the system-level prompt (usually A> or B>). It sees these characters as soon as you press the Enter key. The command processor first tries to match the characters with the resident commands. If there is no luck there, it then looks for a file on disk whose name matches what has been typed.

If you do not include a filename extension (a period followed by one to three characters), the command processor makes a first guess that the extension is .COM and looks for that. Its second guess is .EXE, and its third and last guess is .BAT, which is where we come in. If the command processor finds the .BAT file, it passes control to the batch file processor.

The batch file processor has enough logic in it to read the first line (a command) from a batch file, invoke the command, and when that terminates, read the next command from the batch file. This continues until the batch file is exhausted or the user aborts the sequence.

Note: If the command you type in response to the system prompt contains a filename extension, the command processor will look only for files with that specific extension; the batch file processor won't be invoked unless that extension is .BAT.

As far as the user is concerned, the command processor gets a string of characters just as easily from a .BAT file as it does from the keyboard.

Aborting Batch File Operations

You can abort either the current command that has been called by the batch processor or the whole set of commands that are waiting to be executed.

To abort batch file operations, type Ctrl Break. If the program being executed responds to that character, you will see the following message:

> Terminate batch job (Y/N)?

This is your chance to terminate only the current command or quit the whole batch sequence. If you want to forget the current command and move on to the next in the batch file, type N, (meaning no, you don't want to quit the whole sequence). Type Y to terminate the whole sequence.

There is a fly in the ointment when terminating batch jobs. The current command (program) being executed may not recognize Ctrl Break characters. You will discover this after waiting patiently for a few seconds after typing Ctrl Break and seeing no "Terminate batch job (Y/N)?" message. Here you have a chance to exercise your knowledge of the program being run; give it the command that normally makes it quit. After you have done that, you should get the terminate message. Then you can proceed as usual, giving a Y or N answer.

Because termination of batch job sequences depends somewhat on the good behavior of the program being executed, results of aborting batch job sequences are not always predictable.

Dummy Arguments

An important additional feature exists within the batch processor—that of dummy arguments. To make a batch file's range of applications more flexible, dummy arguments can be indicated using the percent (%) sign. The dummy arguments are filled in at the time the command they are associated with is executed.

In versions 1, nine unrestricted dummy arguments are available. They are %1 through %9. The examples of how to create a batch file expand upon the use of dummy arguments and show you the purpose of the %0 dummy argument.

CREATING A BATCH FILE

A batch file is a file containing one or more lines of text. That's all there is to it. You can create a batch file using EDLIN or another editor, as you would create any file of text. You can also use the COPY command.

You might use the COPY command to create a simple batch file that you are sure does not already exist, or that you don't mind overwriting.

Complex batch files will usually have to be edited, so you might as well be in the editor initially for these files.

For demonstration purposes, we will use the COPY command method here; its format is

COPY CON: XXX.BAT

where XXX is a filename of your choice, up to eight characters in length. Here are several examples of batch file creation using the COPY command.

Example 1—Automatic Program Execution

A disk speedup program, called SPEEDUP, circulates among users of PC-DOS version 1.0 who have not yet taken the $40 plunge and moved on to PC-DOS version 1.1. The SPEEDUP program speeds up disk accessing by reducing the time used by the disk routines to wait for the head to settle after a track-to-track shift. Because the modification to speed up the disk accessing has to be installed every time version 1.0 PC-DOS is booted, the popular solution is to include a call to SPEEDUP within AUTOEXEC.BAT, the batch file that the system executes (if it can find it) on startup.

Assuming that no AUTOEXEC.BAT file already exists (if it does, use an editor to add lines 2, and perhaps lines 3 and 4, of the following sequence), this sequence will cause SPEEDUP to be called on system startup:

COPY CON: AUTOEXEC.BAT
SPEEDUP
DATE
TIME
<F6> (or Ctrl Z)

Note: *Beware of using the COPY command to create an AUTOEXEC.BAT file.* Any such file that already exists will be overwritten—a lot of good work may be lost. Once a complex or pleasing AUTOEXEC.BAT file has been created, you might keep a copy of it in AUTOEXEC.SPR (not .BAK).

Example 2—Abbreviation of a Command

To abbreviate the CHKDSK command to CK, enter

COPY CON: CK.BAT
CHKDSK
<F6>

After this is done, each time you type CK, the CHKDSK program will be invoked. For an expansion of CK to check both drives, assuming A is the default drive, use

```
COPY  CON: CK.BAT
CHKDSK
CHKDSK B:
<F6>
```

Example 3—Abbreviation with Dummy Arguments

Dummy arguments are used here. To abbreviate the RENAME command to the letter R, use

```
COPY  CON: R.BAT
RENAME %1 %2
<F6>
```

If you then type

```
R  BILL  WILLIAM
```

the batch file processor will replace %1 with the first argument, BILL, and %2 with the second argument, WILLIAM. The command processor will see

```
RENAME  BILL  WILLIAM
```

The file called BILL will be renamed WILLIAM.

Let's look at dummy arguments in a little more depth before moving on to the next example.

More on Dummy Arguments

Recall that in versions 1, nine dummy arguments are available, %1 through %9. In addition, %0 will always be replaced with the filename of the batch file; this is useful for repeating an operation indefinitely, as shown in the next example. In version 2.0, thanks to the introduction of the SHIFT command, you can use more than nine dummy arguments.

Example 4—Repetitive Action with Prompt

The REM and PAUSE commands can be included in a batch file to make the action of the file more clear to the user and to serve as a prompt when one is required. To see directories of several disks without having to call for the directory each time, create a batch file by typing

```
COPY  CON: DIRS.BAT
PAUSE Load next disk into drive b:
```

```
DIR B:/P
%0
<F6>
```

This batch file displays the directories of a series of disks placed in drive B. Note that the batch file is passing control, in its last statement, to itself. It is daisy chaining, not calling, so stack overflow is not a concern. The /P option tells the DIR command to pause at the end of each page of a directory listing.

When the batch file processor sees the REM statement in a batch file, it displays the text of the REM statement and goes on to process the next line of the file. If the batch file processor encounters a PAUSE statement, the text of the PAUSE statement is output, followed by the message

> **Strike a key when ready**

The batch file processor waits until a key is struck before processing the next command in the file. In the above example, the user would strike a key after inserting another diskette in drive B. Now that we have seen a few examples of versions 1 batch facilities, let's look at the improvements version 2.0 brings.

BIGGER, BETTER BATCH FILES WITH VERSION 2.0

Five new batch commands have been introduced with version 2.0— ECHO, FOR, GOTO, IF, and SHIFT. We will look at these commands one by one, then go through a sample batch file to see how the new commands can be used. At the end of this section we will examine some of the limitations to the power of batch operations in version 2.0.

The ECHO Command

The batch file processor displays the commands in the batch file as it executes them. The ECHO command, which takes the arguments ON and OFF (and message), can be used to suppress that display. Batch files that contain the ECHO OFF command appear cleaner in operation; they don't muddle the screen with extra chat.

If ECHO is OFF, the messages associated with the REM and PAUSE commands are also suppressed (although you do see the "Strike a key . . ." part of the PAUSE command). You may still want some messages to appear, which is where the ECHO message command comes in. Whatever the ECHO status, the message part of an ECHO message command will appear.

FOR Loops in Batch Files

Version 2.0 has introduced simple FOR loops. In BASIC and other languages, FOR loops typically operate by incrementing a variable at the end of each iteration; they terminate when the variable reaches a specified value.

The batch FOR command takes its variable from a list included in the FOR command, and terminates when the list is exhausted. The result is the same in both cases—repeated execution of the same command, but the batch FOR command is quite restricted. A sample FOR command is

FOR %%y IN (1981 1982 1983 1984) DO Summary %%y

where Summary is a program that takes the year (%%y) as an argument.

Batch's version of the instructions in the FOR loop, which is the part of the instruction that follows the DO, can contain only one command. The one permissible command can be another batch command (except FOR), a program to be executed, or a DOS command. The FOR loop cannot contain another FOR command or the name of another batch file. Another sample FOR command is

FOR %%e IN (2 3 4 5) DO IF ERRORLEVEL %%e GOTO Exit

The IF Command

With the IF command you can test for three different types of conditions: (1) that two strings are the same (IF string 1 = = string 2), (2) that a command or application program returned an error condition equal to or greater than a number (IF ERRORLEVEL 5), or (3) that a file exists (IF EXIST filename.ext). The example after the SHIFT command section shows several uses of the IF command.

The GOTO Command

Because conditionals are included in version 2.0, the GOTO command, or something like it, becomes necessary. The GOTO and IF commands, together with version 2.0's facility for returning numbered error indicators from applications and some systems programs, turn the batch command processor into an interpreter of a minor programming language.

GOTO goes to the line following the label. A label is a line beginning with a colon. The example that follows later shows the use of a GOTO command, and how labels can be used to document the batch file. The text of the label is the characters (no more than eight) that follow the colon, up to the next space or the end of the line.

The SHIFT Command

If you need more than nine dummy arguments (also called dummy parameters), version 2.0's SHIFT command lets you get at those beyond nine. It can also serve as a way to process an indefinite number of arguments. The SHIFT command moves the arguments down each time it is used; the, say, fifth argument becomes the fourth argument after the shift command is executed. The %n dummy argument becomes the %(n − 1) argument, and the %0 argument is lost. Let's examine a sample batch file that includes the SHIFT, IF, GOTO, ECHO, and FOR commands.

A Sample Version 2.0 Batch File

Here is the example. The name of the file is SHOWDUE.BAT. It is invoked by typing

Showdue (Month) Martha Jason

where (Month) is one of the months of the year. For example:

Showdue June Martha Jason

The purpose of the file is to enable someone who runs a day-care center (with the help of two assistants, Martha and Jason) to see if the monthly bills for each child in her care have been paid. The file is run with Ctrl PrtSc in effect (the output is echoed to the printer).

The file SHOWDUE.BAT is shown in Figure 12.1. A sample run of that file is shown in Figure 12.2; another sample run is shown in Figure 12.3.

This batch file is far short of an elegant and practical program, but it does serve to illustrate several version 2.0 capabilities. Let's examine it.

The owner of the day-care center celebrates Christmas by not charging her clients for the month of December. Line 2 takes care of that; the resultant output is shown in Figure 12.3.

The owner (Angelica Sanchez) is planning to add more assistants, so she has used the SHIFT command in line 6 to step through all the assistants' names entered on the command line. Each SHIFT instruction moves the next assistant's name into the %1 parameter. A file for each assistant (xxxx.ast, where xxxx is the assistant's name) has been created so that line 7 can be used to determine when the list of assistant's names has been exhausted. Angelica asked her friends if there was a better way to find out when the SHIFT command exhausts the parameter list, but her friends, including me, did not know of one.

Lines 7, 8, and 9 each show a different use of the %1 parameter.

In lines 10 and 13, the rest of the line beyond the label (the label is Martha in line 10, Jason in line 13) has been used to make each of those lines a

```
 1      ECHO OFF
 2      IF %1 = = December GOTO FreeMnth
 3      ECHO This is the %0 list for the Month of %1
 4      ECHO The following children's %1 bill(s) have not been paid:
 5      :NextAsst
 6      shift
 7      IF NOT EXIST %1.ast GOTO End
 8      ECHO %1's Group:
 9      GOTO %1
10      :Martha 's group
11      FOR %%c IN (Jonathan Mary Joy Joey) DO IF NOT EXIST
          %%c.pd ECHO %%c
12      GOTO NextAsst
13      :Jason 's group
14      FOR %%c IN (Ashley Grendl Susan Hud) DO IF NOT EXIST
          %%c.pd ECHO %%c
15      GOTO NextAsst
16      :FreeMnth
17      ECHO This is the free month!
18      :End
```

Figure 12.1: The Version 2.0 SHOWDUE.BAT File

```
A> Showdue June Martha Jason

A> ECHO OFF
This is the Showdue List for the Month of June
The following children's June bill(s) have not been paid:
Martha's Group:
Jonathan
Mary
Joy
Jason's Group:
Ashley
Grendl
Susan
```

Figure 12.2: Output of the SHOWDUE.BAT File

```
A> Showdue December Jason Martha

A> ECHO OFF
This is the free month!
```
Figure 12.3: The Christmas Season Output of SHOWDUE.BAT

comment. (The temptation to be slightly clever was irresistible.) Note the space between the end of the label and the "comment." That space terminates the label, and in this example makes the line appear a little odd.

The FOR instructions in lines 11 and 14 look for a file with a filename of a child's name and an extension of .pd (for example, JOEY.PD), for each child in the group. Each month, before running this batch file, Angelica creates the .pd files for each child whose monthly bill has been paid.

Now let's look at Figure 12.2, the output of this batch file. For the month of June, only Joey's and Hud's parents came up with the day-care money on time. Figure 12.3 shows the batch file output for the Christmas season.

In this example, only a few variations on the use of batch commands have been demonstrated. It can be fun to experiment with others.

Batch File Powers and Limitations in Version 2.0

Software users can almost always see where a software package can be improved to meet their needs, whether or not the package was designed for the purpose they have in mind. Let's summarize the high and low points of the version 2.0 batch commands.

What's New and Powerful

The ECHO command allows us to add remarks without cluttering the output of the batch file operations. The %%variable in the FOR command can include the wild-card characters * and ?, which means that many files can be processed by one FOR command. The string-matching part of the IF command can be a handy feature. The SHIFT command gives us a way to process an indefinite number of replaceable parameters, adding another dimension to what can be done with batch files.

Limitations

The batch language that version 2.0 provides lacks true variables, which would be very nice to have. The power of the FOR instruction is limited to one instruction in the FOR loop. Other batch files cannot be executed as subroutines, although two or more batch files can be chained together. As with EDLIN, the reach of the batch capability is short: when specifying a file to operate on, path names cannot be used.

A NOTE OR TWO ABOUT BATCH FILES

Remember, when creating batch files, to put them on the disk that will be the command disk when they will be needed.

The F6 key is the same as Ctrl Z (unless, with version 2.0's keyboard key reassignment capability, you have changed its meaning). <F6> is the termination character to the COPY command.

Do use this facility for disk backup. Figuring out how to organize the batch file for backup will help you organize your disk files so that backup is relatively simple. This in turn will encourage you to actually *do* the backup operation, which may save you some later agony.

Keep the batch file facility in mind. It can make your use of the PC simpler and more sure. The charm of the batch file facility is that it can be tailored to a variety of your unique requirements.

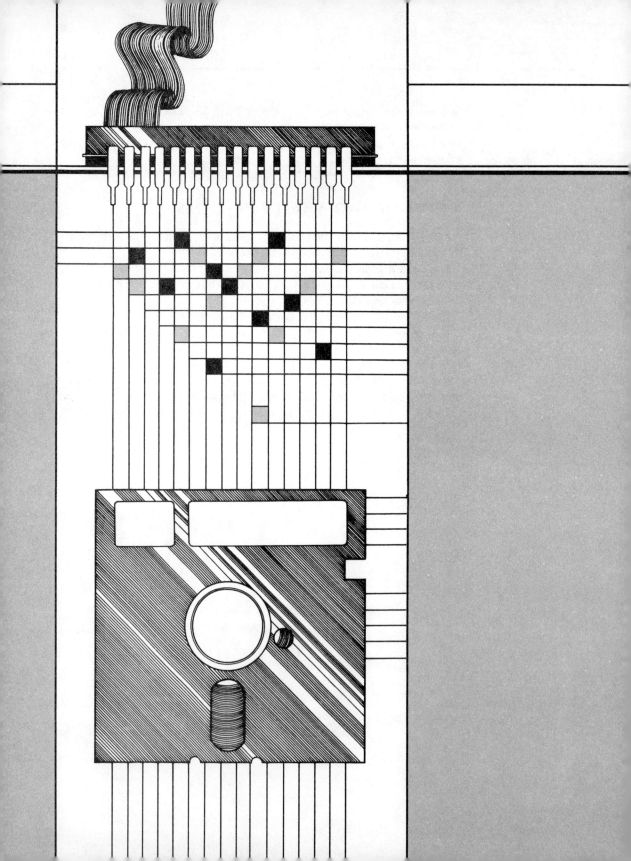

The Monochrome and Color/Graphics Screens

INTRODUCTION

This chapter discusses the two video display options that IBM offers with its PC, showing their characteristics and the differences between them. These options are (1) the monochrome display and adaptor and (2) the color/graphics adaptor (any display).

The chapter will begin with a description of the monochrome display and its adaptor board; we will then move on to the broader subject of the color/graphics adaptor board and the different types of displays it can drive. We will examine both the alphanumeric (A/N) and graphics (APA—all points addressable) modes of the color graphics adaptor. Included in the text is a section on the mixture of alphanumeric character output in graphics mode. The somewhat odd procedure for color selection is described, and tables listing the colors available in the text and graphics modes are provided. The chapter ends with a comment on choosing a monitor and a section on why not to match the color/graphics board with IBM's monochrome monitor.

You may want to know how to program the output of characters to the screens, and how to choose the right character attributes to achieve the desired color, reverse video, blinking, or other effects. Read this chapter first for the necessary background, then refer to Chapter 5, "Output to the Monochrome and Color/Graphics Monitors."

THE MONOCHROME DISPLAY

The standard PC display device is the IBM Monochrome display, a high-resolution, high-persistence green phosphor monitor. This monochrome monitor has a sufficiently high resolution (720 × 350) to support a pleasing and clear character set, presented in 25 lines of 80 characters each. The characters are made from a 7×9 matrix of dots within a 9×14 box. The monochrome monitor is addressed via a monochrome display adaptor board. (This IBM board includes a parallel printer adaptor).

The monochrome monitor is easy to work with, and its appearance blends well with the rest of the IBM equipment. However, the price for the adaptor board and monitor together is a little high, and color is not available; some people have not purchased this adaptor board and monitor combination option and use the color/graphics display option instead. Be aware, however, that many commercially available software packages will run only on the monochrome monitor (and some run only on the color/graphics board!). As usual, let your software needs dictate your hardware selection.

THE COLOR/GRAPHICS CAPABILITY

Probably for marketing reasons, the path to both color and graphics displays is provided entirely independent of the monochrome capability. Killing several birds with one stone, IBM offers a reasonably priced adaptor board that can be used for both color and graphics. This board can be purchased in addition to, or instead of, the monochrome display and adaptor board.

The color/graphics adaptor board can be used to drive a high-resolution IRGB monitor, a black-and-white monitor, or a color television (for those with economy in mind). An IRGB monitor has separate control lines for each of the colors red, green, and blue, and it responds to an intensity modifier. The board will also drive an RGB monitor, but the extra eight colors provided by the presence of the intensity signal will not be available.

The color/graphics adaptor board has a variety of different output options, which between them dictate the appearance of characters on the display and the type of display hardware that the board is addressing. Color and graphics are both available (hence the name of the adaptor board), but not necessarily at the same time.

The board operates in one of two modes: text, alias alphanumeric (A/N) mode, and graphics, alias all points addressable (APA) mode. (Note: There is opportunity for confusion when using the word mode. If you have looked at the ROM BIOS mode setting function, you may have noticed that it accepts as an argument one of seven modes. To integrate that idea of seven modes with the two we are discussing here, consider the following: the first four of the ROM BIOS modes all belong to the alphanumeric mode; the other three belong to the all points addressable mode.) Let's look first at the alphanumeric mode.

The Alphanumeric Mode (A/N) of the Color/Graphics Adaptor

This is the text mode. In it, all 256 characters in the 8-bit ASCII set are representable on the screen (as is true with the monochrome adaptor). The adaptor board contains a ROM character generator that creates about the same set of characters as are available with the monochrome adaptor, except that they are formed from a 5 × 7 matrix in an 8 × 8 box.

In A/N mode the board can create either a 40-character-per-line image or an 80-character-per-line image. In both cases there are 25 lines per screen. The 40-character mode, which doubles the width of the character (but does not change the height), is useful for low-resolution monitors and necessary for almost all televisions. If you use a television set as your display device, you will also need an RF modulator, such as the SUP'R'MOD by M & R Enterprises of Santa Clara, California.

The memory for the characters that are displayed on the screen is contained on the adaptor board. 16K bytes of memory are available in all, since in the high-resolution graphics mode 16,000 bytes are required to represent all points on the screen. The alphanumeric mode does not need, but does take advantage of, all this memory. It divides the 16K bytes into eight pages of 40 × 25 screens, or four pages of 80 × 25 screens. In making sense of that allocation, it helps to remember that in the IBM PC each character requires an attribute byte to describe how it should be displayed, so an 80 × 25 image requires 4000 bytes.

The Graphics or All Points Addressable (APA) Mode

As the name implies, in this mode any point on the screen is directly addressable. The number of points on the screen is determined by the resolution chosen. Three resolutions are offered. In IBM terminology they are low, medium, and high, which are 160 × 100, 320 × 200, and 640 × 200, respectively. The 100 or 200 figures refer to the vertical lines of resolution. Only medium- and high-resolution graphics are described here. In both of these modes, it is possible to produce quite exciting three-dimensional representations of multiple wave forms over time, to mention just one of hundreds of possible applications.

Character Output in APA (Graphics) Mode

You may want to annotate a graphic image with text. Unlike the A/N mode, APA offers no character generator hardware in graphics mode; any characters output to the screen have to be made up by specifying the individual dots. This has the advantage that you can make up your own character sets, which offers much opportunity for creativity; and you don't even have to be limited to the 8 × 8 matrix.

The disadvantage is that making up your own character set is a lot of work. However, do not despair of character output in graphics mode. If you use the PC's ROM BIOS to address the screen in APA mode, some character generation is done for you.

ROM BIOS has defined within it the dot patterns for the first normal-sized 128 ASCII characters. (Note: You can look at those definitions in the character generation table in the ROM BIOS listing found on page A-75 of the Technical Reference manual.) ROM BIOS also includes the routines to put them out to the screen dot by dot.

You can create your own set of 128 characters that occupy the upper half of the 8-bit ASCII spectrum (the ASCII characters between 128 and 255 inclusive.) ROM BIOS will output them for you if vector 1FH, bytes 0:7C to 0:7F, points to your table of dot positions.

If you don't want to use ROM BIOS, and you have access to a copy of the Technical Reference manual, there are enough clues there to make it fairly easy for you to write routines that output characters to a screen when the adaptor is operating in graphics mode.

Let's now see what color choices are available with the color/graphics adaptor in its various modes.

COLOR SELECTION
WITH THE COLOR/GRAPHICS ADAPTOR

This is where we introduce you to the color choices and slightly odd color selection methods offered by the color/graphics adaptor board. A brief piece on the available colors is followed by the specifics of color selection when the adaptor board is operating in A/N mode. The section that follows, on what can be done with color in the APA (graphics) mode, also talks about the memory space on the adaptor board and how that affects the bits available for color choice at the different resolutions. The section on color ends with a summary of the color options available in medium- and high-resolution graphics modes.

Colors Available with the Color/Graphics Adaptor

(Note: In the text that follows, white, black, and gray are considered colors.)

Sixteen colors are created by the adaptor from three basic colors. These basic colors are the adaptor's versions of red, green, and blue. The 2 × 2 × 2 possible combinations of the three basic colors produce eight colors, including black and white. Each of the eight colors can be modified by the high-intensity attribute, to give the set of sixteen colors shown in Figure 13.1. In this figure, the red, green, blue, and intensity components appear alongside the resulting color.

I R G B	Light Magenta
0 0 0 0	Black
0 0 0 1	Blue
0 0 1 0	Green
0 0 1 1	Cyan
0 1 0 0	Red
0 1 0 1	Magenta
0 1 1 0	Brown
0 1 1 1	Light gray
1 0 0 0	Dark gray
1 0 0 1	Light blue
1 0 1 0	Light green
1 0 1 1	Light cyan
1 1 0 0	Light red
1 1 0 1	Light magenta
1 1 1 0	Yellow
1 1 1 1	White

Figure 13.1: The Color/Graphics Adaptor's Sixteen Colors

Let's now see how these colors are used in the text (A/N) mode.

Color Choices in the Text, or Alphanumeric, Mode

The color of a character and the color of its background are both defined by the attribute byte associated with the character. (Note: If you wish to read more about the attribute byte, see Chapter 5, "Output to the Monochrome and Color/Graphics Monitors.") In the text mode, color selection offers much scope for experimentation.

The character itself may be any of sixteen colors, and the background any of eight colors. The attribute byte devotes four bits, one each for red, green, blue, and intensity, to the foreground color, hence the choice of sixteen colors. The background color is allocated another three bits, again one each for red, green, and blue, but no intensity bit. Hence there are eight possible background colors. Filling the attribute byte out to eight bits, the high-order bit is devoted to making the character blink (every two-thirds of a second) if set. Figure 13.2 shows the coding of the attribute byte for color selection in alphanumeric mode.

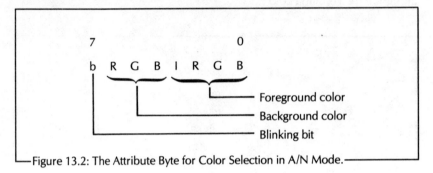

Figure 13.2: The Attribute Byte for Color Selection in A/N Mode.

As you can see, a character can be displayed in any combination of eight background and sixteen foreground colors—that is, 128 possible colors. Some of those combinations will not produce a very clear character, especially where the foreground and background colors are the same.

Color Choices in APA (Graphics) Mode

We need to talk about points on the screen, so we'll take a slight digression here into the name of the point on the screen at which the color is applied. Other names for this point are dot, pixel, and pel. *Pixel* is derived from picture element; *pel* is a contraction of it. Pel is used in the IBM Technical Reference manual. Why pel is a better choice than dot is made clear in the description of medium-resolution graphics. For now we will use whichever of the four names seems most appropriate.

Color Choices and Graphics Resolution

The color choices in graphics mode can be related to the number of bits used to represent each point on the screen. To figure out the number of bits per pel available for color specification, we should first talk about how many pels there are in a full screen, and how much memory there is on an adaptor card to hold a screen image.

Color Choices in High-Resolution   In high-resolution mode the adaptor can address

$$80 \times 25 \times 8 \times 8 = 640 \times 200 = 128,000$$

points; that is, 80 columns in each of 25 lines, with each row/column position being filled by an 8 × 8 rectangle of dots.

With 128,000 bits, at 8 bits per byte, it takes a little less than 16K bytes to store one screen image. The color/graphics adaptor contains 16K bytes of RAM, so it can support only one bit per dot. This allows no spare bits to define the color of the dot, so high-resolution graphics is in black and white only.

Color Choices in Medium Resolution   Given the 16K memory on the adaptor board, medium resolution (320 × 200) can use two bits per pel. These two bits can assume four different values. A value of 0 makes the pel assume the background color, i.e., it is the equivalent of off. The values 1, 2, and 3 are each a different color.

So with medium resolution we see that three colors, plus background, are available for the dot. Now the question is, which three of the sixteen colors do the values 1, 2, and 3 represent? IBM has decided that for us; it has given us a choice of two sets of three. They are as follows:

> *Set one*:   Cyan, magenta, and white
> *Set two*:   Green, red, and brown

The designers of the adaptor board extended the color capabilities beyond the three colors for the dot (apart from the background color) by including an additional 1-bit color set switch. This one bit dictates which of two color sets the three colors will be chosen from. It applies to the three (nonbackground) colors for the whole screen. The two color sets are defined by the adaptor board and cannot be changed.

You may be wondering about the possible choices for the background color, which applies to the whole screen; there is wild freedom here. The background color can be any one of the sixteen colors available on the adaptor.

Graphics Mode Color Choice Summary

Let's now review the options we have for color in graphics mode.

- *In high resolution* (640 × 200) only black and white are available.
- *In medium resolution* (320 × 200) four colors are available: any one of sixteen colors for the background, and a choice between two sets, each of three possible colors, for the foreground pels; *set one* is cyan, magenta, and white; *set two* is green, red, and brown.

The process for selection of color in medium-resolution graphics mode goes as follows:

1. Choose the background color, any one of sixteen.
2. Choose one of the two predefined three-color sets for the foreground colors.
3. Choose each pel's color from the selected three-color set.

The Best of Pels, Points, Dots, and Pixels

Earlier in this chapter we promised to explain why pel is a better word to use than dot or point. Medium resolution is obtained by this adaptor board by drawing a line, left to right, between even- and odd-numbered high-resolution points. So in medium resolution, what appears on the screen is not a point—it is a small horizontal line, more naturally called a picture element, or pel.

A SMALL PUZZLE FOR SOFTWARE WRITERS

Those of you familiar with the contents of the attribute byte may be wondering what happens when a character attribute originally designed for the monochrome display is sent out via the color/graphics adaptor. What will the character look like?

Reverse video still works; however, it affects only black-and-white characters. The attribute bit setting for the underline feature in monochrome results in a blue character when processed by the color/graphics adaptor. The reverse translation takes place when blue characters are output via the monochrome adaptor.

Table 3 in Chapter Two (on page 2-55) of the Technical Reference manual gives more information on this subject.

CHOOSING A MONITOR

The somewhat extensive subject of choosing color monitors is not within the scope of this book, but at least one comment is appropriate. The color/graphics adaptor has the capability for specifying high-intensity output on a character-by-character basis. Some color monitors do not support this high-intensity feature. You can live without it, even though the programmers of much existing software (the WordStar program, for one) seem to be fond of using it.

MIXING AND MATCHING

You might wish to try using the color/graphics adaptor board to drive the monochrome monitor, or the monochrome board to drive an ordinary black-and-white monitor. The basic message of this section is *don't!*

Important technical differences exist between the electrical output of the color/graphics and monochrome adaptor boards, which prevent successful long-term driving of the monochrome screen by the color/graphics board. Smoke accompanying monochrome monitor damage has been reported as the result of one such attempt.

There are adaptor boards offered by other manufacturers that can provide true graphics capabilities (not just block character graphics) on your IBM monochrome display unit. However, the software that drives the color/graphics adaptor will usually have to be changed before it will produce graphics on your monochrome monitor.

SUMMARY

We have seen that two display options exist for the IBM PC: (1) an easy-on-the-eyes, high-resolution monochrome display, driven by the monochrome adaptor board, and (2) a color or black-and-white monitor with poorer character resolution, driven by the color/graphics adaptor. In addition, we discussed the options that exist for choosing color and creating graphics on monitors driven by the color/graphics adaptor. By now, your grasp of the IBM PC's unique and confusing approach to displays may be improved.

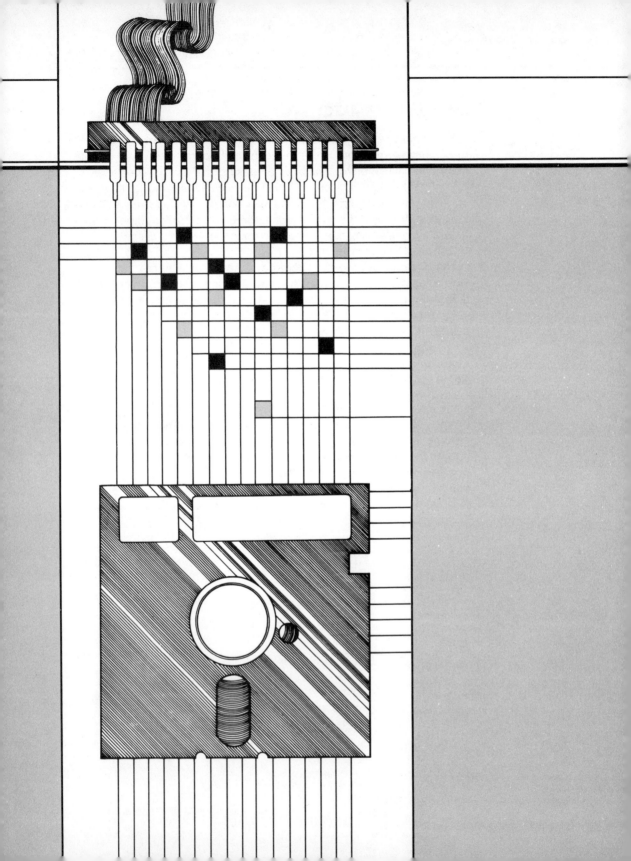

Using the Serial Port

INTRODUCTION

This chapter shows how to use the serial port, alias the asynchronous communications adaptor, that may be installed in the IBM PC. The serial port is your link with the world beyond your desk top. With a serial port, a modem, the right software, and the use of a telephone, you can gather and exchange information with bulletin boards, data banks, perhaps your own bank, Western Union, assorted vendors, and other computer users. Used in a more utilitarian way, the serial port allows you to use letter-quality printers that have only serial interfaces, by redirecting output destined for the parallel port to the serial port.

We will begin the chapter with a brief discussion of the communications capabilities within PC-DOS at the user level. We will give examples of how to use these capabilities to run either of two letter-quality printers, continuing with a note on how success is not always hard to obtain. We will discuss the RS-232 "standard," and cover details of cabling that may be relevant, including what is meant by a "null modem." We will show how to connect with information retrieval services, using The Source as an example.

The serial port in the IBM literature has a grand name, which in PC-DOS version 1.1 the software is beginning to live up to. The board containing the serial port is called the *asynchronous communications adaptor.*

PC-DOS COMMUNICATIONS CAPABILITIES

At the user level, PC-DOS can do a lot for you, if you have the right version. Version 1.0 can, with help, stumble through basic output via the serial port. It won't do it well, and any nonmasochist with a serious interest in communications should buy version 1.1.

Version 1.0 Communications Capabilities—The Basic Offering

We will spend very little time on communications in version 1.0, as it is just not worth devoting a lot of time to. The magazines have published various how-to-do-it articles on serial communications for PC-DOS version 1.0. Perhaps the most useful article is in Volume One, Number Three of *PC Magazine* (June/July 1982), which contains the fairly short listing (on page 153) of a BASIC program that redirects printer output to the serial port.

Version 1.0 offers the COMM.BAS program, which some people have developed an enthusiasm for. This program serves as a framework for communications software. It allows you to specify baud rate, parity, word length, and the number of stop bits, thus dealing with the bare necessities of serial communications; it is therefore of some value.

The MODE command in version 1.0 has no communications options. (Its two options are (1) change the default lines per inch and characters per line on any of the three parallel printers, and (2) set the number of columns per screen on the color/graphics-adaptor driven monitor.) Let's move on to discuss versions 1.1 and 2.0 serial I/O handling at the user's level.

Versions 1.1 and 2.0—Now You Are Talking

The authors of PC-DOS have put a lot of work in version 1.1 into beefing up version 1.0's MODE command. The post-version-1.0 MODE command is a good piece of work and is an essential ingredient in the task of moving files of data across serial ports at the command level.

In version 1.1, two additional options are provided for invoking communications capabilities. Option 3 initializes the serial port, and option 4 redirects parallel printer output to the serial port.

(The first two options in the MODE command in version 1.1 are the same as in version 1.0. In version 2.0, option 1 includes the /P option for continuous retry on timeout, and option 2 is much improved. When options 1, 3, or 4 of the MODE command are invoked in version 2.0, the resident portion of PC-DOS expands by about 256 bytes. In version 1.1, the extra code required is put into the upper half of the PC-DOS communications area at 0:500. Let's examine options 3 and 4.)

Version 2 also includes the CTTY command, which allows you to run PC-DOS from a remote terminal connected via the serial port. The MODE command is used to initialize the port, then the CTTY command is invoked to switch control to the remote terminal.

Initializing the Serial Port

Option 3 of the MODE command allows you to specify baud rate, parity, word length and the number of stop bits, which are the basic hardware- and software-controlled factors that vary according to the device communication and the software driving it.

Option 3 also includes an option (/P) that must be used when initializing the serial port for accepting the output that normally goes to the parallel printer.

The trick to the successful use of this command is to know what to tell it. More on that later. The DOS manual is clear about the options you have and gives useful examples.

Redirecting Parallel Printer Output to the Serial Port

Option 4 of the MODE command allows you to use printers with serial interfaces. It tells PC-DOS to switch the output destined for one of the three parallel printer ports to either of the two serial ports. Again, the DOS manual is clear on how to use the command. Let's look at a couple of examples of printer output redirection.

USING TWO LETTER-QUALITY PRINTERS WITH SERIAL INTERFACES

We will look at the specific MODE commands for using two different letter-quality printers with serial interfaces. The first is the Smith Corona TP-1; the other is the Diablo 630. (Note: the Smith Corona can be ordered with a parallel interface.)

Output to the Smith Corona TP-1

The commands to achieve this redirection (output to the Smith Corona TP-1) are as follows:

```
MODE COM1:300,N,8,1,P
```

followed by:

```
MODE LPT1:=COM1
```

The Smith Corona accepts data at 300 baud, uses no parity, and accepts 8-bit words with a single stop bit. The P is necessary because the Smith Corona's buffer fills faster than the printer can print the characters. When that state occurs, the Smith Corona sends a not-ready condition to the serial port. When the serial port sees the not-ready flag, it has the option of abandoning the communication in progress, or retrying on the assumption that the not-ready condition will soon clear up. The /P option tells the software to hang in there, even if it gets a not-ready condition.

Output to the Diablo 630

The only difference (as far as the MODE command is concerned) between this printer and the Smith Corona is the baud rate at which they operate. The commands are

        MODE COM1:1200,N,8,1,P

followed by

        MODE LPT1:=COM1

as you would expect. If all this seems quite easy, you may be correct. A number of things can, however, go wrong with this process, and at the risk of turning some readers into serial port hypochondriacs, here is a discussion of some of them.

POTENTIAL PROBLEMS WHEN USING THE SERIAL PORT

Let's assume for the moment that you are attempting to use a printer with a serial interface. The problems you might experience center around one or all of the following: cabling, lack of information about the printer characteristics, and the ROM BIOS version 04/24/81 nondetection of printer not-ready bug.

Cabling, or What Do These Guys Think RS-232 Means

The serial port uses the RS-232 standard. So do many letter-quality printers. "Good," we conclude, "the two devices can talk to one another." That conclusion is not valid. In my experience with high-tech Silicon Valley companies, when a new device needs to be connected to the outside world, the engineers think "Well, how shall we implement the RS-232 standard this week?" Their problem (and ours) is that the RS-232 standard has to deal with a wide range of communication complexities. For connecting simple devices (say, truly dumb terminals), only a couple of links are necessary. For more complex communications requirements, a greater number of signal paths is required. That means more expense for the builder and the customer, both for the more bulky cable and for the more complex devices required to drive the communications. The engineers are under pressure to reduce expenses, so they choose to implement a convenient variant of the RS-232 standard. You can see that the RS-232 standard has history working against it; the standard has been widely ignored, because it dealt with communications complexities far greater than were necessary at the time.

Programming is just crawling out of the primeval slime of everyone choosing convenient but short-sighted implementations, and there are indications that engineers who design the communications capabilities of a device are getting used to the cheapness and reliability of greater device intelligence and are planning for it. In the meantime, the most you will need in order to figure out how to connect a printer to your PC's serial port are

- engineering drawings of the printer interface and the serial board;
- complete knowledge of the software operating the devices at each end;
- an oscilloscope and the ability to use it;
- cable, connector parts, and a soldering iron;
- imagination and patience;
- and, lastly, lots of experience.

Lack of Information about Printer Characteristics

This has long been a problem, but there is hope. The previous diatribe ignores some of the good work that is being done these days by some printer manufacturers. Although many printers are shipped without adequate information on how to make them work with specific computers, sometimes the IBM PC connection is documented. IBM has open specifications on the PC, so printer manufacturers can build to suit either the PC's asynchronous or parallel communications. The manufacturers may also provide documentation from which you can find out what baud rate, parity, word length, and number of stop bits to use.

Cabling the Serial Port

The number of connections between the serial port and the device it will drive will vary according to the needs of the device and the sophistication of the software driving the device. By far the simplest approach to successful cabling is to find another PC user who has successfully done what you want to do, in terms of an exact match both in software and hardware. Once you have found such a user, ask him or her who supplied the cable, and to print the command sequences used to get the device going.

It may be that the experience of reaching the correct cabling and command sequence solution was very painful. In that case you may detect a slight hesitation in their willingness to part with such dearly bought information, just for the asking. Offer them a weekend in Reno or Atlantic City. This shows them how much you value the information they have to offer.

The Technical Reference manual section on communications has a page entitled Asynchronous Communications Adaptor Connector Interface Specifications. (In IBM's German language manuals that page title is probably all one word.) It's page 2-151 of the July 1982 edition. The diagram on this page shows how IBM has interpreted the RS-232 standard in the PC.

The only pin number greater than 9 that you may need to connect is pin 20, data terminal ready. Current loop connections are used where the cable length is great, say, over 500 feet in noisy electrical environments, or over 2000 feet in quiet environments. Ring indicate, pin 22, probably will not be used except by software designed to control autodial modems.

If you can't find a cable supplier who can prove to you that the cable you are buying will work for the exact situation you have in mind, and you have found no one who has done what you want to do, check the documentation that is supplied with the device you are connecting to the serial port. Look for pin connection diagrams. As a last resort, call the manufacturer. They will surely show interest in supporting people who use such a popular computer as the IBM PC.

A Null Modem

If you have two IBM PCs that you want to talk to each other, and you don't want to use modems and the telephone to connect them, you will need a null modem. A null modem is a device that connects one PC's transmit data line (pin 2 on its serial port) to the other PC's receive data line (pin 3 on the other PC's serial port). Another matching pair of lines are data terminal ready (pin 20) and data set ready (pin 6). Request to send (pin 4) and clear to send (pin 5) need special handling. Figure 14.1 shows a set of pin connections that serves as a null modem.

Pins 4 and 5 are jumpered together at one end, so both connect with pin 8 of the other serial port. (In Figure 14.1, lines that cross in the central part of the figure are not electrically connected.) There are other variants of null modems. For example, pin 8 may not be used and pins 4 and 5 may be cross-connected just like pins 2 and 3.

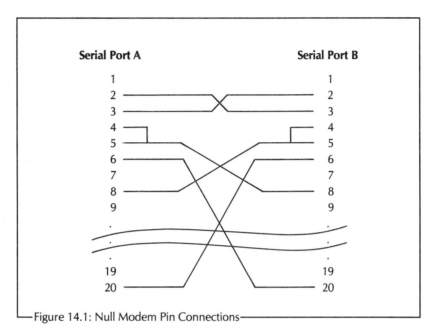

Serial Port A   Serial Port B

Figure 14.1: Null Modem Pin Connections

The Serial Output Bug in ROM BIOS Version 04/24/81

There is one bug in the 04/24/81 version of ROM BIOS that is related to output to the serial port. (Note: You can use the following command in DEBUG to examine the ROM BIOS version date: -d f000:fff5 L8.)

The bug appears when the interrupt routines detect a device timeout condition while sending characters out via the serial device. The wrong error bits are set (50H instead of 80H), so the routine that is using ROM BIOS to send characters will not see that the device is not ready. The net effect of all this is that some characters that should appear on, say, the printer, will not. When you see that there are characters missing from the output stream, this bug is one, but not the only, possible cause.

CONNECTION WITH INFORMATION RETRIEVAL SERVICES

To connect with the outside world, you will need a modem, the serial port, a cable to connect the two, a telephone, and some communications software. We will assume that you have all the hardware.

Communications Software

IBM supplies with PC-DOS a BASIC program called COMM.BAS. COMM.BAS contains the essentials for communicating with information retrieval services. IBM also sells the Asynchronous Communications Support package, which includes a manual as well as asynchronous communications software.

The function of either of these two programs is (1) to establish the communications protocol appropriate to the information service being accessed, then (2) to transfer the characters typed at the keyboard to the serial port, and send characters received from the serial port to the screen. These two communications programs will work for you, but they lack the sophistication that would make them more reliable and more flexible.

Well-written communications software will normally keep at a distance all the messy details of communications such as baud rate, number of stop bits, half- or full-duplex operation, etc. There may be times that you will need to know about these details—well-written communications software usually has a mode where you can specify parameters. You may also be able to use option 3 of the MODE command to initialize the protocol parameters.

Several good-quality communications packages are available from sources other than IBM. One package in particular can be recommended for two reasons: (1) it works well and is well documented, and (2) you pay what you think it is worth to you. The package is PC-TALK from FREEWARE. It is available from most IBM PC user-group libraries.

The PC-TALK documentation encourages you to copy the program, and, if you like it and use it, send money to the program's author. The suggested amount is $25. The way PC-TALK is distributed is an experiment. This FREEWARE experiment has so far produced some well-written software packages. It would appeal to one's sense of social progress to find that authors of freely distributed, high-quality programs could live reasonably well on the proceeds.

Connecting with The Source

Because the COMM.BAS program is available to all users of PC-DOS, we will use it as an example to show how to connect with The Source. It's a simple procedure.

Call BASICA, load COMM.BAS, then run COMM.BAS. You can do this even if the modem is not connected. You will see a message showing you the options available. Connect the modem to the serial port (don't dial the number yet), and select option 5. Have ready your log-in command text, ID number, and password. Follow the instructions that appear after you select option 5.

The Source will break the connection (politely) if there are problems. Don't be afraid to try more than once.

SUMMARY

We have learned how to use the MODE command to redirect output to a serial printer. We have seen how the physical connection between the serial port and the external device may not always be easy to establish, and how another person's successful experience is valuable. We have seen that communications software is necessary to connect with the outside world, and that such software is available from a variety of sources.

Now we'll change directions completely. We will forget the outside world and look at DEBUG, a program that lets us look into the innards of PC-DOS.

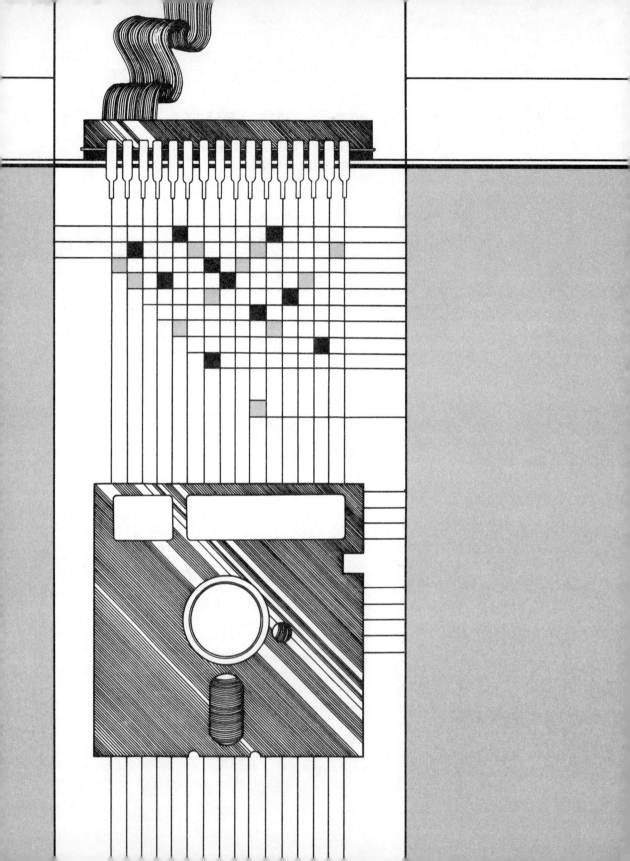

15

The Delights of Debug

INTRODUCTION

DEBUG is your window into the workings and wonders of PC-DOS. It also has the less spectacular but equally powerful function of helping you find bugs in and patch your programs. This chapter is directed to those who have had little experience with debuggers; that is, it is an introduction to debugging, containing little for the experienced assembly language programmer.

In this chapter you will learn what the DEBUG program is, how it works, how to use it, how to patch a program with it, and what ventures of exploration you might undertake with it. DEBUG is a powerful tool for reviewing and changing software at its deepest levels; it is therefore appropriate to issue a few warnings about treading carefully in the software undergrowth. Let's begin with a look at the DEBUG name.

WHY "DEBUG"?

The original bug was a moth, stuck in the works of a huge early computer full of glowing valves. The program running on that computer would not run correctly. The programmers didn't know that the problem was a bug until they found the moth, whose slightly compressed body was preventing the closure of an electro-mechanical relay. Once the programmers had found the moth and removed it from their walk-through computer, they realized they had de-bugged it.

The story has been told many times, and perhaps it wasn't a moth. Most of us differentiate little between the thousands of small crawling things that provoke reactions in us disproportionate to their size. Bug is a suitably expletive sort of name for them, especially when found in computers or sleeping bags, fellow creatures though they are.

So when a program doesn't work as planned, it has become natural to say it needs debugging. Programmers build tools called debuggers to help them find and remove bugs. Let's look at what PC-DOS's debugger can do for us.

WHAT DEBUG CAN DO FOR US

The DEBUG program is a tool we can use to check that our software operates as planned. DEBUG allows us to watch the execution of a program's logic, step by step, whether each step represents a whole module of logic (a subroutine) or a single instruction. In addition to watching the logic flow (or stumble), programmers have an intense interest in before and after views of code and data. Both of these move around in memory, and from disk to memory and back. DEBUG enables us to look at these before and after states in detail.

You can see that one of the major functions a debugging package provides is that it gives us a chance "to see what is really there." It is interesting, as well as useful, to poke around inside the software and look at a disk's contents.

Other facilities provided by the DEBUG package are the ability to patch programs, and to make up small programs in memory and try them out, without having to use the Macro Assembler or other programming language compilers and assemblers. This, of course, applies only to small sections of software. A sequence of anything above 40 instructions (200 in version 2) is probably stretching it. Appendix C shows how to create short programs and save them on disk.

To make full use of DEBUG, you need to have access to descriptions of the assembler language set (see *Programming the 8086/8088* by James Coffron, Sybex, 1983), and be willing to learn something about assembler language programming, if you don't already. You also need to know something of the architecture of the program being debugged and the hardware it is running on. The first thing to understand is how the registers in the 8088 are assigned and used (see Chapter 1).

DEBUG is a powerful tool, and it works best in the hands of an experienced and knowledgeable user. If this is your first experience with a debugging package, don't be surprised if the answers to your questions regarding how a certain piece of software works are not revealed within the first half-hour of using the debugger. You will likely be frustrated by strange and, for that moment, inexplicable circumstances. That's when you either have to learn more or skip that approach and try another. If you don't know much about how computers work, using DEBUG is a little like being tossed into the deep end to learn how to swim—for some unpleasant, for others, (terminally) ineffective.

You may have heard of symbolic debuggers. These advanced debuggers have access to the symbol table(s) of the program(s) being debugged. With them you can debug high-level language programs without having to dig deep into assembly language. DEBUG is not a symbolic debugger, however.

One of the shortcuts to finding out what DEBUG can do for you is to know how it works. Let's explore that topic.

HOW DEBUG WORKS

DEBUG uses debugging-oriented hardware features of the 8088 as well as software to do its job. Let's look over the hardware features first.

A Hardware Assist for DEBUG

In the last few years computers have been designed with better cooperation between the design engineers and the programmers. Intel, along with other chip manufacturers, has recognized that software requires debugging, that debugging is a time-consuming and expensive process, and that if a chip has decent debugging features built in, it will sell more.

DEBUG makes use of the trace and breakpoint features built into the 8088. (Debuggers for earlier microcomputers worked much harder to achieve the same effect, and they had to overcome a variety of problems that had to do with timing and instruction size. These problems, however, no longer exist, thanks to the design of the 8088.)

The 8088 is designed so that when the next command to be executed is a single byte of CCH, an interrupt occurs, execution of the current path of logic is suspended, and control is transferred to the routine pointed to by interrupt vector number 3. All the DEBUG package has to do to get itself called at a specific instruction is to replace the first (and perhaps only) byte of that instruction with the break instruction (a byte containing CCH), and make sure that vector 3 (absolute locations 0CH–0FH) points to itself (the debugging package).

Intel also provides (reserves) interrupt vector 1 (locations 04H–07H), through which control is transferred at the end of every instruction execution if the CPU is operating in trace mode. The CPU operates in trace mode if the trap flag is set in the program status word (PSW).

So you see, there are two easy ways for the debugging software to get control of any stage of program execution:

1. Inserting breakpoint instructions, which replace the first byte of an instruction with the one-byte break instruction.
2. Initiating trace (alias single-step) mode, by turning on the trap flag in the program status word.

Debugging Read-Only Memory (ROM)

You might correctly deduce that the first method cannot be used for debugging or stepping through ROM, because the debugger can't write the break instruction into it. To see what happens in ROM, you should use the second method, single-step, to trace your way through it.

Let's now look at some of the setup operations that DEBUG has to go through to get ready for debugging an existing program.

The Software Components of DEBUG

DEBUG is an envelope around the program being debugged. At the prompt level, when you first call DEBUG, COMMAND.COM loads the debugger. If the name of the program to be debugged has been specified as an argument, DEBUG does again what COMMAND.COM did for it; it loads the program defined by the argument into the memory that is left after DEBUG has been loaded, and it correctly initializes the program segment prefix (PSP), which is the area at the beginning of a program that formalizes its connection with PC-DOS. DEBUG sets up interrupt vectors 1 and 3 and provides the - (dash) prompt. After that, the user is given control.

If no arguments have been specified, the user is given control immediately. The program (or data) loading process can be invoked later by using the Name and Load commands.

Let's look at how to use DEBUG.

HOW TO USE DEBUG

We will begin this section with a very brief introduction to the commands within DEBUG. We will then throw in some perhaps gratuitous advice on what should be in your head when you use it, and then review, again briefly, the commands and facilities worth special note.

A Brief Summary of DEBUG's Capabilities

Figure 15.1 shows in the left-hand column the things you might want to do with DEBUG; the right-hand column lists the commands available. Commands can often be put to good use for purposes other than those shown here.

Function	Command(s)
Program execution control	Go and Trace
Disk access	Name, Load, and Write
Data display	Dump
Code display	Unassemble
Data entry	Enter and Fill
Code entry	Assemble [2.0] and Enter
Status display and entry	Register
Single-character I/O	Input and Output
Search for byte(s)	Search
Compare memory	Compare
Mental aids	Hexarithmetic and Assemble [2.0]

Figure 15.1: DEBUG's Command Capabilities

A more complete summary of the DEBUG commands can be found in Chapter 17.

The Theory and Morals of Debugging

The best debugging tool, if you wrote the program or have well-documented, accurate listings, is your head. A lot of debugging time can be saved if you first think carefully and clearly about the potential sources of the problem. You might be one of those people who tend to get sidetracked by interesting circumstances when digging around inside a program with the debugger. If you are, prepare a well-thought-out search plan first; it will save you a lot of time. This is a recommendation to use your powers of logic and visualization before resorting to the debugger.

However, this recommendation is not always easy to follow. If you want a hero in this field, there is Nikola Tesla, the inventor and engineer who patented the method for generating alternating current. Among many startling accomplishments, he possessed an ability to visualize inventions with great clarity and intensity. Prior to registering his AC power generation and distribution patents, he designed, assembled, ran, then disassembled and examined for wear an AC electric motor—all in his head. There are a few rare programmers who can do the same sort of thing with software. Give it a try!

Now that we have covered the homily of "think about the problem first; use the debugger later," let's return from the world of gods and look at the debugger we are going to need.

Practical Debugging

The first step in any debugging venture is to isolate the problem, i.e., find out when, during the execution of the program, the problem occurs. Doing this will narrow the search to a limited portion of the code. The next step is to see what makes the bug occur, i.e., at which instruction in the isolated group of instructions the performance is not as expected. There is a loose parallel between this two-step debugging approach and the Go and Trace commands in DEBUG.

Go is a good tool for checking your program logic at a modular level. In contrast to the Trace command, it is your coarse-adjustment tool. With it you can follow the program in major leaps until it goes wrong, then back off and examine the last step in smaller increments. At the risk of overstressing a point, when you have narrowed down somewhat the source of the logic failure, take the time to get your head away from DEBUG and think about the program. The bug will often be clear to you long before you can pinpoint it exactly with the Go and Trace commands.

If the bug doesn't yield to the Go-with-breakpoints approach, you may have to resort to the Trace command. The Trace command is useful when a piece of code a few instructions long doesn't do what you expect or what you think the listing dictates.

You need commands to look at the data before the bug occurs, and at the wreckage after the bug has happened. For this, DEBUG provides the Dump, Register, and Compare commands.

Let's take a look at a few of DEBUG's commands, and see how each one can be used.

DEBUG's Commands Reviewed

The DOS manuals give good descriptions of each of the commands in DEBUG. The manuals also have sections on information common to all commands, as well as definitions of the command parameters. There you can find pretty much all you need to know about DEBUG's capabilities. We recommend you read those descriptions; they show you features of DEBUG that are not always available in other debuggers, and that are a pleasure to find. Here are a couple of examples of these features:

1. The ability to mix data in several different formats in the same command line. The manual gives the following example for the Enter command:

    E DS:100 F3 "xyz" 8D

    Starting at DS:100, the five bytes F3H, 78H, 79H, 7AH, and 8DH are entered.

2. The Dump and Unassemble commands keep track of where they were last used, and continue from that point if no arguments are given the next time they are invoked.

The Go Command

The Go command starts or continues execution of the program you are debugging, unless you give it a new address at which to begin execution by using the G=address option. Breakpoint instructions are inserted at any breakpoint addresses you specify. A typical Go command to start the execution of a small program and trap it at one of three places would be

   g=100 10c 116 134

Note that the CS register was not specified; the current value is assumed. If the break occurred at 10C, the next Go command might be

   g 134 147

This continues execution from the 10C breakpoint. Note that it was necessary to respecify the 134 breakpoint. (The example assumes that the 116 breakpoint is no longer relevant; the 10C breakpoint is on a different logic path.)

If you doubt that at least one of your breakpoints will be reached, add the address of the instruction prior to the program's termination as another breakpoint.

All breakpoints are removed when one of them is reached. This wholesale removal of all breakpoints can be annoying in some circumstances. If you want a permanent (for the duration of the debugging) breakpoint, you can set it by using the Enter command to place a CCH at the breakpoint location. Remember that DEBUG won't remove this permanent breakpoint for you.

If you are debugging under version 2.0, run your program with BREAK OFF. If BREAK is ON, that logic gets interwoven with DEBUG's in a confusing way.

The Trace Command

Trace executes one instruction at a time, unless it is given an argument that tells it how many instructions to execute before handing control back to you. You will always get a display of the registers and flags after the execution of each instruction, so this is a very slow way of stepping through a program. The command to trace the next five instructions is

   t 5

The Write Command

The power of devastation is in your hands when you use the Write command. If you are doing anything out of the ordinary, write onto a *copy* of a diskette, never onto an original from which no copies have been made.

The Assemble Command [2.0]

With the Assemble command, which is only available in version 2.0, you can write small routines in assembler language. If you are not going to do anything but minor work in assembler language, the existence of this command can save you the cost of IBM's Macro Assembler. To add instructions at, say, location CS:134, type

        a134<return>

then type in the assembler language instructions.

The Fill Command

Fill is a handy command, occasionally devastating if mistyped. A command to zero all the bytes of a buffer into which you are about to read one sector of a disk is

        F 400 L200 0

where DS:400 is the buffer address.

The Register Command

When you are debugging a program, just after it has been loaded (via the Load and Name commands or as an argument to the DEBUG call), the registers are all set to begin execution of the program. So you can use the Register command to find where the program is loaded in memory.

We have not said much about the Name, Load, and Write commands; let's look at a procedure for patching a program, which is one place where those commands are likely to be used.

PATCHING WITH DEBUG

Patching with DEBUG is quite simple. You need to remember that the program begins at CS:100, not code segment address zero (CS:0000, where the program segment prefix is found). Here are the steps for patching, say, location 273H:

1. Call DEBUG PROGNAME.COM, where PROGNAME.COM is the name of the program you wish to patch.
2. Use Dump or Unassemble to look at location 373H. (Remember, your program begins after the 100H-long PSP.)
3. Use Enter to make the change.
4. Use Dump or Unassemble again to check it.
5. Use Write to write the patched version onto the disk.

Let's look at a more specific, but simple, example. You have written in assembler language a program that first announces itself, then does a variety of small tasks, and then displays all the ASCII characters above 127. The program is very short and the display-loop portion of it looks like this:

```
006A B402      DISP MOV AH,2      ;Display output function
006C BA7F00         MOV DX,7FH    ;Set to start at ASCII 128
006F 42        INCH INC DX        ;Bump to next character
0070 CD21           INT 21H       ;DOS function call
0072 81FAFF00       CMP DX,FFH     ;Done yet?
0076 7EF7           JLE INCH      ;Loop if not
```

Let's assume you want to change the program to display all the ASCII characters, not just the last 128 characters. This can be achieved by changing the word at location 6D to minus one (− 1). If you look at the second line of the display program, the word at 6D is the value of the first character (before it is incremented by one) to be passed to the display output function.

The name of your program is DISASCII.COM. Let's call the debugger. Type the characters following the A> prompt:

    A>debug disascii.com

You will see the hyphen (alias dash) prompt. To look at the code in the area of interest, type the characters following the dash prompt:

    -u 16a

Note the addition of 100H to allow for the program segment prefix. You will see perhaps fifteen lines of your program, the first six lines of which look like this:

```
08F1:016A B402      MOV   AH,02
08F1:016C BA7F00    MOV   DX,007F
08F1:016F 42        INC   DX
08F1:0170 CD21      INT   21
08F1:0172 81FAFF00   CMP   DX,00FF
08F1:0176 7EF7      JLE   016F
```

Check that locations 16D and 16E are indeed the ones that need to be set to − 1. Once you are sure of this, type

    e 16d ff ff

This changes the word at location 16D to − 1. If you have version 2.0, you could instead enter the move instruction again with a different value, as follows. Type

    a 16c

You will see

    08F1:016C

which you follow by typing

    mov dx,ffff

or

    mov, dx, − 1

To check that you made the change correctly, type

    u 16a

and look at the first instruction. (Note: If you are using DEBUG to try out this display loop, you could add, at the end, the following instruction:

    08F1:0178 EBF0 jmp 16a

This keeps execution within the bounds of the display program. Without this extra instruction, careless use of the Go command would send the program into never-never land.)

If the program now looks correct, you are ready to write this patched version onto disk. We will assume that you have another copy of the original program stashed away in case something goes wrong (as mentioned before, the chances of writing incorrect data in the wrong place on the disk are fairly high for beginners, and still high for the experienced, even though DEBUG does what it can to help you avoid this disaster). To write this patched version in the place of the one we read, type

    w

This writes the changed program out to disk, and the job is done. You can see from this example that DEBUG has been written to be easy to use. All sorts of variations in this patch procedure are possible. Read the DOS manual for information on how to patch .EXE files, how to use the Name and Load commands to bring in the file to be patched, and how to use arguments in the Write command to write the patched file to another part of the disk.

EXPLORING WITH DEBUG

DEBUG can be used to look around the programs that make up PC-DOS, and to look around ROM BIOS. With patient exploration, you can learn a lot about programming and operating systems with DEBUG. To begin with, here are a few places of interest that you can look at with DEBUG.

ROM BIOS Version Number

You can check your PC's ROM BIOS version identification with DEBUG. The version date appears at the very end of ROM, at F000:FFF5. To see it displayed, type

    D F000:FFF5 L8

The Interrupt Vectors

The 8088 has the first 1K of memory reserved for interrupt vectors. PC-DOS uses vectors 20H through 27H (and more in version 2.0). See the section "Interrupt Vectors" in Chapter 1 for more information.

ROM BIOS Communications Area

The ROM BIOS data area begins at location 400H. It contains a variety of information, some of which describes the current hardware configuration. Among these values is the equipment flag word at 410H. What else is there is revealed by the ROM BIOS listings found in the Technical Reference manual.

Most programs use the ROM BIOS display output routines (PC-DOS does). These routines use the equipment flag to indicate whether output should go to the screen via the monochrome or the color/graphics adaptor. If you have both devices you can switch output back and forth between the two by changing the value of the equipment flag. Doing this is not without its hazards. One thing to remember is that although you may have patched the wrong value in there and nothing is showing on either screen, keyboard input is handled by a different service routine. If you remember this, faithfully entering the DEBUG keystrokes that reset the screen output to monochrome can bring your system back to conventional life. See the section "Switching Output between Monochrome and Color/Graphics," toward the end of Chapter 5, and the description of the equipment flag contents in Chapter 17.

The PC's Ever-Active Timekeeper

This might not be terribly thrilling, but you can look at the two timer locations in the ROM BIOS data area, at 0:046C and 0:046E. 0:046C is the more active.

Exploring IBMBIO.COM

The first few locations of many programs are jump instructions to particular functions within. IBMBIO.COM is like this. It can be instructive to follow those jump instructions and see what a program does and how it works.

Following the theme of a program is often easy when the program makes frequent use of the interrupt 21H function calls. You can tell what the program is doing by looking at the value of the AH register when it executes the INT 21 command.

Recovering Erased Files

This is for the adventurous. When the ERASE (or DEL) command has done more than you wished, you can recover the lost file(s) using DEBUG and the knowledge you have of the directory structure and file allocation tables.

It is best to have practiced this recovery operation before you need it (or have purchased commercially available software that does it). A bad time to attempt your first recovery operation is late at night when you are tired and angry that a valuable file has disappeared.

The recovery operation has a much greater chance of being successful if no more work was done on the disk after the file was accidentally erased. If this is true, the erased directory entry is the place to begin. The first byte of the name has been changed, but the rest of the directory entry, including the address of the first cluster, is still valid. The blocks belonging to the erased files have been de-allocated, so you will need to reconstruct the FAT entries. It is not sufficient to just fix the name in a directory entry, even if this makes the file reappear. The FAT still thinks that space is free, and the block(s) will soon be allocated to another file. CHKDSK will reveal this incomplete recovery condition.

Once more files have been added to a disk with an erased file, your chances of recovering that file are quite small. Again, CHKDSK will help in determining the recoverability of a file.

If you know about clusters and diskettes, directory entries and FATs, and you know how to use DEBUG, you can recover just-erased files.

SUMMARY

In this chapter we have learned how to use DEBUG to look into PC-DOS and patch programs. DEBUG is a powerful tool in the hands of a knowledgeable programmer; it can be quirkily destructive in the hands of a novice. DEBUG is your window into the system. Have fun.

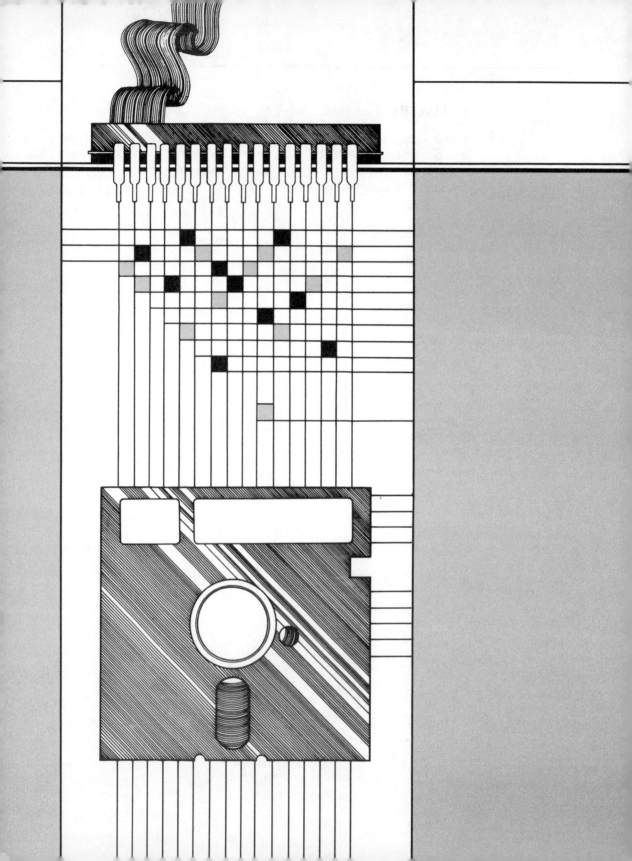

16

A User-Level
View of Version 2.0

INTRODUCTION

This is a chapter about what version 2.0 can do for you. Version 2.0 introduces several important new features. They include the GRAPHICS and PRINT commands (tools that previously were not available from IBM), improvements to nine existing commands, hard disk support (and the commands that make management of all that disk space relatively simple), and the major productivity-related features of I/O redirection, pipes, and filters.

Much of what is new about version 2.0 is discussed in other chapters in this book. For example, the tree-structured filing system is explained in Chapter 11, and the expanded batch and DEBUG capabilities are explained in Chapters 12 and 15, respectively. Here we will first provide a summary of the additions and changes. We will then discuss those new features that are not covered elsewhere in this book. Let's start with a summary of what's new about 2.0 at the user level.

SUMMARY OF NEW FEATURES

Version 2.0 provides these new features:

- Hard disk support and its associated commands
- An expanded batch facility
- Pipes and filters
- I/O redirection
- Print spooling
- Damaged file recovery
- Graphics image printing
- A potential 12.5% expansion in floppy disk capacity
- Modifications to eight existing commands

- 26 all new commands
- Better introductory documentation for the new user
- Cursor control and keyboard key reassignment
- Inclusion of a system configuration file and configuration commands
- Elimination of the use of $<$, $>$, $\backslash$, and $\mid$ in file names

I/O redirection, pipes, and filters tend to be used together. Their descriptions are separate here, but they are illustrated in one example using all three capabilities.

Of the 26 new commands, 11 are associated with disk and file management, and 9 belong in a new category called advanced commands. Of the remaining 6, the two most significant allow you to increase the level of Ctrl Break detection and clear the screen. The new commands are summarized in Figures 16.2, 16.3, and 16.4.

Version 2.0, not surprisingly, occupies more system overhead. It needs 128K to run well; it can get by with some applications in 96K, but 128K is the least you need to make good use of the new facilities.

Now that we have summarized the new features, let's examine them in more detail. We will not devote much space here to those described in other chapters of this book.

HARD DISK SUPPORT

One of the major reasons for the introduction of version 2.0 is to support hard (alias fixed) disks. The PC XT includes a 10MB Winchester disk, and you can buy an expansion chassis for your PC that includes the same 10MB disk. You can find more information on the hard disk in Chapter 3, "Disk Description and Usage."

Once you have all that disk space to play with (it's the equivalent of about 30 320K floppies), you need a better way of managing the files that live on it. PC-DOS version 2.0 provides a tree, or hierarchical, file structure and the tools to manage it. You may have used a tree-structured filing system already. It's the standard filing system found in Unix and Unix-like systems. Even if this type of system is not familiar to you, you will be pleased to see its introduction into PC-DOS. You can find more on the new file management features (the tree structure) in Chapter 11, "Your PC-DOS Files."

THE EXPANDED BATCH FACILITY

So far, five batch subcommands have been introduced: ECHO, FOR, GOTO, IF, and SHIFT. Their use is described in Chapter 12, "Batch Operations." In brief:

- ECHO allows much better control of the commands and text that appear on the screen when a batch file is being executed.
- FOR provides a limited FOR . . . DO . . . capability.
- GOTO and IF provide for branches in the batch program's logic, based on three conditions that can be tested (the existence of a file, the error level returned by a program, and whether two strings are the same).
- SHIFT allows more than ten, or an undefined number of, replaceable parameters to be used.

The new batch subcommands allow for a more productive and satisfying use of the batch facility in PC-DOS.

I/O REDIRECTION

We need to know the meaning of standard input and standard output to be able to understand I/O redirection.

The standard input to a program is from the keyboard. The standard output is to the screen. A program can accept input from sources other than the keyboard, and it can output data to devices other than the screen, but by convention, the standard input device is the keyboard and the standard output device is the screen.

Version 2.0 enables you to redirect the output from a program that normally goes to the standard output device. Instead of going to the screen, the output will go to the device or file that you specify. The following statement redirects the output from the DIR command:

DIR A: >B:DIRFILE

The directory that normally shows up on the screen when DIR is run will be entered, line by line, into the newly created file (DIRFILE) on drive B. (Note that there are only two spaces in the redirection statement shown.)

Version 2.0 also enables you to change the source of standard input to a program from the keyboard to another device or file that you specify. The following statement tells a program that converts all characters it sees to uppercase (UPPER) to accept its input from the file SPARE.BAT instead of the keyboard:

UPPER <SPARE.BAT

A variant in standard output redirection is when the standard output from a command (program) is *appended* to an existing file. The following command will add the directory of drive B to the text of the directory already in DIRFILE (DIRFILE was created by the first example command):

> DIR B: >>B:DIRFILE

The symbol sequence >> means "append the standard output to an existing file." The > symbol, if used with a file name, means "put the standard output into that file, starting at the beginning of the file."

Version 2.0's I/O redirection affects output that normally goes to the screen and input that normally comes from the keyboard. Version 2.0 can only redirect data that is passed through its own screen and keyboard I/O functions.

PIPES

Imagine data flowing through a pipe. At intervals within the pipe are programs that process the data. The data that comes from a program upstream flows into the program downstream, and so on, until the pipe ends.

Version 2.0 allows you to build pipes. Pipes are basically strings of programs where the screen output (standard output) of one program becomes the keyboard input (standard input) for the next program. Here is an example of a short pipe, where the directory information becomes the input to a sorting program:

> DIR ¦ SORT

The ¦ symbol means "take the standard output of the command that precedes the ¦, and provide it as standard input to the command that follows."

Pipes can be longer than the example shown. When you have libraries of programs that do just one thing well, you can use pipes to send data through several of those single-function programs in a row.

The data that is in a pipe is kept by PC-DOS in files called %PIPEnnn. You may see these files in the root directory from time to time. The nnn part of the filename is used by PC-DOS to keep track of which part of a pipe the %PIPEnnn file represents.

Let's look at filters, then see how data can be put through several filters in a pipe before ending up in a file for later reference.

FILTERS

Filters are single-focus programs that are written to do one thing well. They accept data from the standard input device, process it efficiently, then send it to the standard output device.

PC-DOS version 2.0 comes with three filters: the programs FIND, SORT, and MORE. These are all text-oriented filters. They accept text, work on it in some way, then output it. Here are some examples of other text-oriented filters:

- A program that puts each word of a text file on a separate line
- A program that throws away any line in a file that is a repeat of a previous line
- A program that compares text files line by line, creating files for lines seen in one file but not in the other

These examples have not been chosen at random. They lead to the classical example of the use of filters.

If you have a dictionary on disk, one word to a line, sorted in alphabetical order, you can use the SORT filter and the three example filters to create a spelling checker pipe. The pipe looks like this:

WDPERLINE <THESIS ¦ SORT ¦ NORPTS ¦ DIFF DICT >SPELLING.ERS

Your THESIS file becomes the input to the WDPERLINE filter that puts every word on a single line. The output of the WDPERLINE program becomes the input to the SORT program, which puts all the lines (words) in alphabetical order. The NORPTS filter sees the output of the SORT program, and only passes on to the DIFF program a single copy of each word. DIFF compares the dictionary file DICT with the output of NORPTS, and puts any words in output from NORPTS that are not in the dictionary file into the file SPEL-LING.ERS. So your pipe is a spelling checker.

Note that the last example used I/O redirection, pipes, and filters. From it, you can see why the characters <, >, and ¦ are not permitted in file names in version 2.0. (The other newly reserved character, \, is the character that links directories to files or subdirectories in a tree of files.)

The spelling checker pipe could become the first line of a batch file SPELLING.BAT. THESIS would be replaced by %1, so the pipe could work on any text file. The second line of the batch file might be

PRINT SPELLING.ERS

and the third line might be

TYPE SPELLING.ERS ¦ MORE

so you would see a list of spelling errors, one page at a time.

PRINT SPOOLING WITH THE PRINT COMMAND

Version 2.0 will print files while you run other programs. This background printing function operates well, is easily managed, and doesn't put much of a drag on a task that runs concurrently.

The PRINT command will accept a list of files to be printed, put them in a queue, and print them as a background task while other programs are being executed. Options within the PRINT command allow you to

- display the queue (PRINT without any arguments),
- add more files to the queue (PRINT file name(s)),
- delete files from the queue (PRINT file name /C), and
- terminate the whole printing-from-queue operation (PRINT /T).

The queue can hold a maximum of ten files at one time. When you add files to the queue, they have to come from the current directory, but you can change to another directory after adding files and then add more files to the queue.

Of course, you may not use the printer for other purposes while the PRINT function controls the printer. Also, the first time the PRINT command is called, about 3600 bytes are added to resident PC-DOS.

FILE RECOVERY

The RECOVER command recovers data, as best it can, from damaged files. It can be directed to work on either a single file or a whole disk. RECOVER can retrieve undamaged data as long as one file allocation table is intact.

Recovery of Single Files

RECOVER will recover the remaining data from a file that has one or more unreadable sectors. The format for this operation is

    RECOVER A:MYFILE

where MYFILE is the name of the file you want recovered.

When the RECOVER command has finished, you will probably need to clean up what's left with an editor, for two reasons: (1) the data in the unreadable sector(s) will not be in the recovered file; and (2) RECOVER sets the file length in the directory to the number of clusters (alias allocation units) in the recovered file. This will be a multiple of 512, and it is unlikely that, say, a text file would contain an exact multiple of 512 characters.

You have to call the RECOVER command for each file you want recovered. Although the command will accept wild-card characters (* and ?) in the file name, it will only recover one file before it quits.

Recovery of Whole Disks

This option is used when the directory is damaged. The call format is

RECOVER A:

This wholesale recovery operation is quite drastic. In the whole-disk-recovery mode, RECOVER steps through the file allocation table, looking for chains of clusters. When it finds a likely looking chain, it makes an entry in the directory for a file by the name FILEnnnn.REC, where nnnn is 0001 for the first file found, 0002 for the second, and so on.

RECOVER on a whole disk should not be lightly invoked. It is for desperate people. If the disk has tree-structured files on it, the tree will not exist after the recovery operation. All the files will be in a single directory.

GRAPHICS TO THE PRINTER

This is a nice feature to have. It is useful when PC-DOS is operating with the color/graphics adaptor. It has no relevance when PC-DOS is operating with the monochrome adaptor.

Invoking the GRAPHICS command has two effects: (1) resident PC-DOS is increased by 688 bytes, and (2) when operating in any color/graphics mode, the Shift PrtSc keystroke combination prints the image on the screen driven by the color/graphics adaptor.

If the color/graphics adaptor is in 640 × 200 mode, the image is printed sideways, with the image rotated 90 degrees counter-clockwise. The bottom of the screen appears on the right-hand side of the paper.

Command	Change in Version 2.0
CHKDSK	More information available, see description
COMP	Works on multiple files
DEBUG	Includes the Assemble command
DIR	Volume ID and amount of free space displayed
DISKCOMP	Accepts /8 option, for versions 1 diskettes
EDLIN	Block move and copy included, and more
ERASE	Accepts *.* now
FORMAT	/8, /V and /B options added
MODE	Easy switching between display adaptors

Figure 16.1: Commands Whose Features Have Been Modified

MODIFICATIONS TO EXISTING COMMANDS

The commands whose functions have been improved are shown in Figure 16.1. The changes are adequately described in the version 2.0 DOS manual.

THE 26 NEW COMMANDS

This may seem a formidable number of new commands to learn, but breaking them into functional categories helps. We will review them in the following order:

- Disk and disk file management commands
- Miscellaneous commands
- Advanced commands

The new commands are summarized in Appendix A of the DOS manual. Version 2.0 has introduced a new command category called advanced. The advanced commands have their own section in the DOS manual, Chapter Ten. They only include one command with which you might be familiar, EXE2BIN.

Command **Function**

Command	Function
BACKUP	Backs up hard disk files to floppy disks
CD	An abbreviated form of CHDIR
CHDIR	Changes (or displays) the current directory
FDISK	Fixed disk initialization
MD	An abbreviated form of MKDIR
MKDIR	Makes a new directory
PATH	Defines path(s) where command and batch files can be found
RECOVER	Recovers damaged files
RESTORE	Restores floppy disks created by BACKUP to hard disks
RM	An abbreviated form of RMDIR
RMDIR	Deletes (removes) a directory
TREE	Shows the tree for a disk
VERIFY	Toggles read-after-write extra security mode
VOL	Shows a volume's name

Figure 16.2: Version 2.0 Disk and File Management Commands

Figure 16.2 shows the disk and file management commands. All but the BACKUP, RESTORE, and FDISK commands are described in this book. You will need to read the DOS manual to learn about BACKUP, RESTORE, and FDISK.

Figure 16.3 summarizes the new commands in version 2.0 that are neither advanced nor associated with disk and file management.

Command	Function
ASSIGN	Permits use of older programs specific to drives A and B
BREAK	Changes the frequency of checking for Ctrl Break
CLS	Clears the screen
GRAPHICS	Permits printing of graphics image
PRINT	Prints files from queue
VER	Shows the version number

Figure 16.3: Miscellaneous New Commands

Version 2.0 Advanced Commands

These nine commands include three filters (FIND, MORE, and SORT), EXE2BIN (which exists in versions 1), a command to change the PC-DOS prompt, and four others. Figure 16.4 shows the advanced commands.

Command	Function
COMMAND	Invokes another command processor
CTTY	Changes to an auxiliary console
EXE2BIN	Converts .EXE file to .COM file
EXIT	Exits an invoked command processor
FIND	Finds a string
MORE	Pages through a file, screenful by screenful
PROMPT	Defines a new prompt
SET	Inserts strings into the command processor's environment
SORT	Sorts text files

Figure 16.4: Version 2.0 Advanced Commands

The COMMAND Command

COMMAND allows you to invoke a secondary command processor. The secondary command processor will see and interpret what is entered at the keyboard (or the current standard input device) instead of the regular command processor. If you wish to leave that secondary command processor, use the EXIT command.

The CTTY Command

CTTY is useful for directing PC-DOS to accept its commands from another device, such as a terminal linked to the PC via a serial port. Once the CTTY command has been executed, it is the new device that must give the command to return to normal operation. Unless the remote terminal's keyboard uses IBM's Extended ASCII coding for the function and cursor-control keys, those functions will not be available at the remote terminal. For instance, EDLIN's in-line editing functions will not be available.

The PROMPT Command

PROMPT allows you to change what appears when PC-DOS is ready for a command. Instead of the usual A> (or B> or C>), you may have the time and date appear, an anthropomorphic, chatty greeting (such as Hi Honey, What'll it be?), the version number, the current path, or all those in combination with a number of other possibilities.

PROMPT is fun to play with, but it's hard to come up with a prompt that is more than merely informative yet retains its charm after several hundred repetitions.

The SET Command

The command processor has a buffer into which strings can be entered to describe its environment and the environment of any program it calls. The environment includes the path(s) set by the PATH command and other information useful to PC-DOS. It also includes whatever other strings you specify with the SET command. These strings can be examined by a program (their segment address is found at 2C in the PSP). The program's action can be affected by the environment strings.

Type SET without any arguments to see the strings in the environment. To enter a string (that, say, describes a selected accounting method) into the environment, type

    SET A/CMETHOD = CASH

To remove that same string from the environment, type

    SET A/CMETHOD =

THE CONFIGURATION FILE

In versions 1, PC-DOS looks for the file AUTOEXEC.BAT each time it is booted. If AUTOEXEC.BAT is found, the batch file processor is called and the contents of AUTOEXEC are executed.

In version 2.0, PC-DOS also looks for another file—CONFIG.SYS. CONFIG.SYS contains strings that tell PC-DOS how to configure itself. The configurable items are

- the BREAK command,
- the BUFFERS command,
- the DEVICE command(s),
- the FILES command, and
- the SHELL command.

The BREAK Command

The BREAK command has been described briefly already. Normally (with BREAK OFF), only a few functions recognize Ctrl Break. When BREAK ON is in effect, PC-DOS checks for Ctrl Break when any function call is executed.

The BUFFERS Command

The BUFFERS command allows you to tell PC-DOS how many disk buffers it is to maintain. If you have enough memory, and you have applications that do more than sequentially read from one file and write to another (we almost all have such applications), you should use this command in the configuration file.

The default number of buffers is two—not very many. Each buffer costs another 528 bytes (512 plus 16 overhead bytes). Performance increases as you add more buffers, but at somewhere between ten and twenty buffers performance begins to decrease again. At that point it takes the operating system as long to look through all the buffers as it does to get something from the disk. The difference between having two and five buffers is very significant. The difference between having five and ten buffers is less significant, but still a noticeable improvement.

The DEVICE Command

This command is used to tell PC-DOS to include device driver software for devices that are not supported by PC-DOS as being standard. You may have 8-inch floppy disks, or a tape unit, attached to your PC. The chances are that the device will need special software to control it, and that software may be supplied by the device manufacturer. All you have to do is add the line

DEVICE = TAPEDVR

to the configuration file, where the file TAPEDVR has been supplied by the tape unit manufacturer, and your tape accessing programs that run under PC-DOS will be able to operate the tape unit. (This does assume that the tape unit manufacturer supplied adequate software. You may have to make a few phone calls before you receive a version of the device driver that meets your specific needs.)

The extended cursor control and keyboard key reassignment feature of version 2.0 is included in one such device driver, ANSI.SYS. If you want the extended features, the line

DEVICE = ANSI.SYS

must be added to CONFIG.SYS.

The FILES Command

PC-DOS can handle the details of eight different files being open at the same time. It is not often that a program will strain the capacity of PC-DOS to handle simultaneously open files, but when you need more, the FILES command comes to the rescue. With it, you can tell PC-DOS to annex the resident space required to keep track of up to 99 files.

The SHELL Command

If you have written your own command processor, COMPROC.COM, inserting the line

SHELL = COMPROC.COM

in the configuration file will cause PC-DOS when it is booted to call COMPROC.COM instead of COMMAND.COM.

SUMMARY

We have seen how the major new features that version 2.0 has to offer at the user level give us significantly more power than previous versions could provide. The hard disk support, tree-structured files, pipes, filters, and I/O redirection are all powerful features that combine to make PC-DOS version 2.0 an operating system worthy of respect.

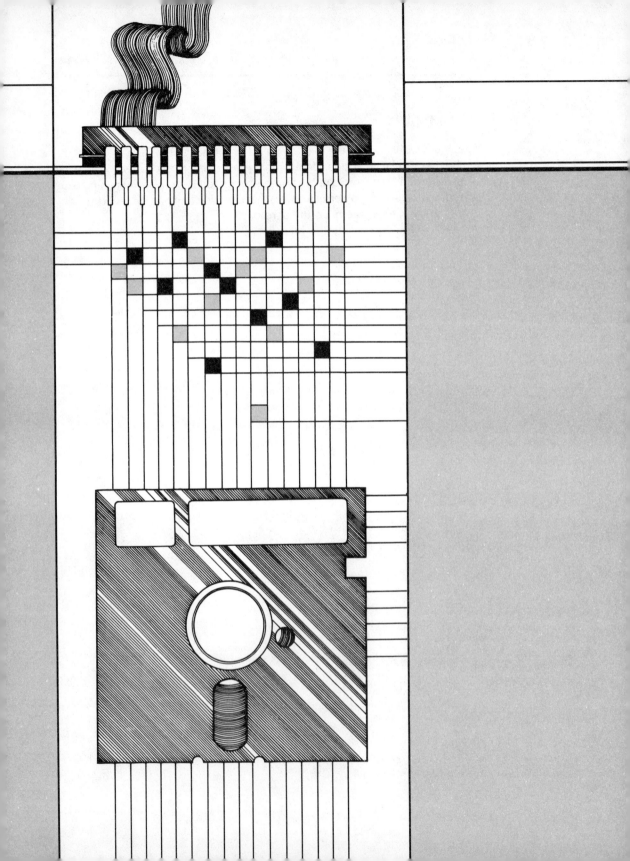

Tables and Maps

INTRODUCTION

This chapter contains all the tables and maps that have been developed to provide quick reference to the features of PC-DOS. They are organized as follows:

ADDRESS CONVERSION TABLES FOR NEWCOMERS

These tables show address conversions for the one-megabyte (1,048,576) address space of the 8086/8088. It takes twenty bits to address one megabyte. The memory is addressed in units of bytes, paragraphs, or segments. A paragraph is sixteen bytes; a segment is 65,536 (64K) bytes.

Conversion within 4 Bits, Single Hex Digit

Hex	Decimal
0	0
—	—
9	9
A	10
B	11
C	12
D	13
E	14
F	15

Conversion within 8 Bits, Two Hex Digits

Hex	Decimal
10H	16
20H	32
30H	48
40H	64
50H	80
60H	96
70H	112
80H	128
90H	144
A0H	160
B0H	176
C0H	192
D0H	208
E0H	224
F0H	240
FFH	255

Conversion within 12 Bits, 4K, Three Hex Digits

Hex	Decimal
100H	256
200H	512
300H	768
400H	1,024
500H	1,280
600H	1,536
700H	1,792
800H	2,048
900H	2,304
A00H	2,560
B00H	2,816
C00H	3,072
D00H	3,328
E00H	3,584
F00H	3,840
FFFH	4,095

Conversion within 16 Bits, 64K, Four Hex Digits

Hex	Decimal
1000H	4,096
2000H	8,192
3000H	12,288
4000H	16,384
5000H	20,480
6000H	24,576
7000H	28,672
8000H	32,768
9000H	36,864
A000H	40,960
B000H	45,056
C000H	49,152
D000H	53,248
E000H	57,344
F000H	61,440
FFFFH	65,535

Conversion within 20 Bits, 1 MB, Five Hex Digits

Hex	Decimal
10000H	65,536
20000H	131,072
30000H	196,608
40000H	262,144
50000H	327,680
60000H	393,216
70000H	458,752
80000H	524,288
90000H	589,824
A0000H	655,360
B0000H	720,896
C0000H	786,432
D0000H	851,968
E0000H	917,504
F0000H	983,040
FFFFFH	1,048,575

CHARACTER ATTRIBUTE BYTES

Monochrome Character Attributes

This table shows the purpose of the bits in the attribute byte as they are recognized by the monochrome adaptor board.

	7	6	5	4	3	2	1	0
	FG	Background			Foreground			
Normal character	b	0	0	0	i	1	1	1
Reverse video	b	1	1	1	i	0	0	0
Underlined character	b	0	0	0	i	0	0	1
No display, black on black	b	0	0	0	i	0	0	0
No display, white on white	b	1	1	1	i	1	1	1

Bit 7 when set makes the character blink
Bit 3 when set makes the character high intensity

The next table shows some of the useful monochrome attribute byte values.

Attribute	Effect
00	No display, black on black
01	Underlined character
07	Normal character, white on black (this effect is also obtained with attribute values 02 through 06)
08	No display
09	Underlined, high-intensity character
70	Reverse video
71	Underline only, not reverse video
78	Reverse video, high intensity, the character appears thinner, more finely drawn
79	High intensity, underlined, not reverse video
81	Blinking underlined character
87	Blinking normal character
89	Blinking, underlined, high-intensity character
F0	Blinking, reverse video
F8	Blinking, reverse video, high intensity, the character appears thinner

Color Character Attributes

The Sixteen Colors

This table shows the bit combinations that make up each of the sixteen colors.

I R G B	Color
0 0 0 0	Black
0 0 0 1	Blue
0 0 1 0	Green
0 0 1 1	Cyan
0 1 0 0	Red
0 1 0 1	Magenta
0 1 1 0	Brown
0 1 1 1	Light gray
1 0 0 0	Dark gray
1 0 0 1	Light blue
1 0 1 0	Light green
1 0 1 1	Light cyan
1 1 0 0	Light red
1 1 0 1	Light magenta
1 1 1 0	Yellow
1 1 1 1	White

Color Selection

This table shows how colors are selected for display.

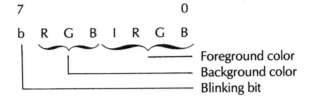

Color Sets in Medium-Resolution Graphics Mode

These are the two color sets available in medium-resolution graphics mode:

Set one: Cyan, magenta, and white
Set two: Green, red, and brown

COLOR/GRAPHICS MODES

The following are the display modes recognized by ROM BIOS.

Mode	Function
0	Text, 40 × 25, black and white
1	Text, 40 × 25, color
2	Text, 80 × 25, black and white
3	Text, 80 × 25, color
4	Graphics, 320 × 200, black and white
5	Graphics, 320 × 200, color
6	Graphics, 640 × 200, black and white

COMMAND SUMMARIES

DEBUG Command Summary

DEBUG commands are single characters, followed by their arguments, typically the range and/or address on which they operate. In this table, commands are presented in alphabetical order.

Command	Notes
Assemble	Assembles your (small) program at the address you specify (this command does not exist in versions 1)
Compare	Compares a range of memory to that at the address specified
Dump	Dumps memory in both hex and ASCII formats
Enter	Enters data into memory
Fill	Fills memory, repeatedly if necessary, from a list of bytes
Go	Executes code, permitting up to ten breakpoints
Hexarithmetic	Adds and subtracts two hex numbers
Input	Reads a byte from a port
Load	Loads programs or data from disk
Move	Moves a range of bytes to an address
Name	Defines the file name for Load and Write
Output	Outputs a byte to a port
Quit	Exits from the DEBUG program
Register	Displays and permits change to registers and flags
Search	Searches for a list of characters over a range of addresses
Trace	Single-step execution
Unassemble	Gives assembler language instructions for the range specified
Write	Writes programs or data to disk

EDLIN Command Summary

Commands are single characters, operating on the current line unless preceded by line number arguments. A line number of # means "one more than the last line (in memory)." In this table, commands are grouped by function.

Command	Format	Explanation
Display commands		
List	n,mL	Lists lines n through m
Page [2.0]	n,mP	Pages through the file
Text modification commands		
Insert line(s)	nL	Inserts line(s) before line n
Edit a single line	n	Line number only
Delete line(s)	n,mD	Deletes lines n through m

Copy line(s) [2.0]	n,m,d,cC	Copies lines n through m to appear before line d, c times
Move line(s) [2.0]	n,m,dM	Moves lines n through m to appear before line d
Transfer (merge) a file [2.0]	nTfilespec	Copies all of filespec to appear before line n

Search and replace commands

| Search for text | n,m?Sstring | Searches for 'string' in lines n through m. If a ? is included, pauses each time it finds 'string'. |
| Replace text | n,m?Rstring1 <F6>string2 | Searches for 'string1', replaces it with 'string2'. <F6>string2 may be omitted. If a ? is included, pauses each time it finds 'string1'. |

Housekeeping commands

End or Exit EDLIN	E	Exits, saving your work
Quit	Q	Exits without saving
Append	nA	Appends n lines from the rest of the file on disk
Write	nW	Writes n lines to disk to make room for more lines in memory

PC-DOS Command Summary

This table is a summary of the PC-DOS command set. All the commands are well described in the DOS manuals. Only a few notes have been added.

Command	Notes
ASSIGN	[2.0] Assigns drive A or B to another drive. This command permits drive-specific versions 1 programs to run using the hard disks (drive C).
BACKUP	[2.0] Backs up some or all of the hard disk to floppy disks.
(BATCH)	[2.0] There are five new batch file subcommands in version 2.0: ECHO, FOR, GOTO, IF, and SHIFT. BATCH itself is not a command.
BREAK	[2.0] Controls and displays level of Ctrl Break detection.
CHDIR	[2.0] Changes or displays current directory. May be abbreviated to CD.

CHKDSK	Checks the directory and file allocation tables. Does not verify the readability of the entire diskette, just the first few blocks. Reports memory installed according to switch settings.
CLS	[2.0] Clears the screen.
COMP	Compares individual files. Useful for checking that two files are identical, or that a few (up to ten) locations contain different values. This command is not useful if one file has one or more extra bytes, except to report the location of the first extra byte.
COPY	Copies one or more files from one diskette to another. Concatenates files on request. Also copies files from one device to another, for instance from console to disk or disk to printer. Because of the file name wildcard (global) characters (? and *), and the /A (ASCII), /B (binary) and /V (verify) options, this is a powerful, flexible command. Do read the manual for this one. The COPY *.* b: command is useful for compressing randomly distributed files onto a new diskette.
DATE	Displays the date and asks for a new one.
DEL	Deletes a file or files. See ERASE.
DIR	Lists all or some of the files in a directory. The filename, extension, size in bytes, and date and time of last alteration are shown.
DISKCOMP	Compares entire diskettes. Useful for verifying the readability of the whole diskette.
DISKCOPY	Copies entire diskettes, byte for byte. DISKCOMP can be used afterwards if you need certainty that the new copy is perfect.
ERASE	Erases (forever, unless you have special recovery software) one or more files. Use with care.
FORMAT	Formats diskettes, single or double sided, with or without the PC-DOS system files (IBMBIO.COM, IBMDOS.COM, COMMAND.COM). You can use DISKCOPY to format unformatted diskettes.
GRAPHICS	When invoked, Shift PrtSc prints the text or graphics image on the color/graphics monitor.
MKDIR	[2.0] Make a directory. May be abbreviated to MD.
MODE	Multifunction command: 1. Sets lines per inch (6 or 8) and columns per line (80 or 132) for a printer. 2. Sets number of characters per line (40 or 80) for color/graphics-driven display. Permits alignment of

image by shifting it left or right and providing a test pattern. In version 2.0, this option permits changing from the monochrome display to the color/graphics display and back again.

3. Serial port control. Sets baud rate, parity, number of bits per word and number of stop bits for an asynchronous channel (serial port). Use the ,P option if directing output to a serial printer.

4. Redirects parallel printer output to a serial port.

PATH	[2.0] Defines search paths for command and batch files not in the current directory.
PAUSE	Used in a batch file to display a message, then wait for any keystroke.
PRINT	[2.0] Prints a queue of files as a background task.
RECOVER	[2.0] Recovers damaged files.
REM	Displays a message from a batch file.
RENAME	Changes the name of a file.
RESTORE	[2.0] Restores backed-up files from floppy disks to the hard disk.
RMDIR	[2.0] Removes a directory. May be abbreviated to RD.
SYS	Puts the DOS operating system files on a diskette that has been formatted to allocate space for these files. Used for transferring the DOS system to application program diskettes.
TIME	Displays, and permits change of, the time of day.
TREE	[2.0] Displays on the screen the tree of directories on a disk.
VER	[2.0] Displays the PC-DOS version number.
VERIFY	[2.0] Sets and displays the read-after-write verify state.
VOL	[2.0] Displays the volume name of a disk.

PC-DOS Advanced Commands [2.0]

Version 2.0 introduced a new category of commands called advanced. They are all new except for EXE2BIN.

Command	Notes
CTTY	Changes standard input and standard output to an auxiliary console. Permits PC-DOS to be run from a remote terminal.
EXE2BIN	Under the right conditions, converts a .EXE file into a .BIN file. The resultant .BIN file may have the format of

	a .COM file and only require a filename extension change to be recognized as such. The .BIN file may require loading at an absolute location.
FIND	Searches files for a text string.
MORE	Displays data one screen at a time.
PROMPT	Changes the appearance of the PC-DOS prompt.
SET	Inserts strings into the command processor's environment.
SORT	Sorts text data.

DISKETTE INFORMATION

Diskette Capacities

A summary of the various diskette capacities appears below.

Single sided/ Double sided	Sectors Per track	Version	Bytes Available (Disk formatted Without /S option)	Bytes Available (Disk formatted With /S Option)
SS	8	1.0	160,256	147,968
SS	8	1.1	160,256	146,432
SS	8	2.0	160,256	119,296
SS	9	2.0	179,712	138,752
DS	8	1.1	322,560	308,736
DS	8	2.0	322,560	282,600
DS	9	2.0	362,496	321,536

Errors Reported by the Diskette Routines

Error	Meaning
80H	Attachment failed to respond
40H	Seek operation failure
20H	Controller failure
10H	Bad CRC on diskette read
08H	DMA overrun on operation
04H	Requested sector not found
03H	Write attempt on write-protected diskette
02H	Address mark not found
00H	Error other than those above

The First Few Files on a Diskette

For all versions (1.0 through 2.0), the first few files are in the same sequence. They occur in the order shown:

File	Lengths:SS,8	DS,8	SS,9	DS,9
Bootstrap sector	1	1	1	1
File Allocation Table—first copy	1	1	2	2
File Allocation Table—second copy	1	1	2	2
Directory	4	7	4	7

If the diskette was formatted with the /S option (which adds the system files to the diskette), the sequence continues:

File	Lengths:SS,8	DS,8	SS,9	DS,9
IBMBIO.COM	4	4	10	10
IBMDOS.COM	13	13	34	34
COMMAND.COM	—	—	—	—

FILE ATTRIBUTES AND HANDLES

File Attributes

This table shows file attribute values that may be found in a directory entry. The number of different file attributes has increased in version 2.0.

Byte	Attribute Meaning
00	Normal read/write file
01	Read-only file [2.0]
02	Hidden file
04	System file
08	Root directory entry containing volume label [2.0]
10	Directory entry containing a subdirectory [2.0]
20	The file's archive (dirty) bit [2.0]

File Handles for the Standard Devices [2.0]

To accommodate I/O redirection, version 2.0 has made files and devices somewhat interchangeable. A handle may be given to both files and devices. The following table shows the handles assigned to five standard devices. These devices are opened by PC-DOS. Your program does not need to open them before using them.

Handle	Device
0000	Standard input device, input can be redirected
0001	Standard output device, output can be redirected
0002	Standard error device, output cannot be redirected
0003	Standard auxiliary device
0004	Standard printer device

Examination of the table shows why the first file opened after the system is booted is given a handle of 0005.

FUNCTION CALL ERROR RETURN TABLE [2.0]

Many version 2.0 function calls set the carry bit to indicate that a function failed. The type of error is returned in the AX register, and may be interpreted from the following table.

AX	Error Indicated
1	Invalid function number
2	File not found
3	Path not found
4	Too many open files (no file handles left)
5	Access denied (file not open for type of access requested, or other condition)
6	Invalid file handle
7	Memory control block destroyed
8	Insufficient memory
9	Invalid memory block address
A	Invalid environment
B	Invalid format
C	Invalid access mode
D	Invalid data
E	(undefined)
F	Invalid drive was specified
10	Attempted to remove the current directory
11	Not the same device
12	No more files

FUNCTION CALL SUMMARIES

Break Detection Control [2.0]

Purpose	Function
Get or set Ctrl Break detection level [2.0]	33H

Character Device I/O

Display (Alias Standard Output Device)

Purpose	Function
Output, with Ctrl Break detection	02H
Output, without Ctrl Break detection	06H
String output	09H

File or Device I/O [2.0]

Purpose	Function
Read CX characters into DS:DX buffer	3FH
Write CX characters from DS:DX buffer	40H

I/O Control Channel Access [2.0]

Purpose	Function
I/O Control, AL dictates subfunction [2.0]	44H

AL	Function
0	Get device information
1	Set device information
2	Read CX bytes into DS:DX buffer
3	Write CX bytes from DS:DX buffer
4	Read CX bytes from BL drive number
5	Write CX bytes to BL drive number
6	Get input status
7	Get output status

Keyboard (Alias Standard Input Device)

Purpose	Function
Input, with Ctrl Break detection	01H
Attempt input (if DL = FF)	06H
Input, without echo or Ctrl Break detection	07H
Input, without echo but with Ctrl Break detection	08H
Get string into DS:DX + 2	0AH
Check status (AL = FF if character ready)	0BH
Clear buffer, invoke 1,6,7,8, or A above	0CH

Printer (Alias Parallel Port) I/O

Purpose	Function
Output character in DL	05H

Serial (Alias Asynchronous Port) I/O

Purpose	Function
Wait for input character	03H
Output character in DL	04H

Country-Dependent Information

Purpose	Function
Get currency symbol, date format, etc. [2.0]	38H

Date and Time Access

Purpose	Function
Get date into CX:DX	2AH
Get time of day into CX:DX	2CH
Set date from CX:DX	2BH
Set time of day from CX:DX	2DH

Disk Access

Purpose	Function
Disk reset, flush file buffers	0DH
Read CX sectors into DS:BX	Interrupt 25H
Select default disk drive	0EH
Write CX sectors from DS:BX	Interrupt 26H

The EXEC Function

Purpose	Function
Execute (or load) a program/process [2.0]	4BH
Terminate a process (EXIT) [2.0]	4CH
Get completion code of terminated process [2.0]	4DH

File Access Functions in Versions 1.0, 1.1, and 2.0

Purpose	Function
Whole file access	
Create a file	16H
Open a file	0FH
Close a file	10H
Delete a file	13H
Rename a file	17H
Sequential record access	
Read a record	14H
Write a record	15H
Random record access	
Read single record	21H
Read multiple records	27H
Write single record	22H
Write multiple records	28H
Finding files in the directory	
Search for first entry	11H
Search for next entry	12H
File size	
Read the file size	23H
Change the file size	28H, CX = 0
Utilities	
Set the Disk Transfer Address (DTA)	1AH
Parse the file name	29H
Read after write verify	2EH
Set random record field in the FCB	24H

File Access Functions in Version 2.0

Purpose	Function
Whole file access	
Create a file	3CH
Open a file	3DH
Close a file	3EH
Delete a file	41H
Rename a file	56H
Reading and writing data	
Read from a file (or device)	3FH
Write to a file (or device)	40H
Move the read/write address pointer	42H
Get file (or get/set device) status	44H
File handle manipulation	
Get another file handle for the same file	45H
Point existing file handle to another file	46H
Finding files in the directory	
Search for first entry	4EH
Search for next entry	4FH
Directory manipulation	
Make a directory	39H
Remove a directory	3AH
Change to another directory	3BH
Get current directory	47H
Utilities	
Get the Disk Transfer Address (DTA)	2FH
Get the disk parameters (free space, etc.)	36H
Get or set a file's attribute	43H
Get the read-after-write verify state	54H
Get and set the file's date and time	57H

Memory Management Functions

Purpose	Function
Allocate BX paragraphs [2.0]	48H
Change size of allocated memory block [2.0]	4AH
Free allocated block (segment in ES) [2.0]	49H

Program Termination

Purpose	Function
Terminate, no completion (error) code	INT 20H
Terminate, no completion (error) code	00H
Terminate, with completion code [2.0]	4CH
Terminate, stay resident	INT 27H
Terminate, stay resident (KEEP) [2.0]	31H

Vector Access

Purpose	Function
Get interrupt vector value [2.0]	35H
Set interrupt vector	25H

Verify Read after Write

Purpose	Function
Get verify status [2.0]	54H
Set verify status on or off	2EH

Version Number Access

Purpose	Function
Get the version number (0 if prior to 2.0) [2.0]	30H

INTERRUPT VECTORS

The first two tables show the first 32 (0H through 1FH) interrupt vectors, their purpose, and their initialized values. The next two show the same for interrupt vectors 20H through 27H. The values are shown to help you look around ROM BIOS, PC-DOS, and BASICA, to see where these programs take on the servicing of different interrupts.

Interrupt Vectors 0H through 1FH

Interrupt Vector	Address (Hex)	Purpose	Notes
0	00–03	Divide by zero trap	
1	04–07	Single step	
2	08–0B	Nonmaskable interrupt	ROM BIOS
3	0C–0F	Breakpoint trap	
4	10–13	Overflow detection	
5	14–17	Print screen	ROM BIOS
6	18–1B		
7	1C–1F		
8	20–23	Timer	
9	24–27	Keyboard	
A	28–2B		8259
B	2C–2F		interrupt
C	30–33	(reserved for communcations)	vectors
D	34–37		
E	38–3B		
F	3C–3F	(reserved for printer)	
10	40–43	Video I/O	
11	44–47	Equipment check	
12	48–4B	Memory size	
13	4C–4F	Diskette access	
14	50–53	Communications	
15	54–57	Cassette I/O	ROM BIOS
16	58–5B	Keyboard I/O	vectors
17	5C–5	Printer I/O	
18	60–63	Cassette BASIC	
19	64–67	Bootstrap	
1A	68–6B	Time of day	
1B	6C–6F	Ctrl Break handling	
1C	70–73	Timer tick	
1D	74–77	Video initialization	
1E	78–7B	Diskette parameters	
1F	7C–7F	Video graphics characters, ASCII 128–255	

Interrupt Vectors 0H through 1FH, with Initialized Values

Interrupt Vector	Address (Hex)	ROM BIOS + ROM BASIC	DOS 1.1 + DEBUG	DOS 1.1 + BASICA
0	00–03	0:0	BF:1501	307:0599
1	04–07	0:0	60:0086	same*
2	08–0B	F000:E2C3	same	same
3	0C–0F	0:0	60:0086	same
4	10–13	0:0	60:0086	same
5	14–17	F000:FF54	same	same
6	18–1B	0:0	same	same
7	1C–1F	0:0	same	same
8	20–23	F000:FEA5	same	same
9	24–27	F000:E987	same	same
A	28–2B	0:0	same	same
B	2C–2F	0:0	same	same
C	30–33	0:0	same	same
D	34–37	0:0	same	same
E	38–3B	F000:EF5	same	same
F	3C–3F	0:0	same	same
10	40–43	F000:F065	same	same
11	44–47	F000:F84D	same	same
12	48–4B	F000:F841	same	same
13	4C–4F	F000:EC59	same	same
14	50–53	F000:E739	same	same
15	54–57	F000:F859	same	same
16	58–5B	F000:E82E	same	same
17	5C–5F	F000:EFD2	same	same
18	60–63	F600:0000	same	same
19	64–67	F000:E6F2	same	same
1A	68–6B	F000:FE6E	same	same
1B	6C–6F	F600:4D34	60:007F	307:15D3
1C	70–73	F600:5744	F000:FF53	307:169B
1D	74–77	F000:F0A4	same	same
1E	78–7B	F000:EFC7	0:570	same
1F	7C–7F	0:0	same	same

*same means same as column to the left

PC-DOS Interrupt Vectors 20H through 27H

Interrupt Vector	Address (Hex)	Purpose
20	80–83	General program termination
21	84–87	DOS function request
22	88–8B	Called program termination address
23	8C–8F	Ctrl Break termination address
24	90–93	Critical error handler
25	94–97	Absolute disk read
26	98–9B	Absolute disk write
27	9C–9F	Terminate but stay resident

PC-DOS Interrupt Vectors 20H through 27H, with Initialized Values

Interrupt Vector	Address (Hex)	ROM BIOS + ROM BASIC	DOS 1.1 + DEBUG	DOS 1.1 + BASICA
20	80–83	0:0	BF:0011	same*
21	84–87	0:0	BF:0015	same
22	88–8B	0:0	307:01DB	2C1:13A
23	8C–8F	0:0	307:01E0	2C1:107
24	90–93	0:0	2C1:0196	307:57C
25	94–97	0:0	60:406	same
26	98–9B	0:0	60:410	same
27	9C–9F	0:0	2C1:182	same

*same means same as the column to the left

MEMORY MAPS

Three memory maps are provided:

1. The full one-megabyte address space map. It shows the major memory allocation at a glance, including the normal locations available for your software, the locations of ROM BASIC and BIOS, the area reserved for the ROMs of your own creation, and the memory areas reserved for other specific purposes.

2. An expanded low address memory map, showing the allocation of low memory (0:0000 to 0:0600) to (256) interrupt vectors and ROM BIOS and DOS data (communications) areas.

3. An expanded view of the ROM BIOS communications area. This is where BIOS maintains its variable parameters. It is also known as the ROM BIOS data area. For contents of special locations, see pages A-2 to A-4 of the Technical Reference manual.

The Whole One-Megabyte Address Space

Hex	Decimal	Contents
00000	0K	Interrupt vectors
	16K	DOS software
	32K	Disk and Advanced BASIC (often)
	48K	Your program(s) and data
10000	64K	
20000	128K	
30000	192K	
40000	256K	
50000	320K	Note there is plenty (at least 98,000 hex or 608K or more than 622,592 bytes) of room for your programs (if you can afford the memory and slot space).
60000	384K	
70000	448K	
80000	512K	
90000	576K	
A0000	640K	Reserved by IBM
		This space claimed for fancy graphics capabilities
B0000	704K	Monochrome display's 4K buffer
B8000	736K	Color/graphics display buffers

The Whole One-Megabyte Address Space (continued)

Hex	Decimal	Contents	
C0000	768K		
C8000	800K	Fixed disk adaptor's ROM	
D0000	832K		
E0000	896K		
F0000		Reserved for ROM expansion	
F6000	984K	Microsoft (cassette) BASIC (F6000–FDFFF, 32K)	R O
FE000	1016K	BIOS (FE000–FFFFF, 8K)	M

Low Memory Map

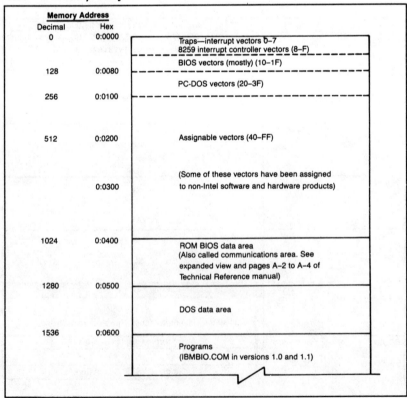

Memory Address: Decimal	Hex	Contents
0	0:0000	Traps—interrupt vectors 0–7 8259 interrupt controller vectors (8–F) BIOS vectors (mostly) (10–1F)
128	0:0080	PC-DOS vectors (20–3F)
256	0:0100	
512	0:0200	Assignable vectors (40–FF)
	0:0300	(Some of these vectors have been assigned to non-Intel software and hardware products)
1024	0:0400	ROM BIOS data area (Also called communications area. See expanded view and pages A–2 to A–4 of Technical Reference manual)
1280	0:0500	DOS data area
1536	0:0600	Programs (IBMBIO.COM in versions 1.0 and 1.1)

ROM BIOS Communications Area—0:400

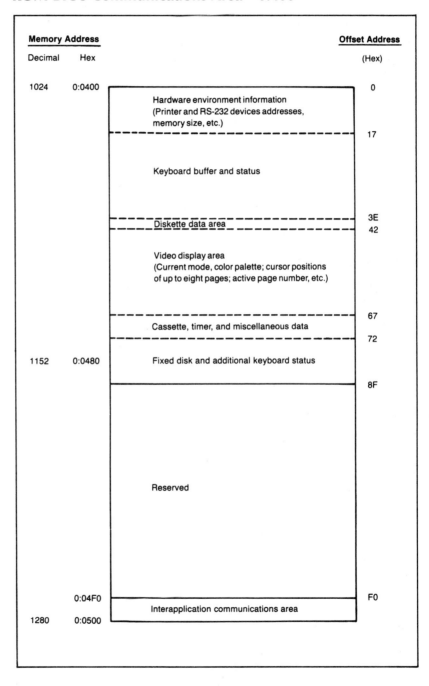

Equipment Flag Values

The meanings of the bits in the equipment flag, where the bits are numbered from low to high order, are as follows:

Bit(s)	Meaning
0	Set if system has diskette drives
1	Not used
2,3	System board RAM size, where 00 = 16K, 10 = 32K, 01 = 48K, 11 = 64K (newer PCs can have up to 256K RAM on the system board)
4,5	Initial video mode, where 10 = 40 × 25 color, 01 = 80 × 25 color, 11 = 80 × 25 monochrome
6,7	Number of diskette drives, where 00 = 1, 10 = 2, 01 = 3, 11 = 4
8	Not used
9,10,11	Number of RS-232 ports attached
12	Game I/O attached
13	Not used
14,15	Number of parallel ports (printers) attached

PC-DOS MEMORY OVERHEAD SUMMARY

Overhead in Versions 1.0, 1.1, and 2.0

This table shows the number of bytes left after PC-DOS has been booted and each of the titled programs has been loaded. For the purposes of comparison we will assume the PC has 64K of memory installed. The last line shows the space remaining when 128K is installed, since systems running with version 2.0 usually have that amount (or more) of memory.

Version	COMMAND.COM	BASIC	BASICA
1.0	53,392	61,384	61,103
1.1	53,136	61,371	61,066
2.0	40,960	61,330	60,865
2.0	106,496	61,330	60,865

Extra Overhead in Version 2.0

The following commands, if invoked, expand the resident system by the amount listed.

Function	System Expansion
ANSI.COM	1664 bytes
GRAPHICS	688 bytes
MODE	256 bytes if options 1, 3, or 4 are invoked
PRINT	3200 bytes
EXEC	17K bytes

RESERVED NAMES AND CHARACTERS

Reserved Device Names in PC-DOS

Device Name	Purpose
AUX:	Same as COM1:, first serial port
COM#:	Asynchronous channel (# = 1 or 2), a serial port
CON:	Console—keyboard and screen
LPT#:	Parallel printer (# = 1 in versions 1)
NUL:	The null device—a bit bucket
PRN:	First parallel printer

Reserved File Names in PC-DOS

Filename	Meaning
%PIPE	Temporary files for data in a pipe [2.0]
@ . . .	Any filename beginning with the character @; used by the auto response file in the linker
BADTRACK	Created by version 1.0 to hold addresses of unreadable clusters
FILEnnnn.CHK	Lost clusters recovered by CHKDSK [2.0]
FILEnnnn.REC	File names resulting from the whole disk RECOVER process [2.0]
NUL	Directs the file to the bit bucket, i.e., to nowhere retrievable
VM.TMP	Created by the linker when there is not enough room in memory for the load module

Extension	Meaning
.$$$	EDLIN, or other, temporary file
.ASM	Assembler source file
.BAK	Deleted and created by EDLIN
.BAS	BASIC program source file

Extension	Meaning
.BAT	Batch file
.BIN	Binary image file
.COM	Command file
.CRF	Cross reference source file
.EXE	Executable file, produced by linker
.HEX	DEBUG assumes this is a hex ASCII file and converts it to binary on loading
.LIB	Source code library files
.LST	Listing file from assembler
.MAP	Linker's map
.OBJ	Assembled object file
.REF	Cross reference listing file
.REL	Relocatable file from the assembler
.TMP	Temporary file

Reserved and Available Characters in File Names

Characters That May Be Used in File Names

- The letters A – Z (if you specify lowercase, the character will be converted to uppercase)
- The digits 0 – 9
- The special characters (left to right, top row of the PC keyboard first):
  ! @ # $ % ^ & ( ) _ -
  { } ~ ` ´

The following four special characters may be used in DOS version 1.0 and 1.1 file names, but not in version 2.0 file names:

¦ < > \

We recommend that you do not use these in earlier versions for the sake of compatibility with version 2.0.

Characters That May Not Be Used in File Names

Of the nonalphanumeric characters on the PC keyboard, those that are not available, mostly mathematical and common punctuation symbols, are

* + = [ ] : ; " , . ? /

Space, tab, and any control characters

A Diskette Directory Entry

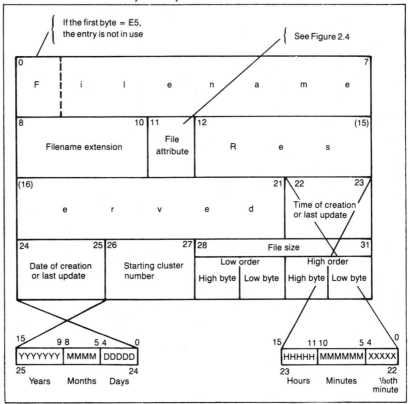

The Standard File Control Block

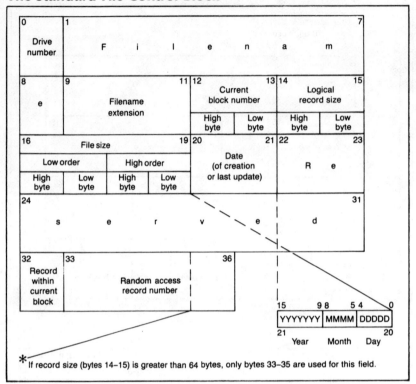

* If record size (bytes 14–15) is greater than 64 bytes, only bytes 33–35 are used for this field.

The Extended File Control Block

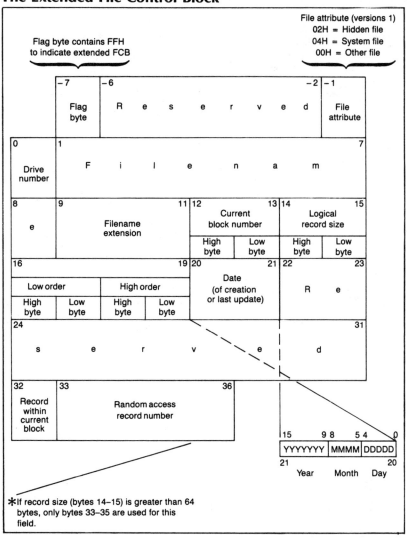

File attribute (versions 1)
02H = Hidden file
04H = System file
00H = Other file

Flag byte contains FFH
to indicate extended FCB

* If record size (bytes 14–15) is greater than 64
bytes, only bytes 33–35 are used for this
field.

The Program Segment Prefix

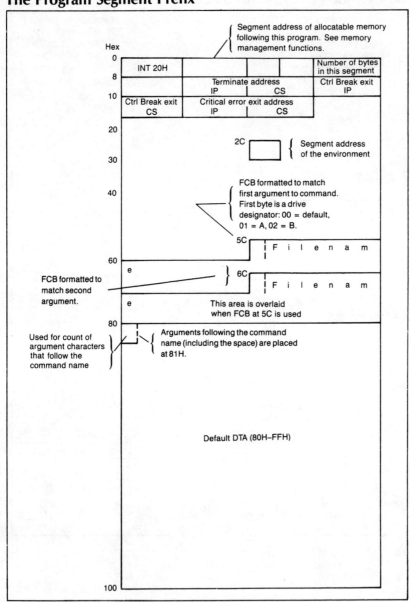

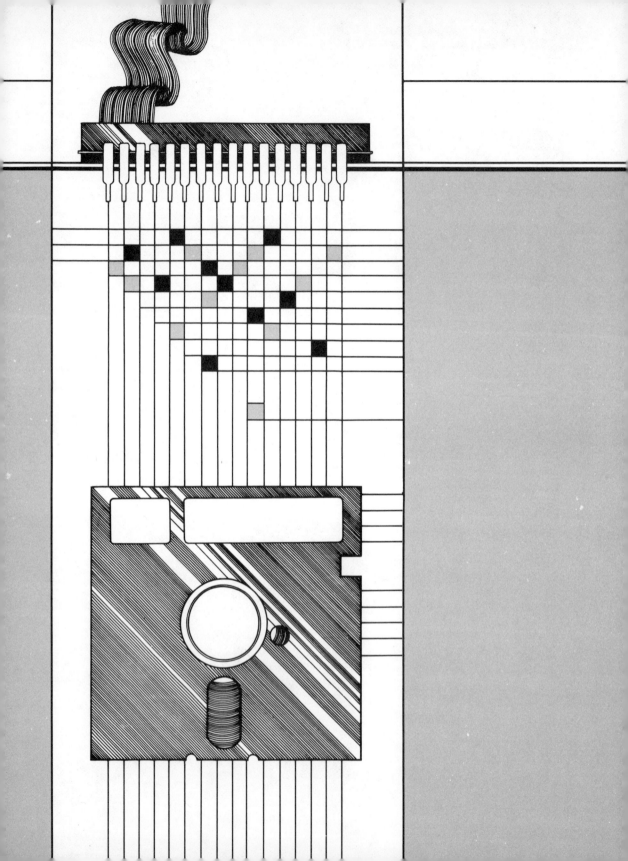

The Difference
Between MS-DOS and PC-DOS

INTRODUCTION

By the time you have finished this short appendix you will know the difference between MS-DOS and PC-DOS. You only have to read to the end of this paragraph to know the important difference. PC-DOS was written for the IBM PC and takes advantage of some of its unique features; otherwise, PC-DOS and MS-DOS are, to an applications programmer, the same—version for version. But do read on.

THE UNIVERSAL OPERATING SYSTEM

Companies that write software for microcomputers would love to be able to write one version of a program and have it run well on any computer. To do this, a universal operating system is required. Such an operating system would, ideally, provide functions calls to do the normal utilitarian things that most applications require (such as output to the screen or printer, accessing the disks, and getting characters or lines from the keyboard). It would have the effect of hiding any differences in the hardware environment from the applications software.

Microsoft's Universal Operating System

Microsoft, with MS-DOS, is attempting to provide the universal operating system for software written to run on 8086/8088-based micros. Microsoft is working toward the time that the MS-DOS operating system is the only environment that any applications program need know about. MS-DOS is a fine system, but it still has a few gaps in it, so its developers continually provide new versions of MS-DOS to get closer to the goal of the universal operating system.

Differences in Each Manufacturer's MS-DOS

Microsoft's customers for the MS-DOS operating system are companies that build microcomputers. IBM, Victor, NorthStar, Altos, and other companies have purchased MS-DOS from Microsoft and offer it to their customers, you and me.

Each microcomputer's equipment configuration is unique, so MS-DOS has to be adapted to each new configuration. In addition, the microcomputer manufacturer can make alterations to what Microsoft provides. The manufacturer leaves the function calls used by independent software developers and other "standard interface" features intact (otherwise the purpose of acquiring MS-DOS would be defeated), but they can and do alter how MS-DOS appears to the user.

The microcomputer company may add commands that are specific to some feature(s) of their hardware, and choose not to provide some of the features that are part of the MS-DOS package offered by Microsoft. The end result of all this customization is that you won't necessarily find the same commands in each manufacturer's version of MS-DOS. Let's look at IBM's version of MS-DOS and how it differs from others.

THE BIRTH OF PC-DOS

IBM asked Microsoft for a version of MS-DOS that would make the most of the PC. The result of that intention is PC-DOS. It has the same internal function calls as MS-DOS, plus easy access to the PC's ROM routines. Let's be a little more specific about the functional similarities and differences.

There Are No Function Call Differences

All the DOS interrupts and function calls are the same—not just apparently the same, but truly so. The arguments are passed in the same registers, the error codes are the same, and the results (file manipulation, character I/O, etc.) are the same.

There Are No File or Disk Management Differences

The basis of MS-DOS is its file and disk handling capabilities. These capabilities do not differ from one host computer system to another. File control blocks are used the same way, and their contents are identical. Disk directory entries are the same.

This does not mean that diskettes written under MS-DOS on, say, a Victor

9000 can be read on the IBM PC. The Victor disk drives are quad density, and unless you have identical quad density drives with your PC, file transfer has to be achieved via a communications link instead of media transfer. (Quad density is an inaccurate but frequently used name for double-sided, double-density diskettes with 96 tracks instead of the PC's 40 tracks.)

The layout of the disk is the same—boot record, two copies of the FAT, followed by the directory or system files. In MS-DOS the two hidden files are called IO.SYS and MDOS.SYS instead of the PC's IBMBIO.COM and IBM-DOS.COM. The name change is appropriate, since much of the work done by MS-DOS in IO.SYS is done by ROM BIOS in the PC.

File names are specified in the same way, except that the nonalphanumeric reserved characters may differ from DOS to DOS. The reserved filenames and extensions are the same, as is the wild-card character (? and *) handling.

Batch File Management Is the Same

Batch files are part of the power of MS-DOS. It would be silly for a manufacturer to extract that capability.

User-Level Differences

At the user level, the commands are a little different. This is a good place to adapt the basic MS-DOS to create an "IBM world," and to tailor the operating system to meet IBM's ideas of how best to serve the user. Different user-level commands also give a strong sense of individuality to the operating system. The MS-DOS command set contains DCOPY, which is called DISKCOPY in PC-DOS. MS-DOS also contains TOD, which is a hangover from the CP/M command for setting and displaying the time and date; it has been replaced by the DATE and TIME commands in PC-DOS.

In MS-DOS the entry of time does not extend to the precision of one-hundredths of a second, just single seconds.

Some other differences are that MS-DOS uses SYSCOPY to transfer system files to another disk, not the SYS command that you will find in PC-DOS. The file comparison routines are included under the command FILCOM in MS-DOS.

FORMAT, EDLIN, and DEBUG are common to both MS-DOS and PC-DOS, though FORMAT in MS-DOS has a few extra options for displaying soft errors and initializing a disk (clearing the directory and file allocation tables, but not formatting the entire diskette). EDLIN appears in MS-DOS, with the same capabilities.

The prompt may differ from DOS to DOS. For instance, the PC-DOS prompt is A> (if the default drive is A). In another manufacturer's MS-DOS it may be A:. The DEBUG prompt is - in PC-DOS, > in another MS-DOS.

CONCLUSION

To date, the differences between MS-DOS and PC-DOS appear only at the user level. To an applications program that avoids the temptation of including code specific to the IBM PC, MS-DOS is the same as PC-DOS.

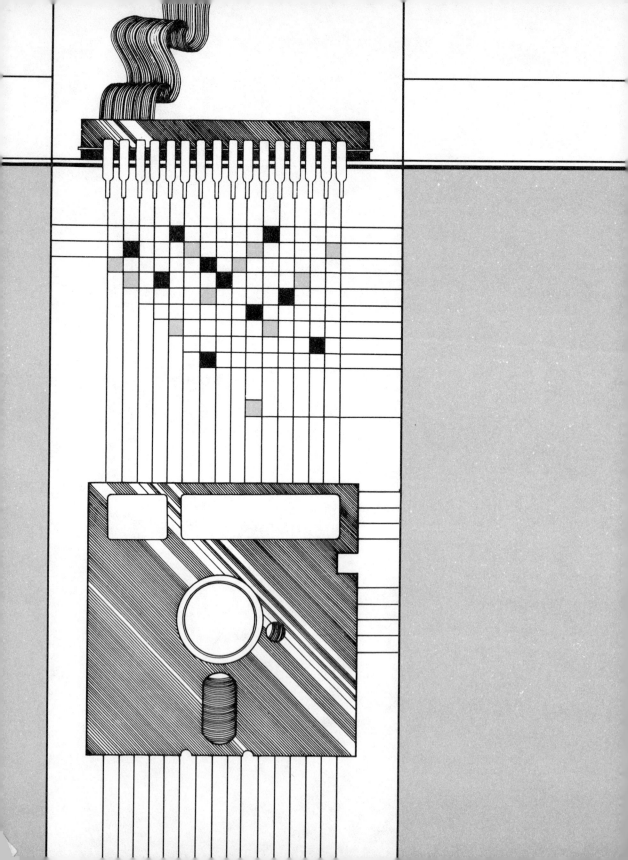

Differences Between
PC-DOS Versions 1.0, 1.05, and 1.1

INTRODUCTION

This appendix points out the differences between the first three versions of PC-DOS: version 1.0, version 1.05, and version 1.1. It shows how version 1.0 is a little buggy, supports only 160K, single-sided disk drives, and is poor at handling serial I/O. It shows how version 1.05 has eliminated a few of the bugs in 1.0, and how version 1.1 is much more satisfactory. (The differences between these versions and version 2.0 are presented in Chapters 8 and 16).

VERSIONS 1.0 AND 1.05

The differences between versions 1.0 and 1.05 exist in BASIC and BASICA. The DOS portion is the same in both versions. About 20 fairly obvious bugs in version 1.0's BASIC and BASICA were fixed. Version 1.05 was supplied free of charge.

Limitations of Versions 1.0 and 1.05

Versions 1.0 and 1.05 support only single-sided disk drives, which is now hard to believe. The TIME and DATE commands are external. Unless the TIME command is included in the AUTOEXEC.BAT file, the TIME question is not asked each time the system is booted.

A file's directory entry in PC-DOS version 1.0 is not time-stamped, only date-stamped.

Support of serial communications is very poor. Redirecting output to a serial printer is highly error prone. Version 1.0 of the Asynchronous Communications Support package is similarly ineffective.

VERSION 1.1

These are the major additions provided by PC-DOS 1.1:

- Double-sided disk support
- Time stamping of files
- Vast improvement in serial communications support
- Faster disk accessing
- Additional capabilities within the COPY command, including file concatenation, the /B option (binary file manipulation), and the /V option (copy verification)
- The EXE2BIN command

These are the minor additions and changes:

- CHKDSK reports disk space and space used by hidden files, user files, and bad sectors.
- The DIR command accepts /W and /P options.
- DEBUG and LINK have been slightly improved.
- LINK cannot succesfully use commas as file separators.
- The size of resident DOS has been increased by about 250 bytes.
- The manual includes a quick-reference card.

The faster disk accessing is obtained by a decrease in the time the disk routines take to wait for the head to settle after a track-to-track move. The new serial communications capabilities are described in Chapter 14. More information on the rest of these changes is available in the DOS version 1.1 manual. The structures of the FAT, the file control blocks, and the function calls are the same in versions 1.0 and 1.1. A directory entry is the same, except that the two bytes used to record the time in version 1.1 are marked reserved in version 1.0.

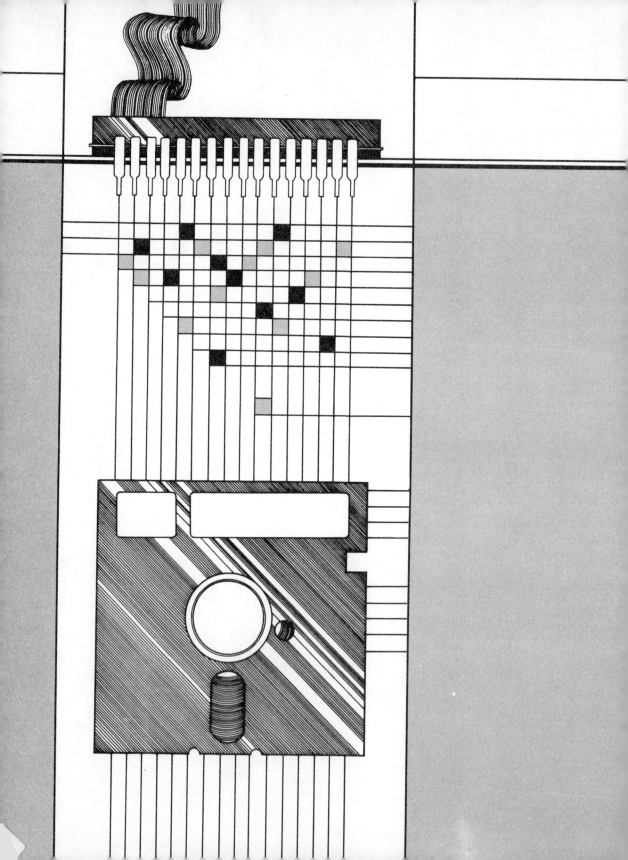

Creating Programs
Using the Debugger

It is easy to create small assembly language programs using DEBUG. It is easier still in version 2.0, where DEBUG will understand your assembly language instructions. We will show you the sequence of operations, then go through an example. To use this method of creating short, useful programs, you need to know a little about assembly language programming, but you don't need to have had experience specifically in 8086/8088 assembly language.

We will use the Name and Write commands within DEBUG to create an executable program (a file) with the name PROGRAM.COM. Once the file has been created, typing PROGRAM in response to the PC-DOS prompt will execute your program (the contents of the file). Let's outline the necessary steps:

- Call DEBUG.
- Use the Name command to specify the name of the program file.
- Create the program, starting at location 100H, and check it out.
- Use the Write command to write it to disk.

As you can see, it is not very complex. Even when we examine the steps in detail, we shall see that most of the work is done for us by DEBUG.

The example program that we are going to write will be called PROGRAM.COM. Its function is to display a message and then quit. Not very exciting, but adequate to demonstrate how easy it is to create (small) programs without buying the Macro Assembler. Although our example takes advantage of the Assemble command available in version 2.0 (which does make life easier), all the other DEBUG commands that are used operate the same way in versions 1 and 2.0. Let's go through the example.

1. Decide on the name of the program. The extension part of the program's name must be .COM.

2. Make sure the disk you want the program written on is in one of the disk drives, and that the disk (and directory) has enough room for a program.

3. At the PC-DOS prompt, type

    debug

4. Use the Name command to tell DEBUG the name of the program it is creating. We will put the program on drive B. Type

    n b:program.com

DEBUG formats the FCB at 5C to match this file name.

5. Create the program. This is presented in four parts, 5a through 5d. Everyone should read parts 5a, 5c, and 5d. Part 5b will be needed by people using versions 1 of PC-DOS, which does not have the Assemble command. In step 5b we show the hexadecimal values for the first three instructions listed in step 5a, and how they can be entered using the Enter command. (Note: If you don't have the Assemble command available, you need to know a little more about 8086/8088 assembly language. James Coffron's book, *Programming the 8086/8088* (Sybex, 1983), will show you how to produce the hexadecimal code for 8086/8088 instructions.)

5a. In this step we assume the Assemble command is available. Type

```
a100
mov ah,9
mov dx,200
int 21
mov al,0
mov ah,4c
int 21
```

The first three instructions (after the Assemble command—a100) display the string at DS:200; the last three terminate our program with a zero (meaning "all is well") return code. In versions 1, the termination sequence would be the single instruction

    int 20

(Note: The program begins at location 100H. This leaves room for the program segment prefix, which PC-DOS constructs, in the first 100H bytes of the program's segment.)

5b. Use this step if the Assemble command is not available in DEBUG. Type

    e100 b4 09 ba 00 02 cd 21 cd 20

These are the hexadecimal values for the code presented in step 5a, where the last three instructions have been replaced by

    int 20

5c. To enter the message that the first three instructions will display, type

e200 'This is a' 0a 'short message.$'

The 0a value in the middle of the message is a linefeed.

5d. Check that all instructions and data are correctly entered by typing

u100

and

d200

The Unassemble command displays the instructions, and the Dump command should reveal the message.

6. Check out the program by typing

g = 100 107

This does not check out the termination portion of the program; it just displays the message. If you check out the termination portion of the program in version 2, you will find yourself back at the prompt, out of DEBUG. All is not lost when that happens. You can recall DEBUG and use the Name command again. The instructions and data will still be there.

7. Set the BX and CX registers to the length of the program. We know that this is a very short program. It begins at CS:100, and its data ends soon after DS:200. We already know that CS and DS are set to the same value, because DEBUG set them that way when we called it in step 3. We know also that only multiples of whole sectors are written to the disk. Our program length is clearly less than 512 (200H) bytes, so we set CX, the low-order part of the program length, to 200H by typing

rcx
200

In our example, BX does not need altering, because it was set to zero when DEBUG was called. If your program is at all complex, there is a good chance that during checkout the BX register was used. If so, to set the BX register to the correct length (0 in our case), type

rbx
0

We don't have to use exact multiples of 200H. In fact, when the program is complete, it is best to be precise about the length of the program.

8. Write the program to disk using the Write command. The length is specified by the CX and BX registers, and the name was specified using the Name command in step 4, so DEBUG knows what to do. Type

w

DEBUG displays a message that tells you it is writing the number of bytes you specified. No address need be specified—our program begins at 100H, which is the default value that the Write command uses if no address is specified.

9. Quit the DEBUG program by typing

q

10. When you see the PC-DOS prompt, type

b:program

You should see

This is a
            short message.

ALTERING AN EXISTING PROGRAM

The procedure for adding to or changing an existing program is very similar. The two differences are (1) when you call DEBUG, you type

debug b:program.com

and do not have to use the Name command (step 4 above), and (2) after DEBUG is loaded and you see the dash prompt, use the Register command and note the CX and BX values. CX and BX contain the length of the program, and they need to be reset to these values (or expanded if necessary) before using the Write command to write out the changed (or expanded) program.

Index

The SYBEX Library

FOR YOUR IBM PC

THE ABC'S OF THE IBM® PC
by Joan Lasselle and Carol Ramsay   100 pp., illustr., Ref. 0-102
This is the book that will take you through the first crucial steps in learning to use the IBM PC.

THE BEST OF IBM® PC SOFTWARE
by Stanley R. Trost   144 pp., illustr., Ref. 0-104
Separates the wheat from the chaff in the world of IBM PC software. Tells you what to expect from the best available IBM PC programs.

BUSINESS GRAPHICS FOR THE IBM® PC
by Nelson Ford   200 pp., illustr., Ref. 0-124
Ready-to-run programs for creating line graphs, complex illustrative multiple bar graphs, picture graphs, and more. An ideal way to use your PC's business capabilities!

THE IBM® PC CONNECTION
by James W. Coffron   200 pp., illustr., Ref. 0-127
Teaches elementary interfacing and BASIC programming of the IBM PC for connection to external devices and household appliances.

BASIC EXERCISES FOR THE IBM® PERSONAL COMPUTER
by J.P. Lamoitier   252 pp., 90 illustr., Ref. 0-088
Teaches IBM BASIC through actual practice, using graduated exercises drawn from everyday applications.

USEFUL BASIC PROGRAMS FOR THE IBM® PC
by Stanley R. Trost   144 pp., Ref. 0-111
This collection of programs takes full advantage of the interactive capabilities of your IBM Personal Computer. Financial calculations, investment analysis, record keeping, and math practice—made easier on your IBM PC.

 **SYBEX**® COMPUTERBOOKS

are different.

Here is why . . .

At SYBEX, each book is designed with you in mind. Every manuscript is carefully selected and supervised by our editors, who are themselves computer experts. Programs are thoroughly tested for accuracy by our technical staff. Our computerized production department goes to great lengths to make sure that each book is designed as well as it is written. We publish the finest authors, whose technical expertise is matched by an ability to write clearly and to communicate effectively.

In the pursuit of timeliness, SYBEX has achieved many publishing firsts. SYBEX was among the first to integrate personal computers used by authors and staff into the publishing process. SYBEX was the first to publish books on the CP/M operating system, microprocessor interfacing techniques, word processing, and many more topics.

Expertise in computers and dedication to the highest quality in book publishing have made SYBEX a world leader in microcomputer education. Translated into fourteen languages, SYBEX books have helped millions of people around the world to get the most from their computers. We hope we have helped you, too.

FOR A COMPLETE CATALOG
OF OUR PUBLICATIONS

U.S.A.
SYBEX, Inc.
2344 Sixth Street
Berkeley,
California 94710
Tel: (800) 227-2346
      (415)848-8233
Telex: 336311

FRANCE
SYBEX
4 Place Félix-Eboué
75583 Paris Cedex 12
France
Tel: 1/347-30-20
Telex: 211801

GERMANY
SYBEX-VERLAG
Heyestr. 22
4000 Düsseldorf 12
West Germany
Tel: (0211) 287066
Telex: 08 588 163